NEOCLASSICAL TOWNS

IN GREECE (1830-1920)

p. 2. Patra, street with neoclassical buildings.
p. 5. Symi, view of houses at Mouragio at Yialos.
p. 6. Symi, view of the sea through a gap between houses.

Photographs: © E. ATTALI fig. 3, 29, 30, 52, 63, 66, 67, 70-81, 84, 86-89, 94, 98, 99, 102-104, 119-124, 126-140, 143, 144, 147-149, 153-161, 165, 168-174, 177, 179-182, 184, 185, 195-200, 205, 235, 237, 238, 240 and p. 2

© V. VOUTSAS fig. 151, 175, 218 and p. 5

© Y. YEROLYMBOS fig. 241, 244-255, 263, 264, 268-277, 295-298, 300-302, 305, 306, 308, 311-315, 319-323

© D. ZIVAS fig. 259, 260

© G. KOUROUPIS fig. 105

© D. PHILIPPIDES fig. 1, 2, 4, 5, 20-25, 28, 31, 40-43, 46, 49, 51, 53, 55, 64, 83, 90-93, 96, 97, 100, 101, 108-114, 142, 176, 186, 189, 190, 192-194, 201-204, 206, 207, 209, 211-217, 219-234, 236, 239, 266, 267, 281-284, 286-292, 299 and p. 6

GENERAL COORDINATION Athina Ragia

TRANSLATION David Hardy

TEXT EDITING Katerina Logothetis

DTP Theoni Soupiona, Kelly Kalogirou

FILMS Toxo

PRINTING Epikoinonia

BINDING George Moutsis

ISBN 978-960-204-278-6

58 Skoufa Street, 106 80 Athens, T. 210/3611692, F. 210/3600865
www.melissabooks.com

DIMITRIS PHILIPPIDES

NEOCLASSICAL TOWNS
IN GREECE (1830-1920)

Photographs
ERIETA ATTALI, YIORGIS YEROLYMBOS

MELISSA PUBLISHING HOUSE

C O N T E N T S

PROLOGUE

When Greece won its independence in 1827, after much bloody fighting, it automatically entered upon a process of rapid modernisation. This 'Europeanisation', as western cultural influences were called at the time, was initially a very thin crust overlying a deep substratum of tradition that had been formed during the Ottoman period. The Greek 19th century was characterised by an uneven struggle between a recent past that was now the object of disdain and a future on which all the hopes of the nation were concentrated.

In these circumstances, the newly founded state, which was itself based on the faithful imitation of western institutions, made a decisive contribution to the Europeanisation of Greek society. The introduction of the model of the neoclassical town was an important element of state policy and marked a decisive turning point in the history of modern Greek settlements.

This imported model was applied in Greece under adverse circumstances, since the country had only just emerged from a gruelling, protracted struggle for liberation. It is difficult today to comprehend the extent of the devastation suffered at that time by the country, in terms of its manpower and housing stock. Virtually nothing had remained standing, while the presence of refugees, uprooted from their ancestral homes, was everywhere painfully apparent. The introduction of the institution of the neoclassical town at this critical stage, through the first steps taken by the Governor Ioannis Kapodistrias as early as 1828, was, as we shall see, tantamount to a revolution that would overthrow every precedent.

The purpose of this account is to examine the neoclassical town in 19th-century Greece pre-eminently as a cultural innovation. Its main feature was the 'Plan', a new mechanism for producing urban space. I shall attempt to show how this innovation was introduced and how it was then disseminated and imposed throughout the entire extent of the country – initially within the, at first, limited bounds of the Greek state and later up to the final borders of the country as we know them today. Taking the view that this mechanism had a profound influence on the life of the inhabitants and also vice versa, that it was itself influenced by the manner in which society was organised and functioned, I shall pay particular attention to the mutual influences between them.

I also take the view that it is not enough to study the neoclassical towns of Greece as a purely historical phenomenon. As one proceeds with their study, challenging affinities constantly emerge with the conditions to be found in Greek towns of the present day. Our ultimate aim is to reveal this connection, however indirect. For what we learn from the study of the neoclassical town is that it forms a perpetual present.

We shall range over nine decades, that is the entire period of the flowering of Greek neoclassicism, from the foundation of the state (1827) to the series of proposals for the redesigning of Athens – known as the 'Miracle Plans' – and the reconstruction of Thessaloniki after the city was burned down in 1917, involving the bold redistribution of urban land. This event brings to a close a major cycle in the history of the modern Greek town.

My intentions are conservative: it is not my aim to contribute new finds in a field in which other eminent scholars have already distinguished themselves, nor even to draw exhaustively on the information available. I seek merely to paint a representative picture, based on large and small settlements, ranging from metropolitan centres to small townships scattered throughout Greece, so as to reveal the great variety of ways in which the model of the neoclassical town has been applied. Since the degree of penetration of this novelty was not everywhere the same, I have also sought to understand the pace of change, not only where it was obvious, in large important settlements, but also in much smaller ones that followed the innovations from a distance and, possibly for that reason, with an understandable simplification. On our itinerary, we shall encounter settlements that were created *de novo* as 'new settlements' by the state, as well as ones that already existed and were subject to individual improvements and extensions.

One basic practical problem in recognising neoclassical towns in Greece today is that after 1920, and particularly after the Second World War, very profound changes took place in the built environment. The neoclassical period of Greek towns paid a high price for these changes, since the later phases were based on the sweeping erection of multi-storey buildings in the old town centres, where the so-called neoclassical buildings were demolished *en masse*. What has survived in the 'historical centres' – as the old settlement nuclei have recently come to be called – that were built in the 19th century is due either to chance, or to the lack of development pressures or, more recently, to the state policy of preserving the neoclassical architectural heritage, and the concomitant shift in public opinion, which has now learned to recognise this heritage as part of the built tradition.

It has proved more difficult in practice to evaluate the urban planning dimension of neoclassical towns. One reason, as we have seen, is the reconstruction of towns after the Second World War. It is only in very few cases that extensive neoclassical complexes have been preserved, enabling us to form a clear picture of what these towns were like a century earlier. Inevitably, therefore, we have to rely more on the study of the plans that were proposed or implemented – that that is to say, on the two-dimensional representation of the town as a series of geometrical tracings on the ground. Naturally, the accompanying architecture thus loses its organic connection with the plan. This difficulty contributes to the general lack of clarity that still exists regarding the character and variety of the neoclassical towns of the 19th century, a lack of clarity that may lead to an undesirable schematisation.

In order to avoid divorcing the architecture from the town in the 19th century, and in order to understand the significance of the new model of the neoclassical town in Greece, I shall examine, by way of introduction, the new management mechanisms that were introduced to produce the plans and the radical change in the relationship between the urban environment – that is, the town – and its architecture. After this I shall analyse a selection of settlements within three large geographical units (Central Greece and the Peloponnese, the Islands, and Thessaly and the New Lands).

I would like to express my gratitude to all those who have helped me to overcome the major difficulties and avoid the snares inherent in an enterprise of this nature and who have permitted me to borrow information and images from their publications, particularly Alexandra Karadimou-Yerolympou, Manos Biris, Panayotis Tsakopoulos, Alexandros Papageorgiou-Venetas and Vilma Chastaoglou.

The photographers Erieta Attali and Yiorgis Yerolymbos, who were invited to contribute to the publication, undertook the very laborious task of identifying and then photographing the traces – frequently barely visible – of neoclassical design in the settlements examined in the text; the former for southern and the latter for northern Greece. The original, impressive photographic material they produced, despite the difficulties encountered by them, reveals the level of their abilities and the undisputed quality of their personal perspective. A fairly small number of illustrations is due to the author, who was called upon to make his contribution where there were gaps.

Finally, it would be remiss here not to acknowledge the contribution of Annie Ragia, who had the original idea for this book during a brainstorming session in early January 2007; or that Athina Ragia and her team in the Melissa atelier, Theoni Soupiona and Kelly Kalogirou, shouldered the very difficult task of accomplishing a most persuasive blend of text and illustrations. In terms of the text itself, its integrity is the result of the exceptional editing of the original Greek by Katerina Logothetis and the often heroic efforts by David Hardy, who managed to skirt many translation pitfalls.

Part I

In Search of a Forgotten Century

3

WHAT IS A NEOCLASSICAL TOWN?

The sweeping, exclusive concentration on traditional culture before Greek Independence, which has today acquired the status of legend, incriminated and at the same time downgraded the role played by the new institutions introduced into Greece after the War of Independence. Neoclassical architecture became acceptable (and therefore eligible for protection) only after it was recognised as a legitimate, that is to say Hellenised, part of this tradition (fig. 3). However, this left neoclassical architecture clearly divorced from the concomitant, neoclassical urban design (figs. 4, 5) which is usually described in shades of black as a lost opportunity for creating humane towns in Greece. However much the question has been subjected to expert investigation,[1] this general impression has not been significantly modified. Architecture moreover is a less vague concept than urban planning, which at the present day in particular has acquired a highly complex bureaucratic content and does little to encourage an understanding of its mechanisms.

Modern urban planning practice, however, is rooted in the experience of 19th-century Greece – that is, neoclassical urban planning – with all the achievements and disappointments of that truly heroic age. It is as though we are looking at ourselves in the mirror. By examining 19th-century planning not as history but as a living present – since it is latent all around us – we can better understand what is happening today. First, however, we need to assess the circumstances in which neoclassical urban planning made its first appearance in Greece.

The then tiny, weak state was called upon, without delay, to repair the fearful damage caused by the struggle for liberation and install a new administrative machine of European origins. Everything had to start again from scratch: the administrative machinery had to be set in place, legislation produced, the foundations of the national economy laid, and order introduced into society.[2] And behind order lies urban planning (fig. 6).

Greece was not to return to the previous system of traditional society, even though it was the only tried and tested one at that time. It had to take a fearsome step in time to claim the position of equal in the present of

1, 2. (spread) Hermoupolis, details.
3. Hermoupolis, detail of the side of the church of Ayios Nikolaos.
4. Hermoupolis, view of the settlement from on high. 5. Hermoupolis, characteristic sloping street with steps in the centre.

the civilised nations of the 19th century. This was tantamount to a second revolution, bloodless this time, but one that, led by the European Enlightenment and the principles of the French Revolution, unleashed equally fearsome forces against the recent past. Thus, rushing impetuously into its future, Greek society had to deploy its forces to confront the most adverse conditions, in order to win this very difficult wager.

This book records the moving efforts made by our forefathers to rebuild their native land from nothing, with immeasurably fewer resources then those available today, and through unimaginable deprivation. But also with great optimism for the future, even when this held so many disappointments and defeats. There was also, however, a widespread fervent belief in progress, an unquenchable hope, which can easily be read in many of the writings of the period. In order to give a taste of this, a large number of extracts from writings of the time are included here.

Who were the leading figures in the efforts to consolidate this neoclassical urban planning? First come the politicians: these were frequently visionary but highly inclined to yield to the allure of power, thanks to their privileged position. With their advisors, and with the aid of the state machinery, these men took the definitive decisions (put their signatures on approved proposals and issued decrees) and at the same time examined the broader consequences of every administrative act (amending or revoking, cancelling and occasionally blackmailing). After them come various categories of technical teams: engineers or architects, the contractors and "geometers"[3] of the period, and possibly others, who lacked special expertise – the basic requirement being that they could trace out an albeit rudimentary plan, first on paper and then on the ground. These men were, variously inspired, brilliant or lacking in imagination. Last in the series comes the ultimate recipient – the inhabitant, as a unit and as a collective. Victimised or victimiser, depending on the circumstances. But also an important eyewitness to events and a public advocate or critic. Many of these witnesses are included here, transmitting unmodified the climate of the century of neoclassicism: like an old musical composition played on authentic instruments of the period.

4

5

6

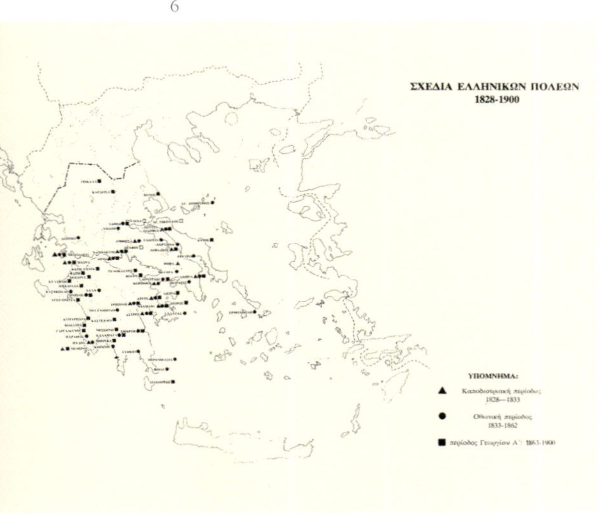

At first the action was virtually monopolised by foreigners (members of missions or expeditionary corps, the retinue of the new monarchy, men who were invited or men who invited themselves) (figs. *7*, 8).[4] There were, however, some exceptions: Stamatis Voulgaris,[5] Lysandros Kaftantzoglou (fig. 9), Stamatis Kleanthis (fig. 10), Theodoros Vallianos and many others, minor or even anonymous civil servants, who provided their services throughout the country. Their work was not easy: at a time when technical means were limited and information non-existent, these men had to work on the spot in order to survey and record what existed and to render it faithfully on maps. Then, again involving time-consuming procedures (since town plans were not reproduced automatically), they had to design, virtually to paint, the desired plan which was followed by the inevitable procedures of 'adjusting', 'smoothing out', 'cutting open' and 'retracing' included in its implementation (fig. *7*).

The town maps produced in this way were either rather like embroideries, containing large numbers of valuable details, or routine maps, that ranged in quality from indifferent to crude (figs. 11-14, 16). They were town maps, however, and this was the important thing at the time, since such maps were a ticket to the future. Even today, the town maps of that period have retained if not increased their value. They provide incontrovertible evidence. The vicissitudes of their discovery and

7

8

9

10

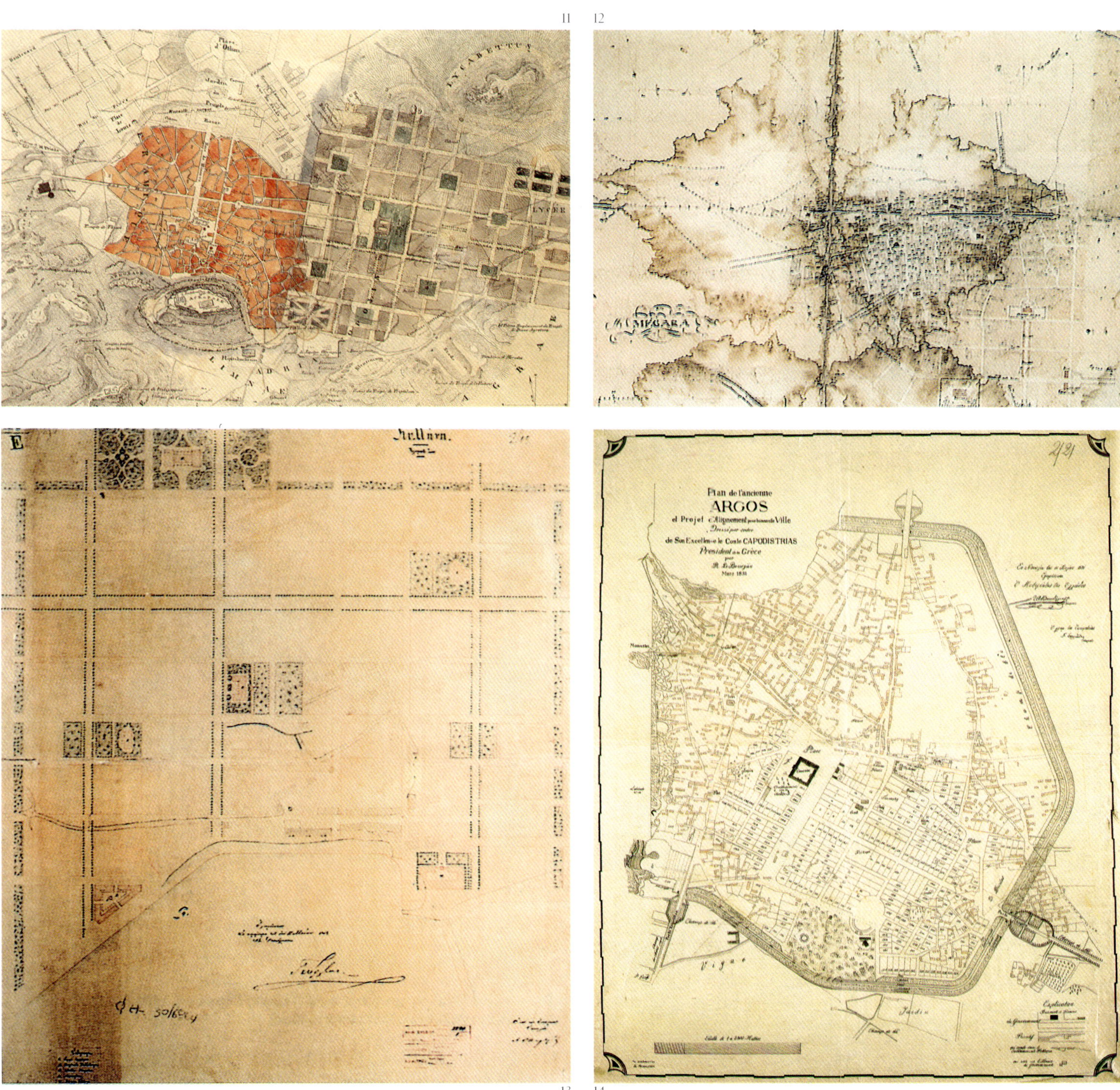

6. Map of Greece showing the settlements for which town plans were drawn up (1828-1900). 7. Leo von Klenze. 8. Eduard Schaubert. 9. Lysandros Kaftantzoglou. 10. Stamatis Kleanthis. 11. L. Kaftantzoglou, counter-proposal for the Plan of Athens, 1838 (source: 1st Ephorate of Byzantine Antiquities of Athens). 12. E. Schaubert, plan of Megara 1836 (source: Map Archive, Ministry of Environment, Planning and Public Works) 13. Plan of Kyllini, 1864 (source: Map Archive, Ministry of Environment, Planning and Public Works). 14. R. de Borroszun, plan of Argos, 1831 (source: Map Archive, Ministry of Environment, Planning and Public Works).

15

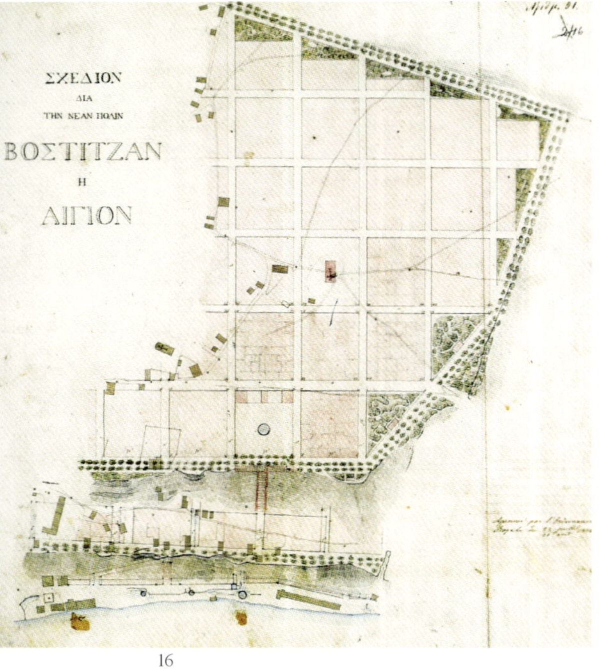

16

15. Topographical map of Monemvasia (Epidavros Limyra). 16. Plan of Aigio (Vostitza) (source: Map Archive, Ministry of Environment, Planning and Public Works).

identification and the exhaustive analysis and interpretation of them occasionally give rise to dispute, and they become the subject of theses, conferences and reports,[6] or fill books.[7] Among these last is numbered a series of general revues, specialised in-depth local investigations, and even biographies of leading agents in the planning process.

For many people, perhaps the majority, the term 'urban planning' brings to mind large spatial concepts embracing the entire area of a town. Even where the plan is nothing more than a faithful record of the existing situation, as in the case of Monemvasia, for example (fig. 15),[8] the sense of the whole is strong enough to compensate for the lack of a radically different vision. If, however, a plan is produced on a smaller scale, simply involving the realignment of a street or adjusting the boundaries between two or three neighbouring building plots, then interest diminishes. Wrongly, of course, since experience has shown that what happens in a town ultimately depends largely on these apparently insignificant minor interventions. The splendid overarching plan presented officially to a king or to a government, has a different aim from the subsequent realistic adaptations of it to the hierarchy of power and the balances between conflicting interest groups in society. We shall have the opportunity to see abundant examples of the latter in what follows.

In 1830 there was another factor that is today completely missing: new towns. These new pioneering installations, which to some extent reflect the circumstances prevalent after the exchange of populations between Greece and Turkey in 1922, are of great beauty, and we shall therefore pay particular attention to them.

The distinction between interventions in existing settlements and the creation of new settlements seems to be a meaningful one, and is valid in a large number of cases, though there are some examples that may be said to fall within both categories. One such is Athens. Chosen as the capital city in 1833, it began its career as an unashamedly new settlement, as is clear from the Plan of Athens by Kleanthis and Schaubert. As we shall see, however, this plan was converted as it evolved, by the amendments made by the Klentze Plan (fig. 18) and by the other changes that it later underwent during the course of its implementation, into what was essentially an extension of the existing settlement, Old Athens; the failure to demolish the existing settlement in order to create an archaeological park transformed the new settlement into an extension of the existing settlement.

Moreover, the original borders of mainland Greece, drawn at the river Spercheios, and the very limited number of the Greek islands within the new state left many regions outside it whose annexation was to take place in a series of later stages. In these regions, indeed, foreign administration, whether Ottoman or other, left behind it examples of urban design in the same spirit as that applied at about the same period in Greece. The delayed annexation of the New Lands of northern Greece and the rest of the islands meant that interventions of Greek origin in these areas were correspondingly delayed and to some extent repeated the steps taken earlier by the Greek state.[9] In Thrace in particular, the towns were not modernised until the end of the 19th century and continued to be "on the well-known Balkan model, influenced only occasionally by the European cultural penetration that followed economic penetration".[10] In the case of Thessaloniki, the plan by Ernest Hébrard of 1917, while later in date than that of Athens, nevertheless belongs to the same family of plans, albeit modified since it is influenced by the strong historicism of the period (fig. 19).

The settlements on the Greek islands exhibit a correspondingly large variety, frequently related directly to the fortunes of the areas of mainland Greece or Asia Minor to which the islands were adjacent. A contributing factor to this variety was the fact that these islands were annexed to the Greek state at different times, a phenomenon also observable in the case of mainland Greece. The study of the neoclassical towns on the Ionian islands, for example, needs to take into account the fact that the transference of these islands to Greece in 1863, was preceded by periods of Venetian, French and British occupation, which had at times resulted in strong exposure to a classicising tradition (figs. 22, 23).

These individual differences, then, combined with the more This is exacerbated by the general tendency to investigate the more remote, traditional character of the earlier settlements as an independent phenomenon, at the expense of the recent, historical dimension regarded, as we have seen, as inferior. These differences have prevented or at least delayed the due recognition of the influences of neoclassical urban planning. A contributing factor in this appears to have been the lack of clarity in our picture of the form taken by the Greek neoclassical towns. While we have all learned readily to recognise neoclassical architecture, with the aid of the (now official) policy of protection of it, we have difficulty in identifying the

17

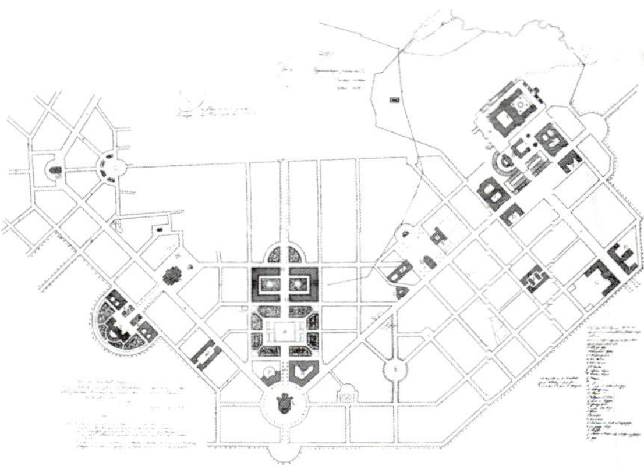

18

17. Aigio (Vostitza), design to reorganise the existing urban tissue (source: Map Archive, Ministry of Environment, Planning and Public Works).
18. L. Klentze, plan amending the original Plan of Athens, 1834.

19

20

21

basic components of the neoclassical town. A factor in this difficulty is the mass reconstruction, after the Second World War, of the earlier Greek settlement nuclei, in the construction of which the highly popular neoclassical forms were used. The presence of a densely concentrated mass of apartment buildings in these nuclei has destroyed the earlier image of these towns (figs. 20, 21). There are, however, tangible signs of the earlier urban tissue, traceable in the street network and the disposition of public monumental buildings, both of which have remained unchanged and may give us an impression, however dim, of what towns looked like at the time – invariably with the assistance of other evidence (literary sources, photographs and postcards, and paintings).

The neoclassical town is, above all, an attempt at the rational organisation of the urban environment, so that its design serves the arrangement of its functions in homogeneous zones. This can be seen mainly in the organisation of the industrial installations – possibly the most important innovation of the period.[11] Despite this, the presence of significant 19th-century industrial installations has until recently been underestimated. This is particularly true for the Aegean, where a number of once idyllic (so it is now believed) settlements were transformed into notable productive centres. Their decline[12] and post-war abandonment, though arrested by recent preservation programs in certain cases,[13] have contributed to the low esteem in which they are held (figs. 24, 25).

19. Thomas Mawson, street plan of Thessaloniki, 1918. 20, 21. Views of Piraeus and Athens (beginning of Panepistimiou Street), dominated by tall modern buildings.

THE REORGANISATION OF GREECE AND THE NEW SETTLEMENTS

During the Ottoman period, the geographical area of Greece was divided between plains where the population was predominantly Muslim, and semi-mountainous or mountainous regions with a Christian population living in smaller communities that enjoyed a partial autonomy. A network of dirt roads and paths serving overland communications linked the two zones. Since there was then no road network suitable for vehicles, of the kind we know today, the great bulk of trade was carried by sea.[14] This accounts for the early development of a coastal zone of harbour-settlements, which were favoured greatly by the new Greek state.

The way in which the urban tissue was organised[15] into neighbourhoods, or *machalades*, remains fairly obscure, as does the way in which the building *insula* was created. Examining the end product with hindsight, we can describe a tightly knit network of spatial and social relations in which private space (the house) and public space (the street) were not differentiated, in terms either of their use, as in the 19th-century towns, or, perhaps more importantly, of their form.[16] For a long period, the urban tissue was only renewed on the occasions of the frequent fires that broke out and led to the rebuilding of entire areas, though without any change in the arrangement of the public spaces.

At first sight, therefore, several differences can be detected between the periods before and after the Greek War of Independence: now there was a uniform planning system for the entire country, not for two separate geographical zones, the plains and the mountains. Town plans were produced that firmly directed their development, in place of the hitherto organic (accretive) method of evolution in accordance with the laws of nature. Finally, there was a radical difference in the organisation of space at the level of the individual building, which was now constructed on a predetermined, privately owned plot of land instead of being incorporated into the complex, 'cellular' form of the traditional neighbourhood.

The first official gesture in this direction was deeply moving: faced with a completely ruined country, the state decided to "contribute to the habitation" of the land and "accelerate its rehabilitation", by making land available on the sole condition that there existed "a plan":

22

23

22. Corfu Town, stepped street in the historical nucleus of the town.
23. Corfu Town, characteristic buildings of the Liston on the Spianada.

24

25

24, 25. Samos, industrial buildings at Karlovasi.

> "*Whereas the war on behalf of justice for the fatherland [...] has resulted in the almost universal destruction of the towns, townships and villages; and wishing to contribute to the habitation of Greece and to accelerate the rehabilitation of the land, as far as possible;*
> *And having heard the opinion of the Senate,*
> *We decree*
> *A. To those wishing to build a town or suburb, where there are now only ruins, or anywhere in Greece on national land, if they draw up the appropriate plan, the land will be made available free of charge, though according to the following agreements [...]*
> *Nauplion, 3 June 1831*
> *The Governor I. A. Kapodistrias*"[17]

This had been preceded, about eighteen months earlier, by a statement of intent:

> "*Considering the need to found social welfare institutions, such as Churches, Schools, Hospitals and Administrative Buildings in the various towns of Greece, and to construct aqueducts, streets, bridges and the like, and to provide the administrative costs [...]*
> *'Considering it necessary, in order to restore the public purse, to find local resources throughout the country sufficient both for a fitting embellishment of the towns and the creation of public establishments, and also for the needs of the public services in the provinces [...] We decree [...]*
> *Nauplion 4 February 1830*
> *The Governor I. A. Kapodistrias*"[18]

Beginning with the large scale, we may note the administrative organisation instituted in April 1833.[19] This was based on the division of the country into 10 prefectures and 42 provinces, corresponding completely with the administrative and economic organisation of the country at the time – that is, Greece as far as the river Spercheios (fig. 26). It is important to keep in mind the mixed character of the system.[20] The institution of the council of elders (at the level of the Municipality) was retained on the one hand, while on the other an administrative hierarchy was introduced with heads of prefectures and provinces (along with the corresponding councils), which corresponded with the organisation of the Greek communities of the Morea (Peloponnese) during the second period of Ottoman rule.

Here there is at once a great affinity, but also a substantial difference: the heads of prefectures and provinces were civil servants, who had no links with the place to which they were assigned and where they served, whereas under Ottoman rule, all grades were staffed at the local level. The system was a mixed one for another reason, too: it was based of necessity on the existing distribution of settlements – that is, on a system that had emerged in different circumstances, during the Ottoman period. This is typical of a transitional phase and one would reasonably expect to find it also in the social and economic structures (organisation of the army, state machinery, and economic system).[21]

In June 1834 a decree "concerning the formation of an Office of Public Economy" within the Ministry (Secretariat) of Internal Affairs created "a special department for the regional-planning and political-economic aspects of its responsibilities", the task of which was "to oversee and strengthen settlement". More specifically, the responsibilities of the new department included the favourable transfer of populations from the "mountains" to the "plain", and the identification of places in which to install "workshops and factories or other industrial establishments".[22]

Twenty years later, some results had been achieved, despite all the problems: the population of Greece had increased from 700 thousand to one million, and "we have constructed from scratch and renewed towns with by no means insignificant buildings and public establishments; we have rebuilt the demolished houses of our villages, and we have added new, notable buildings in many villages."[23] It may also be noted that a little later, in 1859, a relevant bill "granted free of charge to every town and township in the Kingdom a plot of land, from among the unapportioned, available national land, on which to erect a stone food market".[24]

This, however, laid the foundations at an early date of a very familiar structure: the bureaucracy that would of necessity accompany every new organisation aimed at modernising the country. A comment of 1861 summaries one aspect of this, the complexity of the legislation: "The hail of draft laws has barely ceased, and lo!,

26

27

26. Map of Greece with its original northern borders, during the first period of Otto's reign (source: *Istoria tou Ellinikou Ethnous*, vol. 13). 27. Piraeus, view of the settlement towards the harbour, end of the 19th century.

the hail of circulars has begun",[25] while another refers to "the unrestrained mania of civil servants".[26] Not that the efforts were to stop: the new king George declared in October 1863 that it was his aspiration to make Greece "a model kingdom in the East".[27]

The desired balance that emerged from the rationalisation of the administrative system was rapidly betrayed by the uneven distribution of the population and resources, which, it was increasingly clear, favoured the capital. A protest published in a Kalamata newspaper in 1871,[28] to the effect that the provinces were being ignored, clearly reveals the direction in which things would move in the future.

A significant number of the new settlements founded were intended for displaced populations – that is, groups who came from areas ravaged by military operations or regions that in the end remained outside the final borders of the Greek state. We learn, for example, of Cretans (from Sphakia) being settled in the 'fine township' of Adamantia on the Adamas hill in the port of Milos,[29] of the vicissitudes involved in settling Macedonians at New Pella, near Atalanti,[30] of islanders from Psara at Eretria,[31] and of Chiots in Piraeus (fig. 28). Similarly, Maniots were settled at Petalidi[32] and people from Souli in various places.[33] There were also settlements set aside for foreigners.[34] The best-known example is Hermoupolis, in which refugees from many regions congregated after the War of Independence, and which during the reign of King Otto was larger than the then capital. And a review undertaken in 1866 of the progress made so far: 10 new towns had been built and 23 old ones renovated, with a total of 30,000 houses (210 million drachmas).[35]

However, everything in Greece is bitter-sweet. A few years later, in 1872, all this considerable achievement (in terms of the strength of the country) gave rise to a certain scepticism. A conservative newspaper went back to the beginnings of the institution and recalled, through one Euth[yphron], that not everyone was in agreement with the movements of population from the mountains and the islands to the plains that were ordained by the Regency: "to this strange decree the then governor of the prefecture of Lakonia, Ikesios Latrias, replied the following, which has often been repeated in official

28. Hermoupolis, view of the town with Ano Syros on the hill in the background.

28

documents: 'the strength and value of Greece lies above all in the sea and in the mountain areas, to which it is difficult to persuade people to move, and then only out of need. Instead, then, of depopulating the islands and the mountains, it would perhaps be more advisable [...] for government to consider [...] how the people of the islands and the mountains can be maintained in prosperity, through shipping, commerce, and all kinds of arts [...] so that, as it increased, the surplus population would move spontaneously to the plains, if those so moving found advantage and security there.' This would give the government a chance to look more soberly at which abandoned towns are worth restoring and where it should install small settlements of veteran-soldiers."[36]

This kind of text calls to mind two matters that were not, of course, mentioned officially: the directly political dimensions of settlement and the other major incentive in the creation of new towns: love of the ancient world. Two examples are quite eloquent: the settling of Cretans at Minoa, where inhabitants from other neighbouring municipalities in the Argolid were at first enrolled, while in the period 1840-44 they transferred their electoral rights from one place to another in the service of political 'friends';[37] or that of new Corinth, where the political decision "to install a battalion of infantry permanently" was revoked in 1868, whereupon the town lost its "life and movement".[38] On the other hand, we have the example of Sparti, built next to ancient Sparta (now in the form of an archaeological site), which, as we shall see later, illustrates what was meant in those days by the 'resurrection' of towns (figs. 29, 30).

Finally, it emerges that love of the ancient world was itself integrated into the logic of the regular and above all hygienic town – that is of the neoclassical town. Antiquity, as an absolute and undisputed value, gave metaphorical expression to these two central concepts. It was 'order' since it inspired the Enlightenment and created a system capable of directing the present. It was also 'hygienic' since anything alien to it, any later addition or deterioration, was considered to be filthy or an embarrassing mark of barbarity: the Minister of Public Education, Voulpiotis, began the demolition and other work on the Acropolis so that it would "be freed of all the pollution of successive conquests by barbarians".[39]

29, 30. Sparti, views of two-storey neoclassical buildings.

THE NEW WAY OF PLANNING

The enormous changes arising out of the planned movements of population after the Greek War of Independence are striking. Now the state itself undertook to direct the changes, through predetermined procedures: first, the inhabitants decided to unify a number of earlier settlements on a new site. They then submitted a request to this end to the Ministry of Internal Affairs, seeking approval and a plan for the settlement. This meant that they then had the right to request land on favourable terms, and/or loans, so that they could build on the basis of the plan. We should again note at this point the question of making available 'national land', a point of considerable conflict at that period,[40] and also the fact that land was used as payment for services, on account of the shortage of money. This too is something completely new: the 'national land' was that left behind by the Ottoman land-owning class.

Having built their houses, the inhabitants then continued to press for additional funds in order to erect 'social welfare establishments', as they were then called. These, the new towns of the period built in the plains or on coastal sites, radically changed the distribution of the population in a very short space of time, and unified the system that had formerly been split in two. This creation of new settlements is not a new phenomenon in itself, since it corresponded with similar foundations or the movement of administrative centres during the Ottoman period, decided on an individual case basis by the Sublime Porte. Since a decision of this kind involves not only administrative changes, but also regulatory choices affecting the spatial distribution of the population, we may suspect the existence of a corresponding plan; however, this is only attested by observing the evolution of the organisation of the town over time.

Not all the new settlements founded during the reign of King Otto were to develop, or at least the respective expectations were not always confirmed. Not many will have heard, today, of the new town of Voion in Lakonia, since it has since been renamed Neapoli, and remains a rather insignificant settlement. In 1841, however, we learn that it already had a history of seven years behind it, that within two years of the government approval for the creation of a settlement (1838), it had acquired "the regular plan of a new town",

30

31

31. Athens, cylindrical stelai from Hellenistic tombs at Kerameikos.

that 20 houses had been built, and that it was attracting inhabitants from Lakonia and Kythira. In this case, too, we note a familiar connection with antiquity: "Our ancient forefathers knew how to choose good sites for cities. Good villager, wherever you see the ruins of ancient Greek settlement, choose this place for your dwelling, if, indeed, you find water easily." The inhabitants of the surrounding villages who sought an outlet on the Lakonian gulf and, moreover, had "the memory, from tradition, of this ancient city of theirs" were the first to think of this and had the good fortune to be supported by the prefect of Lakonia.[41]

It should not be forgotten, however, that there were other factors affecting decisions, in addition to the rational distribution of the population and activities, or the resolving of outstanding problems, such as that of the refugees. One of these had a strategic character: the future liberation of the other regions of Greece. A report of 1863 provides a general picture of the issue: " We therefore see the Thessalians congregating and dwelling mainly in Phthiotis [...] the Epirots settling in Nafpaktos, Agrinion [...] the Macedonians occupying the islands of the Northern Sporades and dwelling in Atalanti, the Cretans settling in Epidavros Limira, opposite their homeland, and occupying Nea Kriti (Lachanada), Minoa and its environs, and dwelling in Syros, Naxos, Thera and Milos, for the sole purpose of liberating their birthplaces."[42]

Finally, given the political situation, which is known from a large number of references and accusations, it is not strange that decrees were continually being published modifying, transferring or unifying municipalities. On the one hand, problems certainly arose in the implementation of decisions taken at the central level, or as a result of a change in the actual state of affairs, while on the other, pressure was exercised for preferential appointments to posts due to string-pulling. These unethical interventions in decisions concerning urban space should not be ignored, however, precisely because they occurred during a transitional period, and came into direct conflict with existing urban centres.[43] Whatever the cause, a review of these frequent reversals is an unpleasant one: "[...] the continuous changes in administrative laws weaken their enforcement, and this weakness is inevitably followed by a paralysis in the service [...]."[44]

32

33

32. View of Athens, 1873. 33. Athens, view of the area around the bed of the Ilisos River, as seen from the Stadium.

The procedure described above for creating new settlements had a direct impact on the form and content of the space that resulted (fig. 32). This can be noted quite clearly in contemporary documents of the period, in which it is invariably contrasted with the familiar Ottoman model that had been rejected from the start. So, the irregular shapes of building plots and buildings in Athens of 1835 were thought, "in spite of the logic of architecture, to proceed with opposing rules"[45] and in Chalkida of 1837, the postponement of the implementation of the plan perpetuated the "irregularities and damage caused by barbarians".[46] Corresponding references to the Hermoupolis of 1840 speak emphatically of "rhythm and order", of "adjustments", of the "good-taste" of the inhabitants and of the satisfaction of "needs of the soul" thanks to the pleasant life provided by the town.[47] All this, however, was invariably associated, as in Athens, with the existence of social welfare facilities. Schools, churches or a hospital were regarded not only as proof of progress, but mainly of the interest of the inhabitants in the "common good", and therefore of a collective spirit that was generally thought to be a feature only of traditional communities. Thus we are dealing with moral order, as can be seen every time that a misdemeanour on the part of the representatives of law and order is immediately compared with the lawlessness in Turkey: "Are we in Athens or in Karaköy [an area of Istanbul]?" asks one newspaper.[48]

Finally, we may mention a new model of life, as seen in Athens of 1853, where visitors are urged to go for a walk on Patision Street on Sunday, together with the "well dressed", the king riding on his horse, with music playing, or perhaps to visit the antiquities or the countryside by car, or the "agreeable establishments" (refreshment rooms) near the river Ilisos (fig. 33).[49] A similar scene is described a few years later in an area that had hitherto been dilapidated: "The area around the Thiseion has already been embellished so that it can be transformed into a fine garden, and the citizens of the third section [of the plan] come out every evening for a walk in the direction for the public grove, and along the entire avenue there are coffee-houses which are frequented by a large number of ladies [...]".[50]

NEOCLASSICAL TOWNS AND ARCHITECTURE

The image of the neoclassical town

34

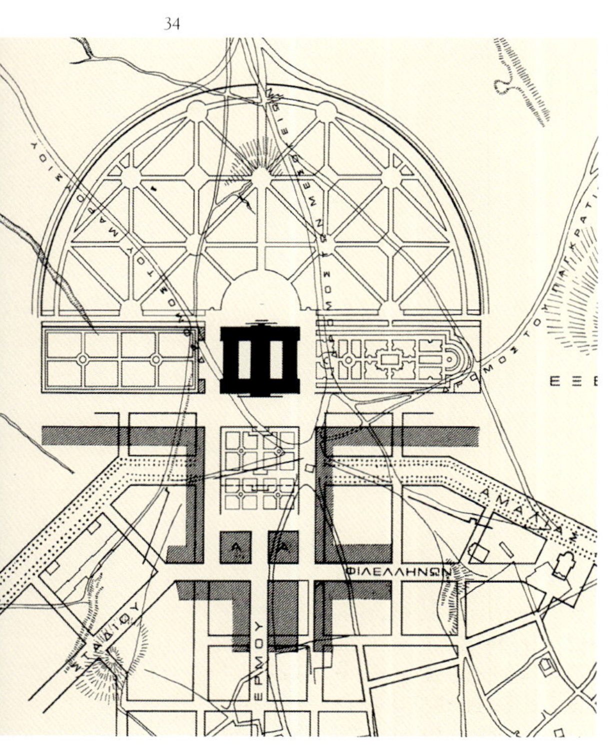

The neoclassical town never acquired a definite, recognisable form, either in Greece or anywhere else in the world; this is not fortuitous. Its name is due to its historical identity: it is neoclassical since it took shape (was formed and supplemented) in a particular period of time which corresponded with the spread of neoclassicism in architecture. A town may therefore be thought to be neoclassical by reflection: because, that is, it provided a suitable field (the planned spatial context) for the development of a specific architectural current – namely, neoclassical architecture, the product of Enlightenment. In general terms, one could note that we all have a concept of the typical neoclassical town as a unique Plan – that is, as something that has been (pre)designed by being drawn on paper – which cannot be random or deformed (that is, without a regular form) but is geometrically defined (fig. 34), and therefore capable of implementation. In practice, of course, the concept of a Plan can be recognised in some but not all neoclassical settlements, as we shall see later.

The difficulty of identifying the neoclassical town with a generally valid model may lead us to the extreme position of asserting that nothing of this kind ever in fact existed, or that the term is misused to include very disparate examples within a single category of urban design. Still, a distinction between neoclassical towns of north and of south Europe,[51] based on climate and history seems plausible.

With regard to this argument, however, we may cite the corresponding difficulty experienced by 19th-century architects in understanding what precisely was the 'classical' character that they were attempting to digest and imitate in their works. The confusion was compounded by the shift from Roman to ancient Greek models, as it was noted that there was a substantial difference between these, despite the use of an identical formal language in their architecture. Symptomatic here is Leo von Klentze's perplexity on the Acropolis,[52] when, anticipating the theory of Konstantinos Doxiadis,[53] he realised that here 'order' had a different logic and did not belong to the established rectilinear regularity. So, too, was his circumstantial understanding of the principles of the typical Italian hill towns that he later wished to apply in his proposal for King Otto's palace on the Hill of the Nymphs in Athens (fig. 35).

35

34. Lieutenant Hoch, plan for the building blocks around the Palace, 1837.
35. L. Klentze, perspective drawing of the Palace, according to his proposal to build it on the hill of the Nymphs.

The distinction drawn by de Sola Morales, who associates outdoor life with the picturesque, is also not adequate, since in practice the existing examples of neoclassical towns belong to different de facto categories, based on their origins, geomorphology, and the way in which they have developed. The already existing historical or traditional settlements (fig. 36) exhibit a neoclassicism of a different type from those created *de novo* in the 19th century; just as those that 'froze' in a fossilised form differed from those that later underwent considerable development; and finally, those that were enlarged by designed extensions differed from those that confined themselves to small-scale, sporadic interventions to improve certain parameters. All the above cases may well not be distinct categories since, as we have already observed, many settlements belong to more than one category – naturally enough when they are examined over time. A typical settlement is defined initially by the definitive Plan drawn up for it, and then undergoes small-scale embellishments (ranging from the erection of public buildings to the planting of rows of trees), or regulatory modifications (shifts in property lines to accommodate changes in the street network).

This use, however, of terms like 'embellishment' or 'adornment' reminds us of the aesthetic approach to the perception of towns, of which we have so far said nothing. And yet this issue can be shown to have predominated in the debate on neoclassical towns in the 19th century, and could indeed be said to have almost obliterated any other factor.

One should also consider the double role played by the aesthetics of the time: as an approach to the object either on the part of those contemporary with the event (architects, politicians and critics) or by those who examine it afterwards, as we are doing now. Study of the way in which the argument was formulated in the 19th century confirms that the overwhelming majority of the references are associated with works of embellishment.[54]

The contrast between the beautiful and the useful may be seen clearly in a comment made in 1852: "The mayor of Athens has constructed new street lamps, which he has placed in the most central streets. This is a fine achievement. But the mayor ought to see to the constructing of underground sewers, which will communicate with the great sewers of the city, otherwise sewage will flood

36

36. Athens, view of the north-east side of the town, 1840. 37 View of the Athens railway, train stopping at Neo Phaliro.

the city."[55] The concept of the beautiful, however, is not confined solely to decoration: the supreme technological miracle of the period, the construction of the railway line from Athens to Piraeus, is also embellishment (fig. 37).[56] So, too, at about the same period, is the laying out of a central drainage network for the city,[57] and two decades later, the constant attention to the unresolved problem of the city's water supply.[58]

As we have seen, embellishment is an inseparable feature of the urban design of the period. Despite this, the contrast between beautiful things and useful things is constantly present. In 1861, for example, there emerges for possibly the first time a certain reservation with respect to what is usually regarded as mandatory – that is, the embellishment of the city. Judged by the criterion of what is socially useful, the road construction and embellishment projects carried out by the government were "vain ostentation", whereas it ought to have been concerned for the "interest of the land", that is to say, functional projects that would promote economic activity: roads to Penteli and Ymittos for the quarries, roads to all the small settlements in the basin of Attiki, reservoirs at the sources of the river Kifisos for irrigation purposes, the dredging of the harbour of Piraeus, and the renovation of the ancient aqueduct.[59] Of relevance here is the criticism advanced in 1883 against a "window-dressing" project – to use a modern expression – that betrays clear political expediency:

37

38

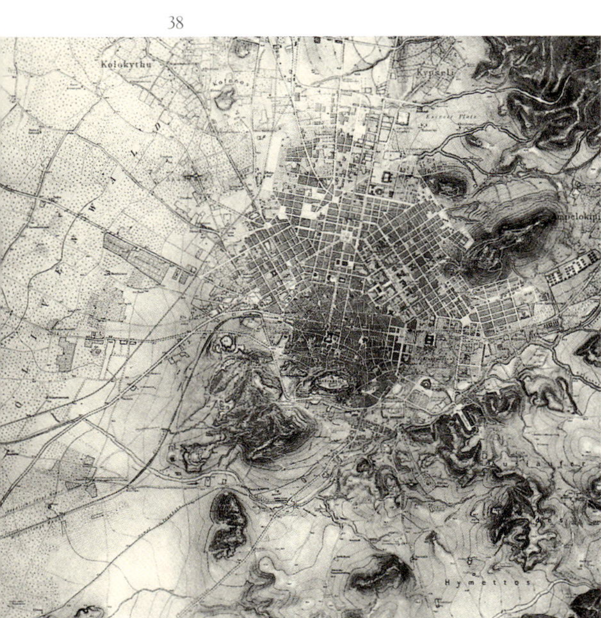

38. J. Kaupert, topographical map of Athens, 1890.

"As we know, most parts of the municipality of Athens were adorned before the municipal elections with fountains, on which no small sums were expended. After the end of the elections, the water was cut off from many fountains that were installed in front of the houses of those who did not faithfully believe in the action on behalf of the mayor, while other fountains were completely demolished [...] and yet, about six hundred drachmas were expended on the installation of these fountains and on the acquiring of them."[60]

The invocation of good taste, at once a slogan and a point of friction, is a metaphor for the malaise of a society that sees itself as inferior to the model, and feels itself ultimately excluded. It would be difficult to find a more pointed example than the (unwitting?) coupling of the scourge of the period, robbery, with embellishment: parallel references to these two issues of concern to society may be observed in a series of articles published in 1856-57.[61]

Given its great variety, the concept of the neoclassical town ceases necessarily to be associated with a specific form, as we have seen, and is reconstructed mainly as process. What makes it neoclassical, that is to say, is the manner in which it is produced and not the spatial form it takes on any given occasion. Particular attention should therefore be paid to all that is concealed behind the founding act of a town, which may be defined by a plan submitted for implementation, and all that inevitably follows, as the management of a plan on its way to implementation. In other words, the neoclassical town is a mechanism, perceived as such not only by ourselves, who have the advantage of a general overview of the century before last, but also – however strange it may sound – by the inhabitants themselves who, participating as they did in these new urban formations, began to live as a 'neoclassical society'.

The neoclassical town in 19th-century Greece represents the purest form of Europeanisation. Participating in this neoclassical adventure, the inhabitants tasted fully of its goods and automatically acquired the European identity of which they dreamed, probably without understanding what they were imitating.[62] The neoclassical town thus became a means of achieving the ultimate goal, that is progress, which was nothing other then complete identification with western models.[63] Any divergence from this was regarded as paradoxical: as early as 1834, a French traveller groaned as he commented that Greece would be a European country within 50 years (fig. 38), resulting in an "increase in needs", which implied loss of "the simplicity of life" and the ages old "customs". His local listener would not understand any of this.[64]

The neoclassical town was essentially a new situation, a new way of life – the charter of modernity in the 19th century. It was the progress of humanity proclaimed by the Enlightenment, translated into an urban environment. In 1834, for instance, the new life found expression in the creation in the capital city of a new institution, the Club. The legendary Club at Nauplion, equipped with French furniture and European novels, had preceded it, but had gone bankrupt.[65]

The neoclassical town represented something new that tended constantly and progressively to improve itself – the urban environment which is continually changing and moves steadily towards its ideal final form. This process is generally interwoven with modernity in the 19th century, tending constantly towards something without ever reaching it. In a way, the neoclassical town represents the disappointment of expectations, just as the visions of the Enlightenment were later defeated.

In more realistic terms, the unfinished nature of Athens was reflected by the lack of clear boundaries to its expansion; these were constantly being negotiated between the government (Ministry of Internal Affairs) with the landowners. The vicissitudes of Athens could well be summed up in the history of the extensions to its constantly revised plan, as a modification of the initial passionate desire for the implementation of the ideal Plan. However fine that provisional plan was, it still offered only a static picture of the city, and this conflicted with the reality, in which the predominant factor was the perpetual disputation about the boundaries of the city (fig. 39). Thus, it was the time required for the approval of an urban extension that became the most crucial factor, not the quality of the plan itself.[66] After a period of twenty years an enormous effort was required before the value of the Plan could be re-affirmed.

39

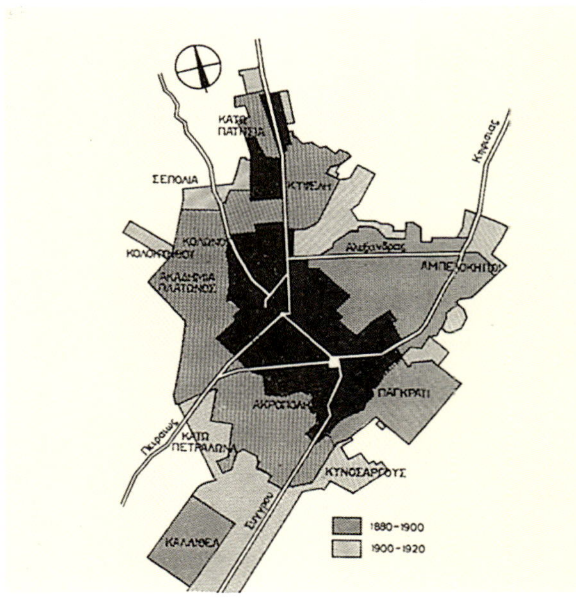

39. Athens, schematic representation of the successive extensions of the city from 1880 to 1920 (drawn by D. Philippides).

40

40. Hermoupolis house at the intersection of two streets.

At the end of the period under study, precisely this incomplete aspect of the city was emphasised as "an anomaly, a convulsion. [...] Certainly Athens has something incomplete about it. It is like a city in process. But when will this end?"[67]

Embellishment, a major tool in the ideological persuasiveness of the neoclassical town, was also deployed in the struggle for inevitable improvement. If one part of this was expressed through design methods, another was addressed directly to the intellectual sphere: it had to do with 'identities'. The restoring of place names, names in settlements, and even names of streets. In a report by a committee dealing with these last in Athens, the recommendation was made "to use the well-known ancient names [...] and the better sounding of the modern ones", and where possible, to replace them with "similar sounding" names (instead of Pseiri Square, which reminds one of lice, Psaron Square, after the small Aegean island).[68] This, of course, was connected with the familiar cult of the ancient world.

This discussion of names was rightly a matter of concern to committees and the government – its importance has been attested, without break, down to the present day, after every historical reversal. However, even the mere assigning of a name is indicative of something: the endeavour of the Municipal Council of Athens to give names to "anonymous streets", 250 in number, indeed, in 1884,[69] indicates the extent at that time of the modification of the plan, resulting in unofficial alleys cut into existing city blocks in order to provide additional plots for construction. Was this problem perhaps a deeper one, connected with the conflict between 'plan' and 'implementation'?

A basic tool in the production of the plan was the geometric tracing of a representation of it on a topographical map, which led, after various intermediate stages, to its implementation on the ground, as a translation of the plan into reality. The rationalist clarity and order of the geometric shapes on paper, as a representation to scale (albeit 1:10000) of a generalised scheme, was thus translated to life size (1:1) for implementation on the ground, after all the individual circumstances that govern the tangible reality had previously been taken into account. A new spatial order was in this way imposed, with the mediation of the plan, on the unformed natural landscape or the existing organic (traditional) settlement. In a similar fashion, the new geometry of the urban space was diffused into the contemporary social process and gave it the features of a corresponding 'order'. Much of the criticism expressed on this question in the 19th century is connected with the lack of correspondence between social and geometric order observable in Greek towns.

Part of the problem may stem from the imposition of this 'schema from above' on the natural or urban space, involving a collision that is particularly intense when the schema is not of local origins but is imported as a novelty. In this case the functional value of the Plan and the management competence of those responsible for its implementation are not of importance. This argument, however, could not have been formulated in the 19th century, which was dominated by the allure of the Plan as a means of Europeanisation that covered everything. Only those who were opposed to progress and modernisation could potentially condemn the Plan.

For the lack of a plan meant chaos, as was noted when a French engineer was asked to give his opinion, whereupon he asked to see it: "We learn officially, then [...] that our capital city, twenty-five years after the founding of its authorities, does not yet have a plan, but is in truth a heap of houses built irregularly and purposelessly, like a place in which the stones from a cultivated field are piled up [...] imagine then, [the Frenchman's] surprise when he was told, in so many words, that no plan was ever drawn up, and that none now exists [...] that there is some arrangement in only two parts of the city, but that, to tell the truth, this is confined to one or two streets". The story was repeated a few months earlier, when the "lighting contractor" asked for the plan but was not given it, whereupon the businessman concerned (Feraldis) was obliged to pay to have a "feasible, suitable plan" drawn up and presented to the local authorities, which "seemingly would be used solely for adornment purposes".[70]

41

42

41. Detail of the side of the Academy of Athens building, by Th. Hansen (1859).
42. Detail of the facade of the National Library building in Athens, by Th. Hansen (1884).

43

THE RELATION OF THE NEOCLASSICAL TOWN TO NEOCLASSICAL BUILDINGS

Faced with such 'shortcomings', so obviously visible in even hastily taken photographs, it is reasonable to turn our attention to neoclassical architecture – that is to say to neoclassical buildings, as a component of this so elusive townscape. The neoclassical building, at least, has all the features that seem to be lacking in the neoclassical town: self-sufficiency, formal order, and clearly distinguishable rules of design (fig. 40). Irrespective of what happens around it, the neoclassical building is an undisputed entity that forms and defines the neoclassical town, moving from the single unit to the collective entity. Given this reasoning, neoclassical buildings are tangible evidence of the existence of the neoclassical town as a receptacle. Neoclassical buildings are incorporated into the plan, as its constituent units. In the best case (fig. 48) the plan makes provision for their presence, prescribes their features (such as houses with a garden) and, with regard to important public buildings, which serve as landmarks, it also notes their precise position and a hypothetical outline. Conversely, when the time comes for the definitive landmark to be designed and constructed, it is presented as an 'image' (figs. 41-43) which 'hovers' in an ill-defined urban space. The building eclipses the town.

The relationship between town and building in the neoclassical town in particular, may thus be considered contradictory. This is due to two changes that occurred almost at the same time: the roles played by the Enlightenment town and Enlightenment architecture both changed. Let us examine them in order.

The content of the town changed as it moved in the direction of a functional machine, a tool that now needed good management. As Yannis Tsiomis observes with great perspicacity: "[...] what is the relationship between the neoclassical town in Greece from 1833 onwards and capitalism? In the end [...] I attribute less significance to the forms of neoclassicism than to *the mechanisms and circumstances of the choice of forms*."[71]

The town is a machine that is constructed by using the relevant technology. One might thus assume that steady progress in the technical sphere will lead to perfect towns. The designer of towns is a scientist, and is thus identified with any technocrat who dreams of miracles, such as the reforms proposed in 1891 by a certain Bastakos, the director of Attic Railways, for an underground railway from Omonia to Piraeus and from there to Palio Phaliro.[72]

The entire debate about the hygiene of towns and their orderly functioning so as to promote the happiness of their inhabitants reflects this change. This is the desideratum, and it is with regard to this desire that the ideal (the Plan) clashes with reality (the built Greek town). As we shall see, all the battles that were fought during the 19th century, and also those that were fought afterwards, with a succession of 'visions', which eventually arrived at the modern pragmatism, are based on this crucial failure of identity.

On the other hand, architecture, with the support of J.N.L. Durand at the theoretical level, descended to the 'mechanical' – that is, it came to be identified with a detailed 'catalogue' of types, from which, in order to compose the desired building, the forms of facades and the designs of spaces were derived by combining different elements. If this is directly transferred to the design of the neoclassical town, we may note a paradoxical feature: while the town is superficially based on a similar typology of individual elements that characterise it as a trademark (rules for hygiene and functionalism), it does not have a similar clarity as an end product. This mechanism is the vocabulary of a unified language. Architecture is designed by mixing elements from an inventory in the same way that, as noted above, using a mechanism to secure the ideal conditions for life creates the town. The wonderful unity of the examples of neoclassical architecture stems from precisely this process by which these examples are produced. Here we can see determinism at work: the Enlightenment promoted rationalism which was to lead to the industrial revolution, and this in turn penetrated every sphere of the human spirit, conquering it or provoking reaction. Nothing was to remain untouched by this sweeping change.

The inclusion of architecture in the rationale for the production of a town, the basic values of which are its functionality and hygiene, may be seen in the composition of the circular "Concerning the penalties for contraventions regarding public cleanliness, issues related to food and building enterprises" (1833), in which

44

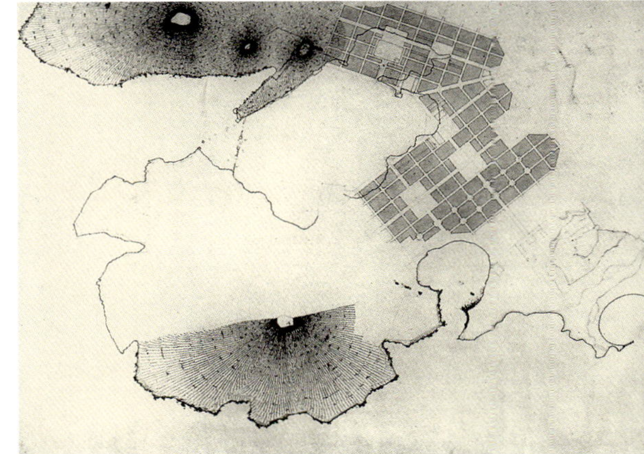

45

43. View of Athens University, by Chr. Hansen (1839), as seen from Korai Street. 44. Unfinished preliminary plan for Piraeus. 45. Painting of the port of Piraeus with the Customs House (left), 1837.

46

46. Karterado on Santorini, the neoclassical school in the traditional island settlement.

these three things (cleanliness, food and construction) exist alongside each other. In order to erect or repair a building you needed "a plan decided and approved by the responsible Authorities for its stability and safety". Anyone who departed from the plan was punished. Anyone who "neglects the maintenance of a building" that might harm another and does not repair it in good time was punished; the same penalty was imposed also on the architect who "neglects the supervision of construction". If the owner of a building neglects it, then "the authorities" either repair the building at his expense or demolish it.[73] In other words the property belongs to the city, and is therefore controlled by the state.

The close affinity between building and town can also be seen in practice in a decree issued by King Otto for building in Piraeus, in which the prices at which plots are made available are defined "on the right part [...] which is reserved for the Chiots". Here we may note that the price takes into account the surrounding public space: "in the calculation of the price will be calculated not only the area of the space for building, but also that of the adjacent spaces, public squares and streets and streets for half their width [...]" (figs. 44, 45).[74]

Similarly, the early building regulation "Concerning the implementation of the town plan for Athens" (1836) was not at all concerned with questions of appearance, which are subject to aesthetic criteria, but insisted on defining the rules of the game in quantitative terms (property boundaries, fronts, heights, partition walls, special regulations for central squares and streets). The only reference to questions of order is the "reform" of the boundaries of building plots after the laying out of streets, to give the buildings a rectangular shape.[75]

However many affinities are identified between the neoclassical town and neoclassical architecture, the buildings that are produced as neoclassical are not of themselves a necessary and sufficient condition for identifying the neoclassical town. It is questionable whether any neoclassical building, even a centrally designed neoclassical school building, built in an old, historical settlement is enough to characterise it as a neoclassical settlement (fig. 46). Architecture alone cannot undertake this role.

Interest attaches to a comment made in 1840, drawing a direct correlation between the embellishment of the city of Athens and the erection of notable buildings, such as churches.[76] Conversely, unfenced ruins were turned into public toilets and rubbish dumps for those who dwelt nearby.[77] A long description of Athens in 1853 entitled *General view of Athens* begins with the observation that it is no longer a Turkish town and ends by listing a series of important public buildings, stressing the new churches, which indicate that "our city will exceed in technical expertise the towns of the whole of Turkey and possibly those of the Ionian islands."[78]

However, quite apart from the formation of a unified formal language that satisfies functional needs, what is the main characteristic of neoclassicism, from even the most accessible aspect of its architectural expression? What are the distinctive features of this language? The geometric clarity of the shapes and the purity of the delineation of the forms follow specific rules of composition and exude a sense of harmony as order. The design, whether architectural or urban, reflects an order of this kind through its regularity and symmetry.[79] Everything irregular or anomalous, formless or distorted, has been removed, or at least has been reduced to a minimum, so as to have only minor value. The importance of this order was understood very early on: "Architects, in the designs for their buildings use square, quadrilateral and rectangular shapes. The Athenians, for their houses, use obtuse or acute angles, polygons, lozenges, trapeziums, and so on."[80]

Given this rationale, the perception of a town as regular and European was directly associated with houses that were built "uniformly and of equal height", just as much as it was with provision for public squares that formed "square gardens".[81] Or with King Otto's wish that Syntagma Square should acquire a building to match the Grand Bretagne Hotel in a symmetrical position, on a plot of land that he himself was prepared to provide free of charge, though in the end no one was found to take up his offer (fig. 47).[82]

Order is certainly one virtue, and a second is cleanliness which is directly associated with hygiene.[83] The neoclassical town is by definition a hygienic one. It was therefore a great blow for such a town to seem to be filthy, because this

47

48

47. Proposal for Syntagma Square, Th. Hansen, 1842. 48. Geographical Service of the French Army General Staff, map of Athens, 1854.

49

49. Hermoupolis, view of part of the old cemetery. Monument to the P. Avgerinos family (by the sculptor G. Vitalis, 1884).

detracted from its artistic value. Possibly the greatest struggle carried out in the 19th century was thus to secure cleanliness in the public spaces of the town, the main problems being dust, rubbish and outdoor urinals.[84] There is no reference, however, to private areas;[85] attention is focused entirely on public spaces. Here there is a distinct contradiction: taste and hygiene, as indicators of civilisation, ought equally to play their part in daily life, but the role of hygiene is not taken into account in the private sphere.

The same combination of order and hygiene is also characteristic of the equally new institution of organised cemeteries, another application of rational design (fig. 49). The decree of 23.3.1834 lays down the conditions for their design as distinct special units some distance from settlements. The dead are assigned to a predetermined zone with an enclosure wall whose height is defined just like that any other urban function, such as industry.

And something else: in a rather unexpected manner, the same inclination to break the rules that is apparent in architecture, with its irregularities, breaches of the regulations and land encroachment, is also found in the town, in which claims and land encroachment play havoc with its boundaries: these were known, in the case of Athens as "machinations about its extension".[86]

As shown on the map recording the gradual implementation of the Athens Plan, the dispersed new structures seem to float freely in space rather than being aligned to the still invisible traces of the main thoroughfares (Akadimias and Panepistimiou Streets) which point to the fact that a Plan exists. Though at the same time, the terrible (by the standards of the time) section cut through the mass of built Athens, by Ermou and Aiolou Streets,[87] which removed entire strips from the 'meat' of the old town, reveals more graphically what is happening here (figs. 50, 51). Ermou Street, indeed, was originally called 'the Main Street'.[88] In other words, the neoclassical town is present in Ermou and Aiolou, but not in Panepistimiou, at least in its first phase. That is to say, what we today regard as a central feature in the tracing of the new town, the almost ninety degree angle between Pireos and Panepistimiou Streets, was at that time not prominent; instead, the dominating feature was the intersection of Aiolou and Ermou Streets – "the cross formed by the two great streets" with *I Oraia Ellas*, the famous coffee-house mentioned by Edmond About, at the intersection.[89]

The desired synthesis was not long in being achieved; an article republished from *The Times* of London, in 1878, heaps hymns of praise on Athens, the panorama of nature around it, the distant views, and of course the city itself: "nothing is more novel than Athens, its wide streets and the majestic buildings of the new town."[90]

50

51

50. Athens, detail of the map in fig. 48, showing the section cut by Ermou and Aiolou Streets through the tissue of the old town. 51. Athens, view of Aiolou Street at present.

ΖΑΠΠΕΙΟΝ

Part II

Central Greece & the Peloponnese

54

CENTRAL GREECE (FORMERLY ROUMELI)

From Athens to Lavrio

The almost inevitable selection of Athens (fig. 56, 57) as capital of the new Greek state, a choice that was "more archaeological than political",[91] and the transfer of the seat of government from Nafplio, was accompanied by a splendid, impressive plan for Athens, the work of the young architects Stamatis Kleanthis and Eduard Schaubert (fig. 60). Alexandros Papageorgiou-Venetas, who has meticulously studied the early cartography of Athens, states that "they had already compiled a detailed measured topographical plan of the old town 1831/32, and this served as the basis for their town plan."[92] Far-sighted and bold visionaries, they thus drew up an "ingenious proposal for the creation of a 'lavishly planted' classicising city [...]," in which "the plan is adapted to the Mediterranean climate and attempts to combine the geometric layouts and the vanishing perspectives and views of monuments associated with central Europe with the building manners and traditional way of life of the South [...]".[93] Here, then, we are not dealing simply with a new town model of the kind founded on various sites in Greece, but with something unique, an innovation at international level worthy of the unique nature of the land in which it was to be implemented. This Mediterranean, "'lavishly planted' classicising city" was based on the "harmonious co-existence of the new town in the North and the zone of excavations, with

52. (spread) Athens, Zappeion Hall, entrance porch.
53. (spread) Piraeus, the coffee-house by E. Ziller, detail.
54. The Athens Plan of Kleanthis and Schaubert, 1833: version in the German Archaeological Institute.
55. Athens, view of part of the centre of the city (from Lykavittos hill).

55

56

57

their rich history, in the South".[94] A plan of this kind was never to be seen again, and it has therefore remained known to history simply as the 'Plan of Athens', without the need for further clarification (figs. 54, 58, 59).

It is worth dwelling here on two texts written by possibly the most important student of Athens, the architect-historian Kostas I. Biris: a study of the first designs for the city published on the thirtieth anniversary of the approval of that fine Plan in 1933,[95] and a later article devoted specifically to the memorandum that accompanied it.[96] The two young architects designed a city "for at least 35-40,000 people" which could be extended on the north, so that "the new town extends around the old like a crescent moon from East to West". This description is of importance, since today we are accustomed to speak mainly of a roughly isosceles triangle that encloses the old town (fig. 61). In the plan there are no curved tracings: everywhere there are intersections between axes set at right or oblique angles – yet the designers saw it as a crescent moon.

The memorandum further notes that in addition to the favourable climate for the new city (there is no mist or fog, and in the summer it is refreshed by the evening wind off the sea – the *batis*), the main feature of new city is that "it still possesses the advantage that the area of the ancient city of Theseus and Hadrian is not built up, and there is free space for excavations." These would have to

56. View of Athens, painting by Jacques Carrey (1674) (source: City of Athens Museum). 57. View of Athens from the area of what is now Syntagma Square, engraving by E. Dodwell (1805) (source: City of Athens Museum).

take place immediately to avoid accusations of lack of foresight being levelled in the future. The value of the antiquities that would be found during these excavations was incalculable. In addition to the monuments themselves, "the soil should be dug down to the level of the ancient city, when, without doubt, one will discern even the position of the ancient streets and squares. Here and there some of the picturesque, ruined churches of the Byzantine Middle Ages could be left, to provide a pleasant contrast with the works of the ancient Greeks. The space between these monuments could be filled with clusters of trees, greenery and gardens, and the groups of trees should be laid out in such a way as to give a more favourable prospect of the monuments, so that the whole will form a museum of ancient architecture, the like of which is not to be found anywhere under the sun."[97] In other words, this archaeological garden, a distant memory of which may be seen in the present excavated area of the Ancient Agora or the Kerameikos, is the antithesis of the geometrically laid-out neoclassical town, the "crescent moon", that surrounds it. The angular shape of the town is supplemented by the creation of a romantic garden, which naturally could not be designed[98] but was only formed in the imagination.

But let us turn to more practical issues. King Otto approved the Plan in July 1833. After a Protocol for the appropriate compensation had been drawn up on 17 September 1833, jointly with

58

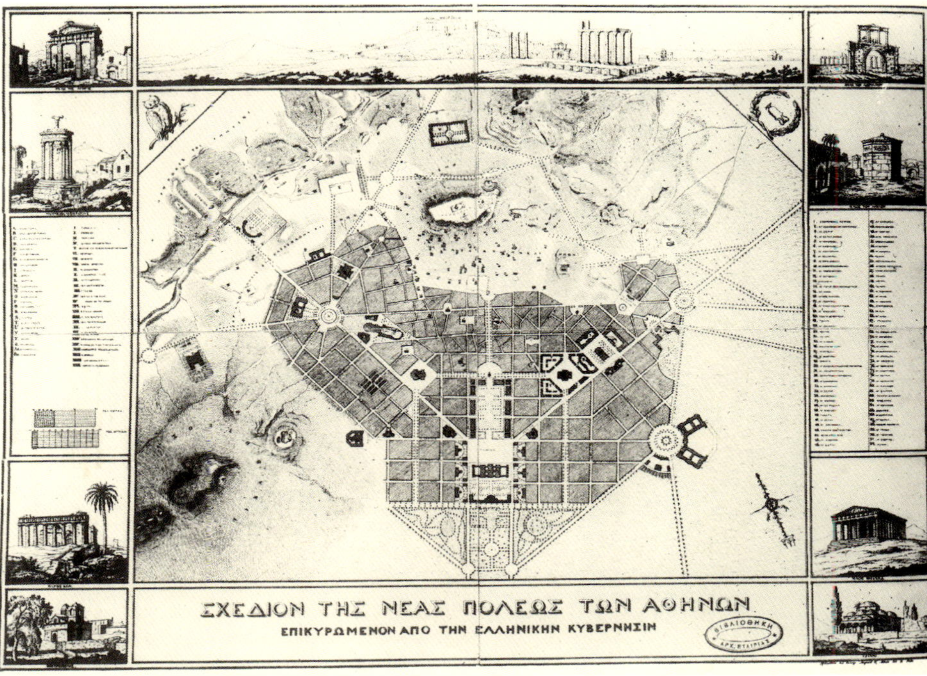

59

58. The Athens Plan of Kleanthis and Schaubert, as approved by a Royal Decree of 1833. 59. Print of the approved proposal for the Athens Plan of Kleanthis and Schaubert, bordered by monuments of the city.

60

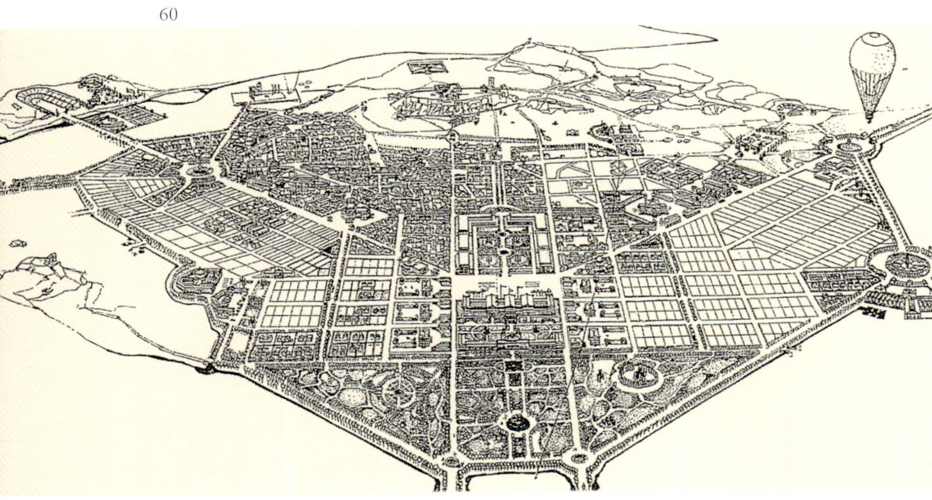

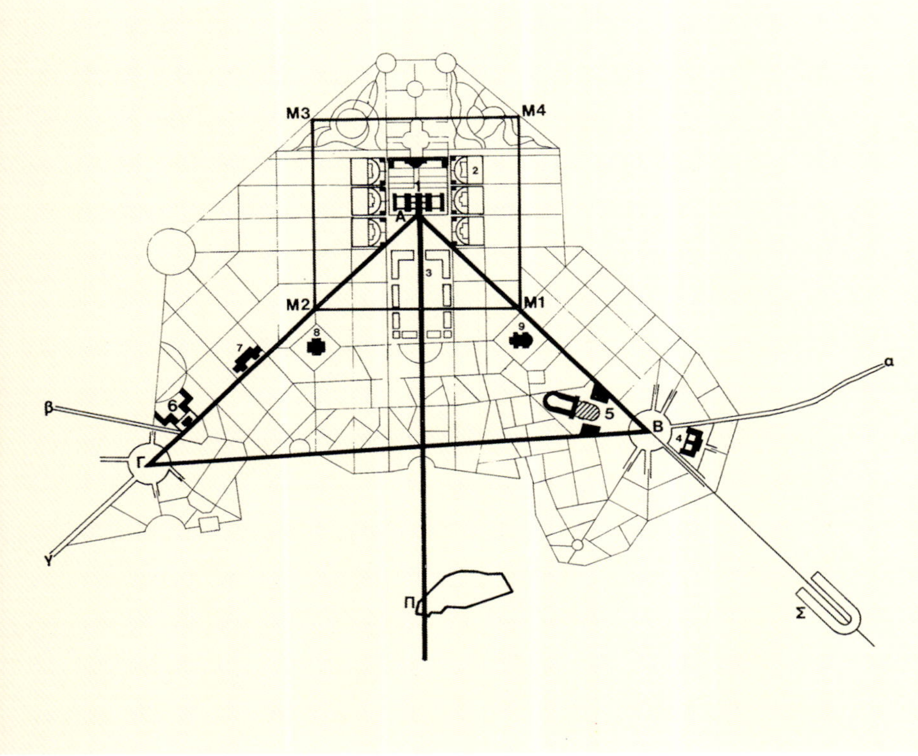

61

the inhabitants of the town, the foundation of Athens was proclaimed by a decree dated 30 January 1834. The Mayor of the time, who happened to own building plots in the new town, made considerable profit by selling them, though he ought to have made them available at lower prices for those who had lost houses or workshops as a result of the implementation of the Plan. Others copied him in this, so that ultimately "one would think that the implementation of the Protocol [...] was a difficult and almost completely impossible matter."[99]

Another crisis arose later: "The Greek architect Kleanthis designed it with broader aspirations. [...] It was a plan, at least, like the present one drawn up by Thomas Mawson. But that plan was judged to be the madness of an extreme visionary. The Bavarians arrived with their practical domesticated ideas, without any flight of artistic fancy, and gave Athens the plan of a village."[100]

It is a great irony of history that the Plan of Athens, which was originally considered over-ambitious (though it was simply inexpedient, thanks to the changes of mind by the interested parties, whose concern now shifted toward profit-making[101]), was ultimately overtaken by events, though it would at least have been more capable of assimilating[102] the later monstrous expansion of the city (fig. 64).

Let us move on now to what followed. The most tortuous problem for Athens, from the very moment that it was selected as capital city, was

60. Perspective rendering of the Athens Plan of Kleanthis and Schaubert, by A. Papageorgiou-Venetas.
61. G. Tsiomis, schematic outline of the basic tracings of the Athens Plan of Kleanthis and Schaubert.

the relationship of the city to its antiquities – that is, with what had been the very reason for moving the capital from Nafplio. The Kleanthis - Schaubert Plan, as we have seen, proposed demolishing the old town in order to carry out excavations and reveal the ancient city, which was to be integrated into a large archaeological park. Seen in this way, Athens was unequivocally a new town laid out next to an archaeological site, such as its neighbour-port, Piraeus, or Sparti and Gytheio in Lakonia.

This was not considered feasible, however, and Leo von Klenze's revision of the Plan reflected a different reality – that is, a city built as an extension of an existing settlement (Old Athens, or Plaka) (fig. 68).[103] What followed thereafter was essentially the result of this highly important change in the basic objectives. In this respect, Klenze's Athens recalled Nafplio or Argos in the Peloponnese.

Given this situation, the development of Athens constantly fell foul of questions relating to its proximity to archaeological sites and the attitudes to them. The respect due to these sites could hardly be expressed in practical terms, particularly where the antiquities happened to be located close to poor-quality buildings – to working-class neighbourhoods, as we would call them today. The amending Klenze Plan did not simply apply the Kleanthis - Schaubert Plan for a new settlement but, as we have noted, revised it to produce a built entity that was uniform,

62

62. J. Kaupert, topographical map of Athens, 1890, detail of the central section (see fig. 38).

63

in which the new was a continuation of the old (fig. 65, 69).[104]

A first consequence of this shift was that antiquities were constantly juxtaposed with the modern city, though with the tacit assumption that antiquity is sacrosanct and beyond dispute and therefore automatically demands respect (fig. 79). The situation is not quite so clear with regard to the Byzantine monuments of the city. Kleanthis and Schaubert meticulously recorded them on a map of Old Athens, since they intended to retain them in the archaeological park, as we have seen.[105] With the rejection of the Plan, however, the fortune of the monuments became uncertain: without an owner, incorporated into the urban tissue, and in the ruined condition in which they were preserved, they constituted an obstacle (or better a source of exploitation) rather than features that would enhance the neoclassical city. When the decree "Concerning ecclesiastical buildings" (20.5.1836) was promulgated, it was clear that many such ruins had already been demolished illegally. The decree attempted to impose some restraint on the impunity in this sphere, though it was unable convincingly to document the artistic value of the medieval monuments. It dealt with them as potential sites, which might, by selling the ruins sitting on them as mere rubble, assist in the erection of the University or new

63. Athens, view of the end of Panepistimiou street towards Syntagma square. 64. Modern view of the centre of Athens from the Acropolis looking towards Lykavittos hill.

64

churches "of a similar spaciousness and splendour".[106] Even several years later, however, public opinion continued to be hostile: if one walked down Ermou Street, "when one sees in the middle of it, instead of a square, the irregular structure of Kapnikarea", one doubts whether it should be preserved.[107]

In contrast, squares were recognised as nodal features of the modern city, and the public paid great attention to their fortunes. The charge was laid, for example, that the authorities seemed to have schemed together to "destroy the town plan and make it entirely Turkish in character. As though there were no place for the city to extend, they have nowhere left any significant square, though there should be squares everywhere, in the interests both of the enhancement of the city and of the health of its inhabitants."[108]

The prestige of the square did not diminish in the following decades; on the contrary, it increased. The contrast between embellishment and "the indolence of the Ottoman period" can mainly be seen where there was a square: "we try to reduce its size in the interests of the supporters of the government."[109] Similarly, the square envisaged in the plan on the site "of a monastery property" on Solonos Street was rejected because "the warden of the monastery [...] calculating the significant benefits that would emerge from [...] the conversion of all monastery property in general into building plots", used his indirect

65. Fr. Stademann, Panorama of Athens from the hill of the Nymphs, 1835. 66. Athens, view of Korai Street towards Klafthmonos Square.

65

66

67. Athens, the building of the Greek Parliament (formerly the Royal Palace), by Fr. Gärtner, 1836.

68

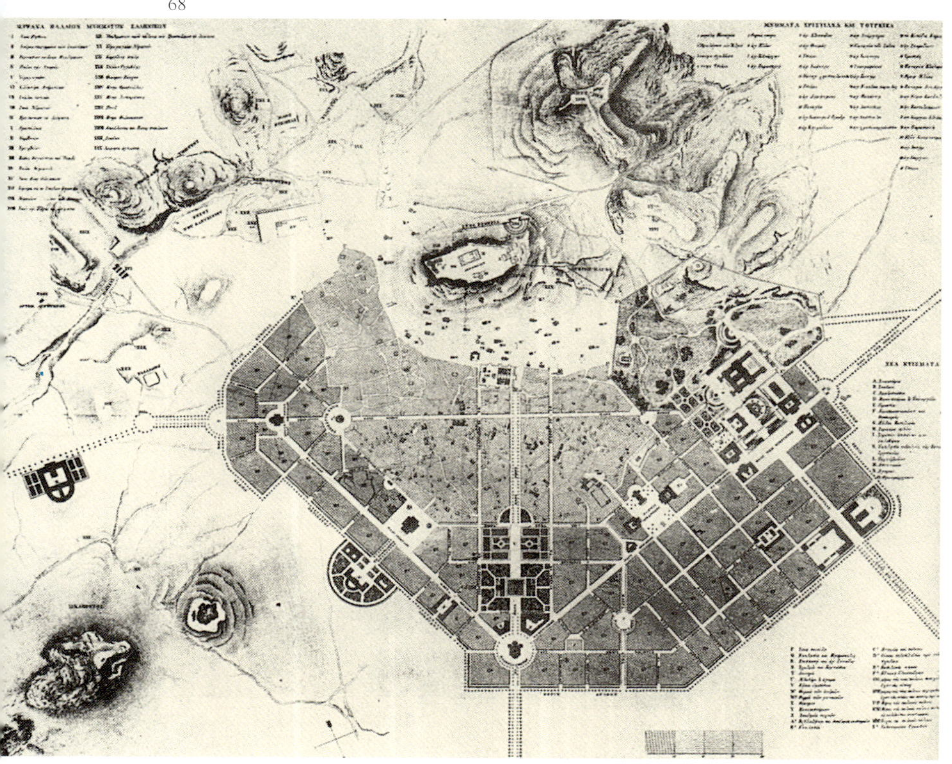

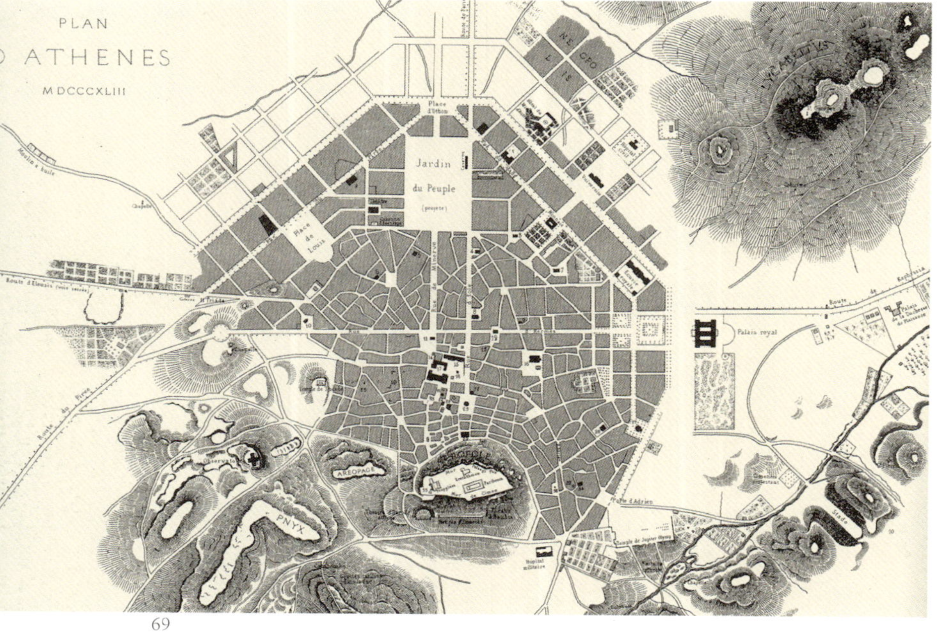

69

influence to secure its rejection – successfully – giving rise to the question: "what social need" was its cause?[110]

Despite all the difficulties, the efforts to improve the Plan here and there, particularly in central areas that functioned as "a shop window" to the city, did not cease (figs. 70-72, 76-78).[111] A description in 1851 is characteristic: "The modification of Othonos Square [i.e., the present Omonoia Square] from a circular shape to a square shape has been approved. Approval was likewise given to the increase in the width of Aiolou Street to 20 Royal cubits from its intersection with Stadiou Street. [...] Approval was given to the extension of the street of the Old Palace [i.e., the first makeshift royal residence] in a straight line to the west, where it ceases to be straight as far as the point where it meets Aiolou Street. Approval was also given to the widening of this street by 15 Royal cubits as far as the point at which it exits into Stadiou Street."[112] Thirty years later the extension of Syntagma square "according to the new plan" was announced, with the trees being pruned so that the Palace would be visible, with passageways "for carriages", with "paving", and with "four iron poles at the four corners bearing chandeliers roughly like those in the square of St Mark in Venice." In this way, the "rectangular square will become roughly square in shape."[113]

Squares, and by extension main streets, continued to be sensitive points of the city. A little later

68. L. von Klentze, amending plan of the Athens Plan (cf. fig. 17). 69. E. Chenavard, street plan of Athens, 1843. 70. Fr. Boulanger and Th. Hansen, Zappeion Hall (1874-88). 71. Th. Hansen, propylon of the Academy of Athens.

72. The Panathenaic Stadium of ancient Athens, which was excavated and restored with marble in the late 19th century to designs by Anastasios Metaxas for the requirements of the first modern Olympic Games (1894).

73

special mention is made of "the Boulevard, a broad street [...]. Civilised Europeans furnish all their cities with such wide streets planted with rows of trees, which not only adorn them and make them pleasant and convenient, but also serve as places where the inhabitants can stroll, clean the air, and bring about health and well-being"[114] (figs. 73, 81). The important public buildings were undoubtedly associated with the squares and streets: "Athens, we have to admit, has undergone enormous development in terms both of large luxury private houses and of the extension of the city. Anyone who left ten years ago and now returned would not know whether in fact he is in Athens. [...] Foreign travellers admit that the capital of Greece is the leading European city."[115] But at the same time the question is posed: "[...] In what European city would one find flocks of goats in the street? [...] Where else would you meet men herding turkeys and carrying a twenty-cubit reed poles passing through the main streets of the city?"[116]

As we have noted, the great problem, both ideological and practical, was respect for the glorious past – the great defect of Athens. The ancient ruins were threatened by inappropriate functions, by illegal settlers, and by rubbish: "If this profane behaviour continues, we shall in a few years see wineries, coffee-houses and residences being erected on the Acropolis itself, and the sacred territory being in demand for private buildings. The Pnyx began to be

73. Athens, view of Vasilissis Sophias Avenue from Rigillis Street looking towards Syntagma Square.

covered by small houses, the Areopagos was captured by assault, lamentable and filthy little dwellings have been built beneath the ancient fortification walls in contravention of the town plan and with the criminal connivance of public servants, the Stadium will soon be covered by private houses, and these historic parts of Athens are vanishing, since for years now they have been made inaccessible by the rubbish accumulated on them."[117]

And a little later, a similar protest: "What authority has ever shown any passion or zeal to rescue our heirlooms that are buried beneath rubbish and dung? And I ask these questions with regard to the ruins that have recently appeared and are gradually being covered: what is one to say about all those antiquities from the Kerameikos to the columns of Olympian Zeus, that are smothered with piles of little houses on the point of collapse, yet never demolished? All the area around the Acropolis, all the district of Plaka conceals priceless treasures [...] No public official has ever been sent to preside over the digging of the foundations of a house under erection [...]"[118]

To this climate belongs one of the brilliant ideas of Charilaos Trikoupis, the charismatic Prime Minister – that of "the progress of Athens through the discovery of the dead ancient world", since a city of this kind, "with the pretensions of a European megalopolis" but without any trade or industry, had no other

74, 75. Groups of neoclassical buildings in the historical centre of Athens.

way of attracting foreign visitors.[119] This apparently contradictory linking of the future with the past was to be repeated by an early, visionary town planner, Pavlos Vakkas, who argued that, since the state "gives the profits from an entire state lottery to the Archaeological Society for it to uncover the past", it could give five times as much for the future: "in any case, in many places the excavations would go hand in hand with the new street layout."[120]

It is worth dwelling on the above coupling of ancient and modern Athens by the perspicacious Trikoupis. Up to this point, the ancient city had been a reconstruction and, in practice, an archaeological park (the vision of Kleanthis and Schaubert, as noted above), or at least a view of the Acropolis as the supreme symbol of the city. It was now realised that the ancient city underlay the modern city, for which it was the unknown, mysterious "mould". If at the turn of the century the future ("the Athens of the Future") was accessible and measurable (figs. 74, 75), the ancient, hidden topography still remained undefined.[121] This ambiguity, which was to continue down to the present day, helped to delineate the 'modern' character of the city, as something completely down to earth, associated with vague prospects. This indeterminate nature of the contradictory aspects of the city gave birth to an ill-defined nostalgia for the old days, as a reaction against the speed of change. Its expression was the concept of Old Athens, already

familiar even at that time, as something that had once existed but was now lost; its tool was the auction room, with its "well-known types of second-hand dealers" – that is, what we now know as the Flea Market at Monastiraki or Yousouroum.[122] At the very end of the period under examination a pronounced trend to acquire "old objects [...] of embroidery or pottery" made its appearance"[123] as a consequence of the general turn of attention towards Byzantium attendant on the Megali Idea (the Grand Vision of Greek Irredentism). An ephemeral and frivolous trend of this kind would have had no importance had it not been connected with what was happening at the same time in 'Byzantine' Thessaloniki, as we shall see below, where the committee seemingly in a deliberate way introduced the new master plan as 'Byzantine'.

I cite three characteristic views from about the turn of the century of a Dream-Athens, which expressed the climate of obsessive optimism then prevalent that led directly to the so-called "Miraculous Plans" within a few years.

Each of these views gives prominence to some particular point: the first (1898) to the role played by private initiative while the public authorities proved incompetent; the second (1899) to two significant embellishments of Stadiou Street which were to influence the image of the city; the third (1902) to the splendid city as a whole, which would cover the entire Attic basin after two centuries.

76. Athens Town Hall in Dimarcheiou Square, named after it, by P. Kalkos, 1872. *77.* The modern Athens University Club at the corner of Akadimias and Massalias Streets.

76

77

78

"[...] The vitality of the Greek People, which has created the truly glorious, scintillating, dazzling, electrifying Athens, in everything connected with private initiative and activity [...]." When the population reaches 500,000 "it will certainly be the most original of cities, because it will truly be an Outstanding City, [...] truly a dream-city, between blue and green, between gold and violet."[124]

"New embellishments of the pampered Stadiou Street are impending." The National Press and the Royal Stables were leaving and on the former plot was to be built a new ministry, while the second "will be transformed into a spacious cross-shaped Arcade, with shops, restaurants, coffee-houses and a theatre, perhaps like the arcade in Naples or Milan. This embellishment will give Athens immense beauty and an abundance of life"[125] (fig. 80).

Finally, as the writer sails along the Attic coast, a vision of Athens two or four centuries later: "Athens, a coastal city, queen of the sea, as the ancients dreamed of her when they built the long walls, follows the up-to-date notions of a modern city, advances uncontrollably, occupies plains, gardens and hills, unites the Acropolis with Piraeus and the two Phaliron areas in a single entity. [...] Imagine all this beautiful semicircular coastline fringed by wide pavements of white marble, adorned by gardens and flower-beds, flanked by rows of columned white mansions reflected in the blue water and stretching to

78. Athens, the Bank of Greece building, between Panepistimiou, Omirou, Stadiou, and E. Law Streets, by M. Zoumboulidis and K. Papadakis (1933-35).

infinity behind, occupying the olive-grove, proceeding through the suburb to the foothills of Parnitha and extending to the right as far as the ridge of Hymettos."[126]

The bombast of the 'Megali Idea' is present in all these references, as a conscious endeavour to embellish reality, effacing any black marks, which had earlier been emphasised with great elation, almost sadistically. Now the position is reversed: embellishment loses its material aspect and is elevated to the sphere of a phantasmagoria, where it remains until the sudden awakening of 1922 (the defeat of the Greek army in Asia Minor). When 1900 is compared to the present day, it certainly seems idyllic; if it is compared to 1834, however, the distance is truly dizzying.

Athens was at the interface and its volatility is excellently symbolised by the 'scandalous' competition for the Court House in 1901. This monstrous building, symbol of the most extreme chauvinism, was to arouse much opposition;[127] again, it is not at all curious that a 'spectre' of this kind constantly moved from site to site within the city.[128] This kind of exorcism, of course, did not completely obliterate reality, but shifted interest elsewhere. It takes a man who knows the city as well as the reporter Theothoros Vellianitis to remind us of the wounds of the 'unknown' Athens: "Athens is not only the city of Stadiou Street, and of the squares of the Zappeion and Old and

79. Athens, Plaka, the choregic monument of Lysikrates surrounded by neoclassical buildings.

New Phaliron."[129] This indicates that the city had already been divided into two parts, the open (and acceptable) and the secret (and unacceptable). Such a division in the perceptible image of the city is associated at a more profound level with a split personality – split between realism and the unattainable dream of Europeanisation.

A few years later, in 1911, Ludwig Hoffmann advanced his proposals for the complete redesigning of Athens.[130] Only one year later came oblivion: "Plans are the easiest thing to make and the easiest thing to forget. Do you remember the fine plans that were drawn up once upon a time for the "Chain"? [an area on the northern outskirts of the city] Groves here, squares there, streets, greenery, trees and so much else that one fainted with exquisite pleasure as one reflected on how the suburb would eventually be [...]".[131] Three years later, the "grandiose" plan of the "famous English architect" Thomas Mawson was submitted, but was adjudged impossible to implement, whereupon a committee of seven experts from the prefecture undertook to study the matter.[132] Things did not end there: Mawson returned in 1919 to advocate his proposals, and give an interview in which he identified the future of the city with reference to two parameters – green parks and the distribution of functional zones – in an endeavour to speed things up, despite the opposition of his 'rivals'.[133]

80

80. Athens, view of the City Link Complex, formerly the building of the Army Share Fund, between Panepistimiou, Voukourestiou, Stadiou and Amerikis streets, by L. Bonis and V. Kassandras (1928-38).

This was the last attempt to promote a proposal from a 'saviour'; hereafter, the work would be assigned to large, naturally sterile, committees. From April 1920 to the beginning of 1921, the Supreme Technical Council of the state was convened and charged with the duty of discussing and expressing an expert opinion on the master plan and on a range of practical issues; it remained divided, however.[134]

After all these attempts to revise the Plan, it proved, in the end, impossible to make progress in practice. Perhaps all that remained, after the numerous previous failures, was the taste of the unattainable, combined with sharper criticism of the existing situation. The dreams of reform did not solve any problems but they did dispel the myths, and people came down to earth abruptly. On the one hand, there was a feeling that the problems were increasing rather then being controlled: "[...] How will the Athenian streets cope with the rapidly increasing number of motorcars?"[135] And on the other hand was the familiar old theme: "The capital must be put in order, must shed its eastern aspect and appear presentable [...] the time has come to give some semblance of order to the appearance of Athens, which is in danger of acquiring the appearance of a Turkish town."[136] The solutions advanced are invariably the familiar tried and tested ones, following the line laid down by Trikoupis; the celebration of the centenary of Greece was to be accompanied

81. Athens, view of the beginning of Vasilissis Sophias Avenue looking towards Syntagma square.

Πειραιάς
Peiraias
Γλυφάδα
Ομόνοια
Omonoia

82

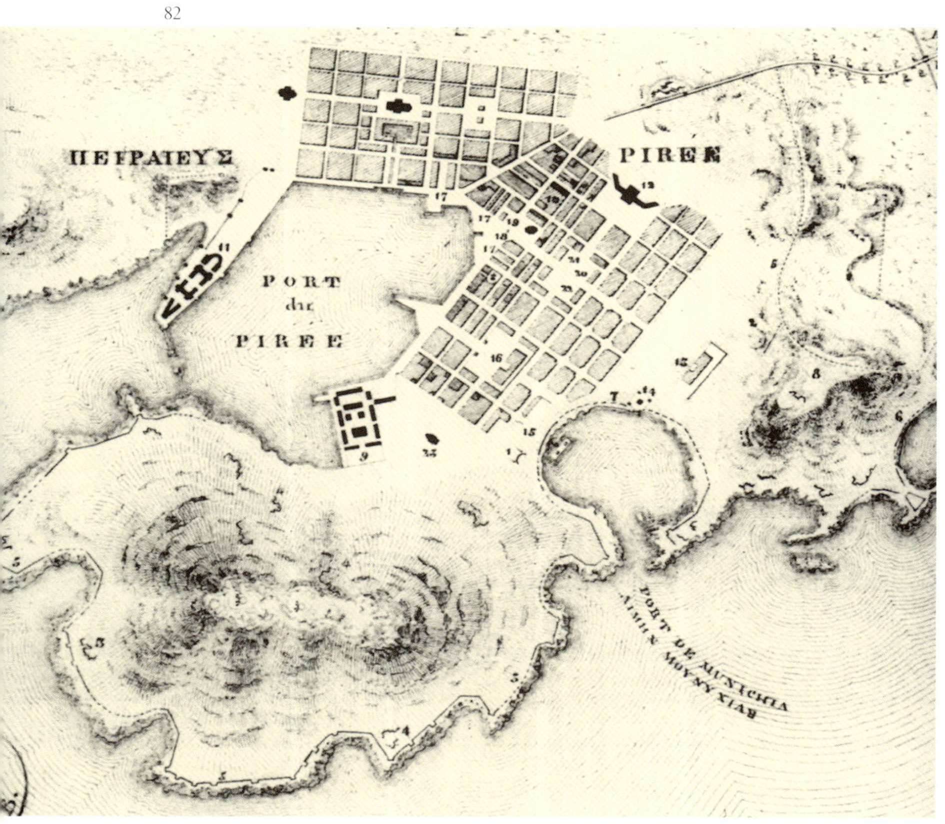

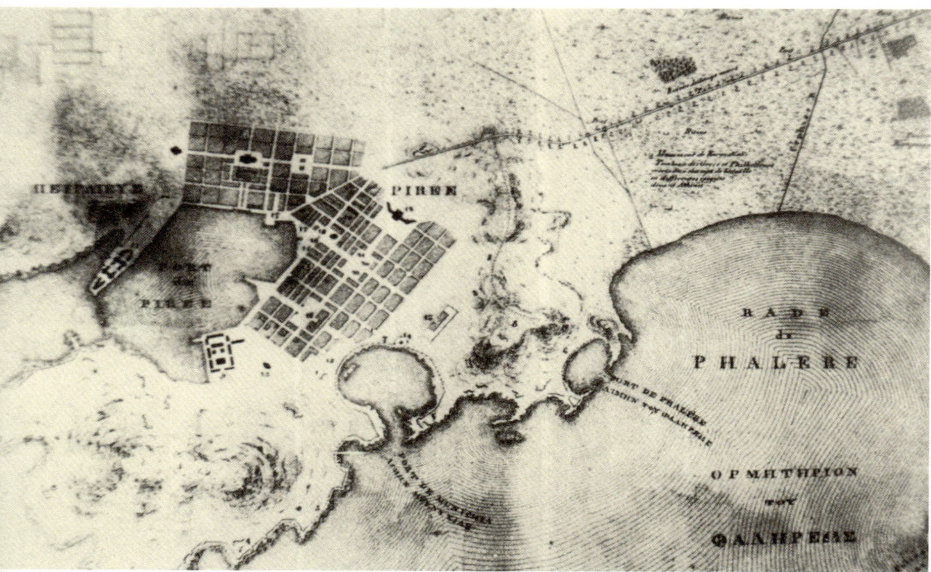

later by the announcement of archaeological excavations directed by Alexandros Philadelpheus, the Ephor of Antiquities for the Acropolis and Attica.[137]

In comparison with Athens, Piraeus has a distinctive feature of a different kind; it came into being in the form of an independent new town, functionally (though not in terms of its town plan) linked with the capital of which it was the harbour (figs. 83, 84).

The relationship between the two settlements was a symbiotic one from the outset: Piraeus was the productive centre while Athens, as we have seen, was the administrative centre and lacked an economic base. Thanks to the rapid development of both towns, each for different reasons, Piraeus was fairly quickly unified with Athens, without losing its distinctive character,[138] and the two towns surpassed all the original projections of their corresponding plans.

The beginnings of Piraeus, then, were typical; in 1835 it was announced that building plots would be made available to any interested party: "The Secretariat of State for Internal Affairs Proclaims [...] 2. Anyone who has requested, or intends to request a plot of land in Piraeus, should present himself or appear through his representative before the civil architect in Piraeus, to review the town plan of Piraeus and show on it the place he wants to receive the building plot. [...] I. Kolettis, Secretary of State."[139] The town plan that he was to "review"

82. Detail of a general map of the basin of Attiki, showing the new city of Piraeus by F. Altenhoven, 1837 (above) and (below) by Curtius (1862). 83. Piraeus, view of the buildings in the area of Akti Moutsopoulou on the Peiraïki peninsula. 84. (next page) Piraeus view of Zea harbour from Phreattys.

ALPHA BANK
A 234
ΣΧΟΛΗ ΝΑΥΤΙΚΩΝ ΔΟΚΙΜΩΝ

85

was that of Kleanthis and Schaubert,[140] which was finally approved on 11.8.1834: "The two architects are designing a neoclassical town, with important open spaces and wide avenues lined with trees, a considerable area, and large building plots, emphasising its commercial purpose and allowing it to be extended essentially only in the direction of the capital and on the north-west. At the same time they preserve the surviving antiquities.[141] That their plan of Piraeus is identical – with only a slight deviation – with the plan of the Classical town deserves detailed investigation."[142] All these tactical moves sound very familiar (fig. 82).

The new settlement was intended for dispersed refugees from the island of Chios, although they did not show any particular interest, despite all the sermonising: "Speech of N[eophytos] Vamvas to the meeting of Chiots on the settlement [...] We sought to erect a commercial city near the Capital of free Greece [...] It only remains for us Chiots to justify this great favour [...] and build a home for ourselves and our children."[143] From the beginning, Piraeus had a mixed content: it was to be a new commercial town next to the capital city: this was translated in practice into the provision of plots of land suitable for industrial installations.[144] However, the seasonal flooding of the river Kifisos created a swamp that caused a malaria epidemic and deferred the distribution of building plots in Piraeus.[145] A year later attempts were made

85. Piraeus, the first buildings erected in the town on a map of 1870 (source: *Atlas des Ports Étrangers*).

to reclaim and clean the area of the swamp in the hope that this would encourage "Chiots and others" to settle in Piraeus.[146] At this point we may cite its description by Ludwig Ross in 1836: "By way of a spacious anchorage, the traveller arrives on dry land and finds a small (for the time being), but well-organised town with well-built houses and other buildings. Shops on both sides of the street are inviting [...]".[147]

In a decree dated 1836 "Concerning the settlement of Chiots in Piraeus" we read: "The whole of the right part of Piraeus is granted to the Chiots so that they can settle here [...]". The rules follow: 10 houses must have been built in the first six months and another 40 in the second, and if by the end of 1837 two fifths of the total have not been built, the state will auction off those plots of land that have not been disposed of.[148] Since, as we have seen, there were not enough Chiots, other settlers were invited, and Piraeus is referred to for the first time as "a settlement of people from Hydra and Chios" in the following comment: "[...] and this Piraeus, of great name, is being settled under the most favourable portents for a brilliant and happy future."[149]

A protest of that period (1836) reveals that the person who was granted a site to build a market and houses was responsible for filling the plot with rubble in the case of 8 of these 12 houses.[150] There were also other problems:

86

86. Piraeus, detail of the side entrance of the church of Ayios Nikolaos, on Tombazi Street.

87

'certain people' (i.e., Kleanthis and Schaubert, who proposed to fill in part of the Kantharos harbour) sought to fill in the harbour of Zea: "If Hippodamos were alive [...] he would not, of course, fill in Kantharos, nor would he allow profiteering from land filling [...]. But Hippodamos was, as can be seen in Aristotle's *Politics*, not only a great engineer but also a wise politician. And he who designs Greek towns should not be a foreigner, nor simply an engineer."[151] In a strategy that is today quite familiar, the excesses of the Piraeus plan were finally legalised in 1842,[152] supplementing the previous, tactical moves of a decade.

The main advantage of Piraeus was, ultimately, the view of the sea (figs. 87, 89); one A. G. writes to a friend: "I do not go up to town, because Piraeus provides me with greater pleasure, particularly now that it is being embellished."[153] Piraeus soon began to take shape ("it is already becoming more attractive"), and "the Chiot merchant princes from abroad are now coming to visit their native land and their home town."[154] Within a year, work began on the erection of a church,[155] while the accusation was levelled that certain interested parties, with houses in the east part of the settlement, "have succeeded [...] in moving the site of the market to be near them, thus turning the citizens of Piraeus upside down [...]".[156] In 1842 we read a decree setting

87. Piraeus, view of Kastela area from Akti Dilaveri.

a deadline "for the construction of building foundations on the plots of national land purchased in Piraeus,"[157] which recalls the continuing delay in the settlement of the town.[158] However, "a large number of merchants and shop sellers, handicraftsmen of ancient type and small builders, all of them professionals who worked on the creation of the capital," soon settled here.[159] Within four decades (1840-80), even without the proper planning, the coastline of Piraeus was transformed into a harbour complex, and the work was completed by the railway link with Athens (1868).[160]

With regard to the unrivalled value acquired by squares in a neoclassical town, as we have already emphasised, Piraeus offers a further example, which demonstrates that squares were not simply a question of embellishment but also had significant benefits for those who built on them. So, in an article of 1851, those who felt themselves wronged declare: "The right to have our houses on the square and not behind other houses is a right no less sacred and inviolable; for we purchased the plots of land *under this explicit condition*."[161] And a later relevant comment compares the squares of Athens, which are very few, small and tend to be divided up into building plots, with those of Piraeus which are large and fine.[162]

As the general state of the economy prevented a more rapid rate of development in Piraeus,

88. **Piraeus, the Municipal Theatre on Kolokotroni Street.**

88

the town turned to the kind of embellishment characteristic of the capital: "The Municipality of Piraeus is daily progressing, being beautified and becoming more European thanks to the good taste of the Mayor, Mr. Omiridis and the Municipal Council [...] In addition to all the other goods, we see with pleasure that two squares have already been formed strewn with sand, each of which has a reservoir and two splendid busts of King Otto and Themistokles."[163] By the middle of the century, despite all the difficulties, this coastal town had succeeded in acquiring a romantic image: "This most amphitheatrical coastal town, all new with its splendid quay, with large numbers of boats and sailing ships and steamships [...]."[164] Two decades later, this optimistic atmosphere was more confidently expressed; Piraeus is a "European town", the like of which the Turks do not have.[165] At a more practical level, efforts were then being made (1880) to plan the extension of the town, which was already being described as "Manchester of Greece":[166] "The Municipal Council of Piraeus has decided to extend the plan of the town in the direction of Phreattys and Vavoula [...] this measure has been made necessary by the increase so far and the future increase of the population and the expansion of the buildings in this most commercial of cities."[167] A little earlier approval had been given to the industrial zone, which was to be legally recognised in 1892 and was to determine the fortune of the city thanks to its position and size.

89. Piraeus, coffee-house opposite Alexandras Square, on the turn towards Akti Koundouriotou, by E. Ziller (cf. Fig. 53). 90-93. (next page) Details of houses in neoclassical Piraeus.

90

91

92

93

94

94. Piraeus, a house above Tourkolimano, a mixture of romantic and modern forms.

The growth of Piraeus was now visible on all sides. While the other large ports of Greece went into decline, Piraeus made progress: if it was threatening Hermoupolis in 1880, it finally overtook it in 1893, after the opening of the Corinth Canal. It was assisted in this by its strategic location in relation to the national rail network. In the meantime a number of important social welfare institutions were added, such as the Tzaneion (1860-76) and the Chatzikyriakeion (1889-1904), and landmark buildings such as the Stock Exchange (1873) and the Municipal Theatre (1883-95) (fig. 88).[168]

By 1903 the evidence of the progress made by Piraeus had already passed to a radically different level, leaving far behind the descriptions of typical urban embellishments. Piraeus was neither beautiful nor ugly, but was now a statistical chart on which was recorded the economic progress of the town: shipping, commerce and industry[169] would henceforth be the language of the progress of this major urban centre. After the Second World War, Piraeus was to find itself the object of many attempts at regeneration, as indeed was Athens. We may single out a proposal to create an archaeological park at the urban gates of (ancient) Piraeus, the result of an architectural competition which is now at the implementation stage.[170]

95

Lavrio – the modern town, not to be confused with the ancient – "is a company town by Greek standards" (fig. 95). [171] We do not know who drew up the first town plan of Lavrio in 1867, when it was still called 'Factories'.[172] The proposed plan presents a symmetrical design centred on the harbour and two squares associated with it, and incorporates the few installations that already existed near the jetty. The plan attempts to add quality to an industrial installation but has two basic disadvantages. The axis of symmetry leads nowhere, and provision was made for a large (main) square in front of the jetty, at the centre of the harbour, with factories around it. The plan was therefore not implemented.[173] In the "Diagram" that followed in 1875, any attempt at composition was abandoned (and it was therefore no

95. Lavrio, view of the installations at Lavrio in the last quarter of the 19th century, with the harbour, factories and residential areas (Serpieri collection). 96. Lavrio, neoclassical school complex in the settlement.

96

97

97. Lavrio, view of the harbour. 98. Lavrio, the Municipal Market (Fish Market).

99

longer called a plan), but there is a clear extension to the north-east, in the direction of Athens, with provision for a square that was later to be called Serpieri Square, after the entrepreneur who had acquired the local mines. This isolated the town visually from the industrial zone.[174] The implementation of the plan would require large land-fill projects, but this made it possible for it to incorporate the area of Nychtochori, albeit as a wedge of urban blocks of irregular outline, which was already being built up illegally and "presents the appearance of an unkempt village".[175] This can be seen clearly in the following plan of 1880.

Five years later, the railway link between Lavrio and Athens was completed and in 1896 two zones of extension of the settlement can be made out, one an extension of the original 'Factories', and the other, called Neapoli, at the west, again involving an attempt to integrate its illegal houses into the plan. The entire town, finally, can be seen in a plan of 1899, "which has no aesthetic extravagance, but does have cohesion, order and organisation, with wide parallel and perpendicular streets."[176]

The area that is missing from all the previous plans is Kyprianos (figs. 100, 101), which was under the jurisdiction of the French Mining Company. There is little difference between the plan of 1899 and the street plan of 1967: the basic directions are retained, with new extensions in all directions except to the west.

99. Lavrio, abandoned neoclassical building on the way to Athens.

100

101

A refugee settlement has been added to the south of the previous basic units.[177]

Since Lavrio is a purely industrial town, it is important to observe the way in which what might conventionally be called its urban, residential area is combined with the units of production that form its economic base. In the end the industrial installations "cannot be regarded as isolated from the other functions of the town, but at least they do not occupy any of its central points" (fig. 102). The Greek Company was on the southwest side of the harbour while the French Company was to the north of the town, on the road to Athens (fig. 104). The mines were outside the town, mainly at Plaka and at Kamariza. The railway, the importance of which is evident from the fact that it was the first line to be constructed in Greece, had to link the mines with the factory and the town, and inevitably, therefore, sundered the unity of the urban tissue.[178] Since these installations dominated the life and growth of the town in the 19th century, it is evident that the strong fluctuations in the local economy (foreign intervention for the rights to mining residues, stock exchange crash)[179] had a direct impact on its composition and the way it evolved. In any case, the survival of the town depended on its constant adaptation to new opportunities, an example being its conversion into a bunkering port in 1911, which attracted considerable traffic to the port.[180] As we shall see, this flexibility was not to be found in other

100, 101. Lavrio, view of the residential area Kyprianos from the hill above the facilities of the French Mining Company. 102. Lavrio, industrial building at the centre of Neapoli, now a cultural centre. 103. Lavrio, complex of working-class houses in rows at Neapoli.

104

104. Lavrio, view of the facilities of the French Mining Company.

provincial industrial towns of Greece, which therefore entered into decline and were abandoned. The most recent development in the industrial installations of Lavrio, indeed, involved the conversion of the facilities of the French Mining Company into a Technological and Cultural Park,[181] which has the potential to transform the town yet again.

In its final form the town of Lavrio has five squares, a "garden with trees", a Market (Fish Market, 1885) (fig. 98) and a few landmark-buildings, such as the Serpieri residence, the Association of Lovers of the Muses, a Railway Station, and the administrative building of the Society of Metalworkers – all in keeping with its size and history. It is certainly a neoclassical town with some distinctive features: its architecture belongs to the general category of neoclassicism, with 'vernacular', 'bourgeois' and moderately monumental buildings, invariably conforming with the context of a small labour town (figs. 96, 100, 101, 103) to the appearance of which a certain attention has been paid: "It has the appearance of a spacious modern industrial town, with very wide avenues and a working-class neighbourhood with identical houses".[182] Just as the trends of neoclassicism in their simplest form are recorded in the general image of the town, so the variety and changes of character found in the individual neighbourhoods reflect the strong fluctuations experienced by its economy, mainly in the 19th century (figs. 97, 99).

From Chalkida to Eretria

The emergence of Chalkida (named Negreponte by the Venetians, or Egripos, after the name of the Straits) in the free Greek state was connected directly with its position as an important harbour on Evia (fig. 105), which to an extent preserved its importance down to the eve of the Second World War, with "a lively import and export trade", mainly in agricultural produce.[183] This accounts for the successive attempts to dredge the straits of Evripos in 1843 and again in 1849,[184] and the great interest shown by the Voulgaris and Miaoulis (1856-59) Governments in continuing the work (since 1853) of excavating and bridging the straits of the Evripos, where Evia draws close to the coast of central Greece opposite, using dredging operations and overland structures (the mechanisms connected with a metal drawbridge).[185]

While all these projects, of great benefit, were being carried out on the straits, the medieval (Venetian) fortification walls of the town (figs. 106, 107) still survived a short distance away on the Evia side. The town itself had not suffered from military operations during the War of Independence and remained unchanged; according to Ludwig Ross's description: "This town [...] gives a good idea of the interior of Turkish towns, with its narrow oblique alleys, its tall, irregularly built houses, and its slender minarets."[186]

The only work carried out before the construction of the new drawbridge was the demolition of the now useless fort on the opposite coast of Boeotia.[187]

105. Chalkida, view of the coast looking towards the strait of Evripos (aerial photograph by G. Kouroupis).

106

107

The retention of the fortification walls of the castle at Chalkida was to be repeated at other towns, where, for a series of reasons, attempts were made to remodel their interiors without affecting the outline of the castle. This conservative attitude on the part of Chalkida may account satisfactorily for why it was originally impossible to produce an adequate new plan. Three relevant news items, at least, attest this from the period 1835-39:

"For three years already [...] the Bavarian architects have been working to draw up the plan for the town of Chalkida, and they have still been unable to cancel the old town plan [...]".[188] In the end the "regular town plan" was completed but it was confined "to a few innovations" and it did not satisfy "the good taste of the majority". The Municipality drew up a second plan "more splendid then the first and at the same time more in accord with public hygiene with regard to the street layout and the width of the streets, since the climate is a very humid one." The new plan was submitted for approval to the Ministry for Internal Affairs, which, while continuing to support the original plan, in the end approved this one. A number of the municipal councillors then discovered that their properties would be affected by the proposed street layout and appointed a committee to estimate the extent of the damage. As a result, "in the interest of petty and twisted interests", the town was condemned "to a lack of good taste [...]".[189] Two years later (1839) there was still no plan, and while public buildings had been

106. Chalkida (Negreponte), view of the Venetian town with its fortifications (de Rossi). The engraving shows the fortifications on the coast opposite the bridge and the moat on the inland side (source: Gennadius Library). 107. Chalkida, the bridge over the Evripos before the demolition of the fortification walls of the town (source: Gennadius Library). 108. Chalkida, the present pedestrian way on the coast, with the neoclassical Town Hall.

108

109

110

erected, the private ones "were still wretched in every respect, and the highways unfortunate and almost insufferable [...]."[190]

The implementation of the legislation relating to building activity – decree of 3.4.1835, specifically the Royal Decree of 9(21).4.1836 – led to the plan of Chalkida of 1839, "in which the form of the new building *insulae* is completely in keeping with the present situation, and requires simply the creation of a few streets, a number of cases of the slight widening of streets, and partial realignments."[191] The plan was finally completed a little later and was approved; naturally with provision for a "*proastio*", that is an extension outside the city walls.[192] The demolition of the castle, however, was delayed. After much debate, the government's decision to demolish the "useless Venetian fortress of Chalkida" was issued in 1872,[193] but it was not carried out for some time (1890-1900).[194]

Forty years later, the general picture had not changed: "[...] we crossed the bridge and walked from the main street, where there were houses with distinctly projecting wooden roofs, rooms that extended above the street, and windows with grilles, to the mosque, a picturesque building with its minaret, surrounded by stone cannon balls. Today it is a barracks. Next to it there is a splendid marble Turkish fountain shaded by palm trees and beautiful deep-shaded pine trees" (figs. 110, 111). Nevertheless, the change had occurred – and it was formally connected with the novelty

109. Chalkida, the Byzantine church of Ayia Paraskevi on Tzavara Street in the old centre of the town. 110. Chalkida, the marble Ottoman fountain in front of the mosque on I. Mavromichali Street. 111. Chalkida, the mosque, now a conservation laboratory of the Archaeological Service. 112. Chalkida, the Court House building, in E. Venizelou and Kriezotou Streets.

111

112

113

of the small square next to the mosque, which "is very pleasant and shady, with stone seats and tables, while at the centre there is a bandstand."[195] Another thirty years were to pass before the completion of the railway link with Athens (1904) – by the standards of the time, the most crucial project in the area of communications. The Chalkida that resulted in the first quarter of the twentieth century is summarised in a few rather condescending phrases: the town presents "particularly in the centre, the aspect of an old town. Its layout is certainly good, with many regular streets, particularly near the coast [...]"[196] (figs. 108, 109, 113, 114).

113. Chalkida, view of the old bridge from the south.
114. Chalkida, view of the old bridge from the north.

114

115

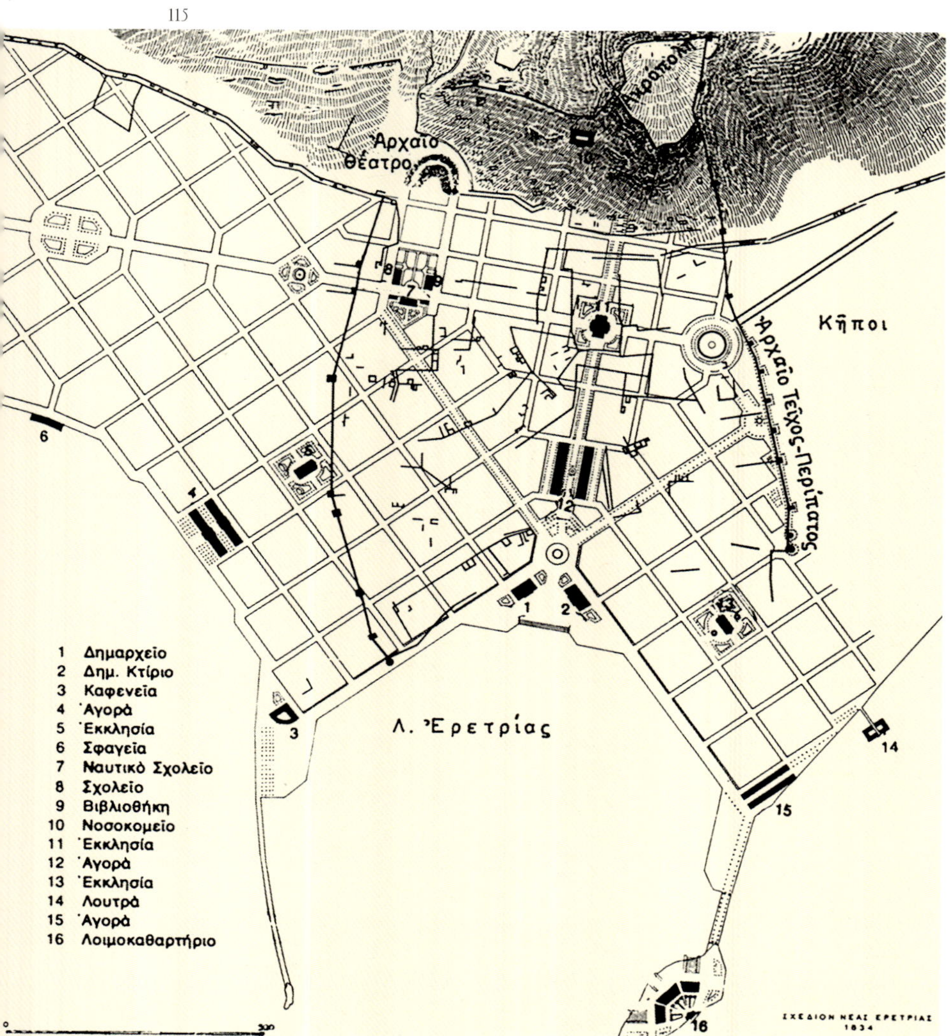

Eretria, like Chalkida, was built above an ancient city.[197] Its traces can clearly be made out in the architect-archaeologist Ioannis Travlos's redrawing of the original town plan (1834)[198] of Schaubert, whose surveyor was J. Beck (115, 116).[199] Its structure is based on two axes intersecting at right angles, one of which ended at the centre of the town harbour. The square building blocks form a continuous row interrupted only in the central zone at the almost isosceles triangle between two tree-lined streets intersecting at right angles. This automatically gives rise to associations with the other two related plans, of Athens and Piraeus, on which Schaubert had collaborated with Kleanthis. That of Athens is the most complex and that of Piraeus the most simple, while that of Eretria seems to be the purest in geometric terms – and therefore perhaps the most successful composition. Whatever we may say about the plan, however, it does not cease to be that of a lesser settlement, which could never compete with the grandeur of the capital. Despite this it was to be built, like so many others, to more or less inspired plans. So we read an "advertisement" placed by the "Committee for the Plan of the Town of Eretria" for the construction of two buildings, a town hall and a school) which are put up for tender by Dutch auction; it ends: "at the same time notice is given that since, generally speaking, the Town is beginning to be built, any masons who come to Eretria will all find uninterrupted work to their great advantage."[200] The development of the settlement, however, proceeded at a very slow pace.[201]

115. Eretria, redesigning of the new settlement by I. Travlos. 116. The left part of the new settlement in a plan of 1834 by E. Schaubert.

116

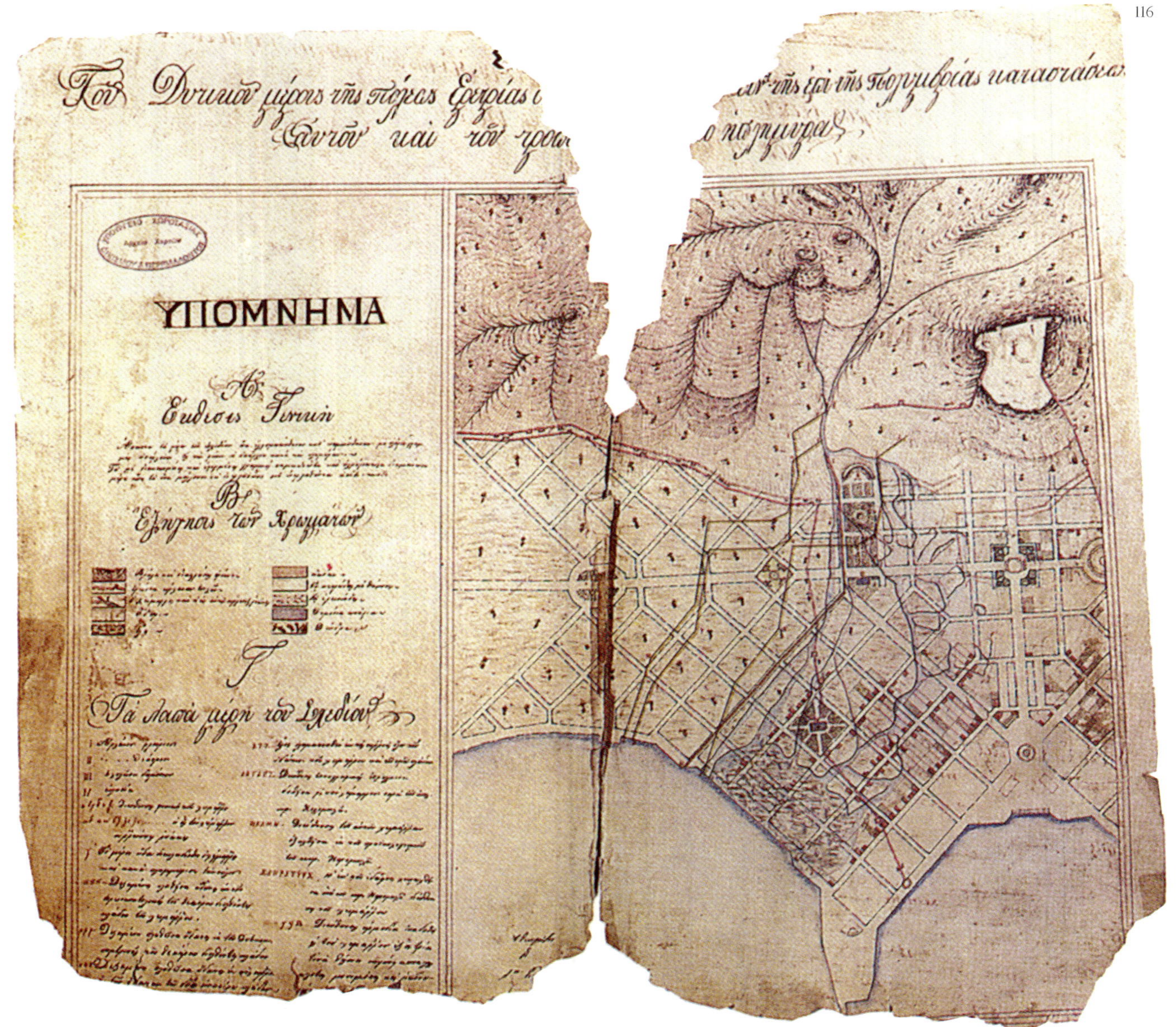

117

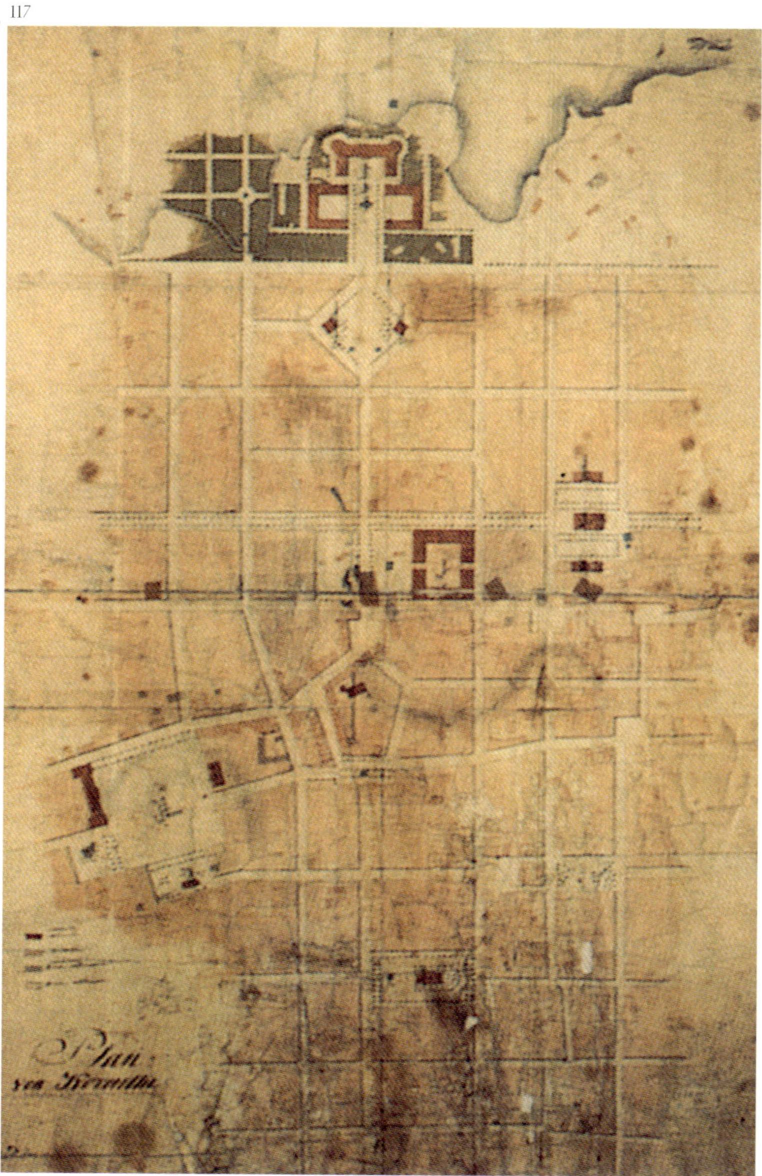

THE PELOPONNESE (MOREA)

From Corinth to Methoni

The Peloponnese (formerly Morea) accounts for the greatest density of town plans drawn up in the whole of the country as it then was.[202] Things could hardly be otherwise, since the Peloponnese dominated free Greece in terms of both its population and its economy. We shall confine ourselves to some of its large settlements, together with some other, smaller ones that have distinctive features.

A new settlement, Corinth, was founded on 10.5.1857 at Schoinia,[203] to house the population of Old Corinth,[204] 8 km. away, and that of the nearby villages that had been destroyed by earthquake (figs. 117, 118). Long before this, however, the site had played an albeit minor role in the debate on the new capital, during the period of Kapodistrias, since it lay at the centre of gravity of the country and since the prospects of digging the nearby canal had already been raised. The proposal was rejected at this time and it was another fifty years before the canal was constructed. This, however, did not prevent those who were implementing the plan of the new settlement, which we shall examine directly, from building a new quay, before the completion of work on a new ambitious port to provide anchorage for steamships – though these never made their appearance.[205]

Work on the construction of new Corinth began in 1858[206] "on the basis of a most perfect plan, one

117. Corinth, ambitious plan for the new town by E. Schaubert (1836) (source: Map Archive, Ministry of Environment, Planning and Public Works).
118. Corinth, later plan for the settlement, 1858 (source: Map Archive, Ministry of Environment, Planning and Public Works).

of the best for that period, with vertical and parallel intersecting wide streets and large tree-lined squares." Another earthquake in 1928 razed the town to the ground, whereupon the Independent Organisation of Earthquake Victims of Korinthia Province was founded, which undertook to rebuild the settlement with anti-seismic structures and with slight deviations from the earlier plan. Apart from its densely built centre, New Corinth followed the principles of 'garden cities'.[207] The rectangular plan is intersected diagonally by the bed of a winter torrent and includes two squares, an open one above the harbour and one at about the centre of the settlement, with the public buildings around it.

It is worth adding a few details here about two other new settlements intended to flank the Corinth canal: Isthmia at its east end and Poseidonia at the west, designed by General Türr, the president of the canal company. Each of these settlements spread on both sides of the canal. The former was intended for the staff and administration of the company, and by the end of 1883 had 98 houses and 10 shops. The latter remained at the design stage.[208]

As we proceed along the west coast of the Peloponnese (prefectures of Achaia, Ilia and Messinia), we encounter a series of harbour-towns founded in the 19th century on old or new sites to serve the export trade to Europe (farm produce, mainly currants) before the opening of the Corinth Canal. Prominent amongst these

118

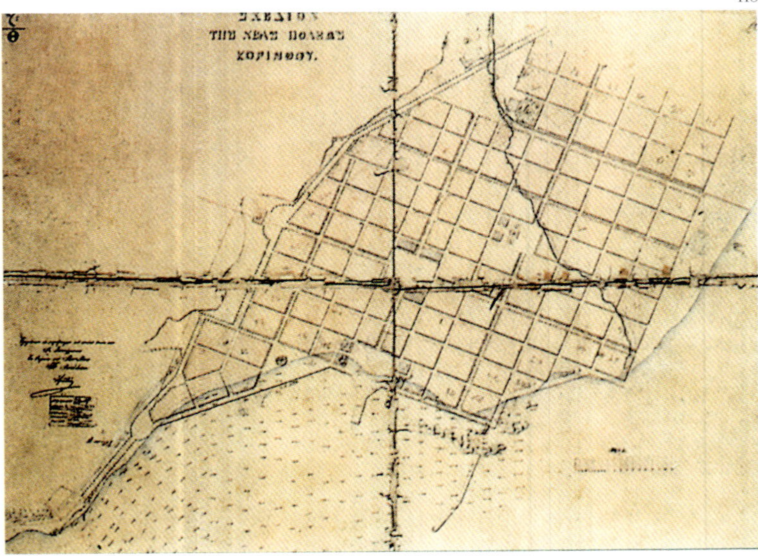

are Patra, now the largest settlement in the Peloponnese, Pyrgos (with the port of Katakolo) and Kalamata. Of these we shall concentrate our attention on the first and on its neighbour, Aigio, before dealing with a number of smaller, distinctive settlements, from Kyllini and Kyparissia to the fine castles of Messinia (Pylos, Methoni and Koroni) and Petalidi. Filiatra and Gargalianoi, south of Kyparissia, are of some interest, though we shall not be dealing with them. In these last three settlements, which were endowed with plans in the last quarter of the century[209] but afterwards experienced only moderate development, it can now be seen that internal alleys were laid out as culs-de-sac in some building blocks of the grid, to enable construction on plots smaller than those originally designed.

Aigio (Byzantine Vostitsa) is from one point of view a miniature Patra, to which it is very close. They share three common features: there was an ancient settlement on the same site, the town is developed on two terraces, and it was also a large port exporting currants. And a fourth coincidence: the square with a distant view and with "a very charming garden" where the locals took their stroll,[210] is called Psila Alonia (Upper Threshing Floors) in both towns. The presence of important buildings by the great architect Ernst Ziller, particularly at Aigio (figs. 119, 121),[211] shows that it once competed consciously with its neighbour, the major centre of Achaia. There are also differences: the Lower Town of Aigio

119. Aigio, the church of the Phaneromeni, by E. Ziller (1890), with modern buildings around it.

120

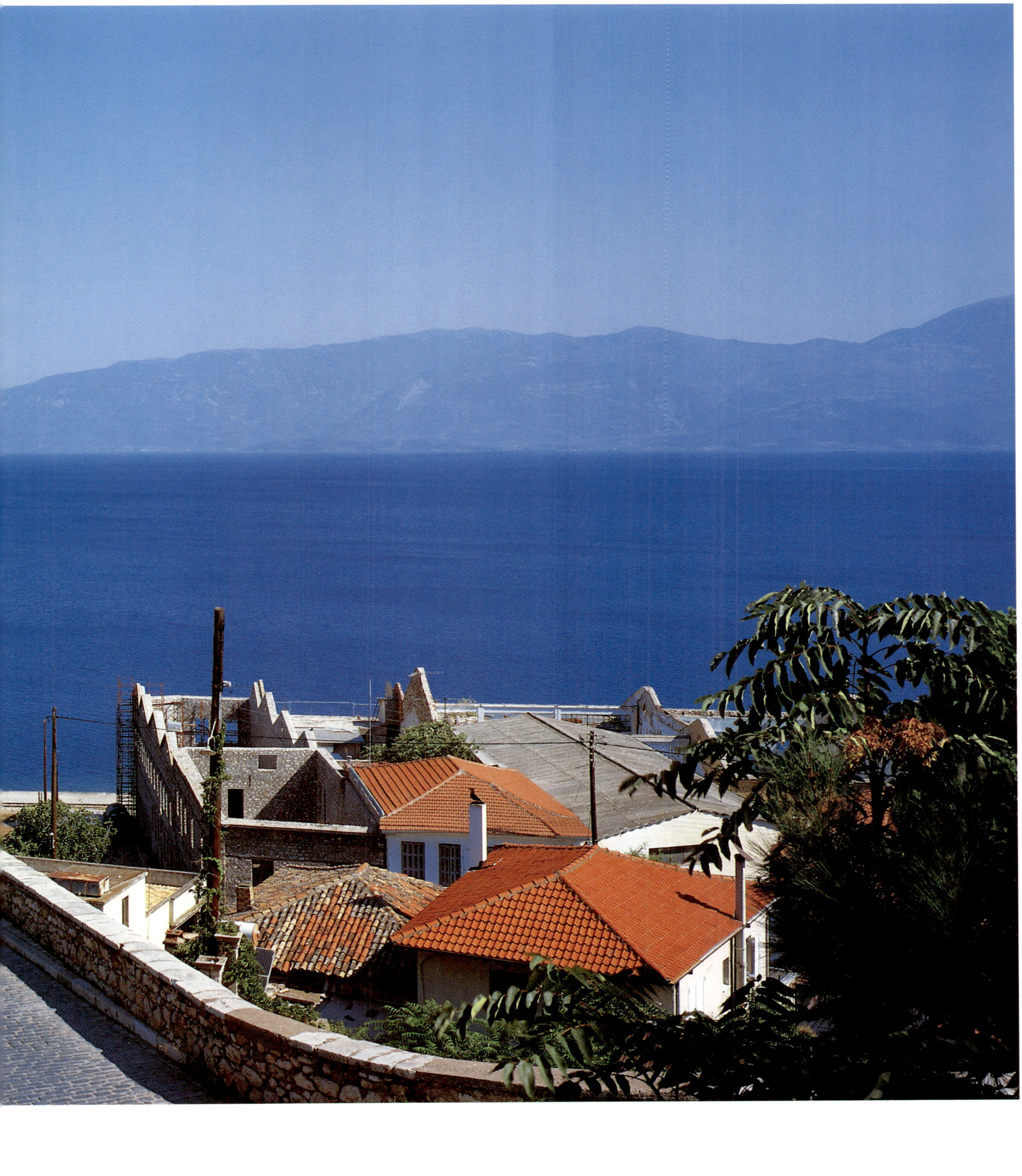

120. Aigio, view towards the sea from the highest part of the settlement.

121

121. Aigio, the present Archaeological Museum, housed in the building of the old Market, by E. Ziller.

covers a narrow strip of land[212] in contrast with the Upper Town, which is the only area capable of being extended (figs. 120, 122-124). In Patra things operated the other way round; the upper (old) town never played a leading role, while the coast had unlimited potential for development.

Although Aigio suffered two earthquakes (1861, 1888) it remained a "fine verdant" town until quite late in the 20th century, with four districts that had a good street layout, with regular pavements, and with the market as its main feature.[213] What it lost in development it gained in attraction. The description of the society of Aigio before the Second World War recalls things that are possibly forgotten today but are close to the image of the neoclassical town that we are seeking to identify here: "The society of Aigio has a tendency to imitate the social customs of the large towns, in a transitional state between provincial township and a town of the first order. The crowds that jostle either in the market, or in Psila Alonia Square, present a mosaic from the point of view of their dress; there are amongst them, that is to say, people wearing their carefully ironed *fustanella* [old peasant dress] or their famous cape, and others dressed in the latest art of the Athenian tailors."[214] The most recent earthquake of 1995 threatened a large part of this charming atmosphere, as summarised in the street with neoclassical buildings that links the church of the Eisodia with the Market (now the Museum).[215]

122

123

124

122-124. Aigio, neoclassical buildings.

125

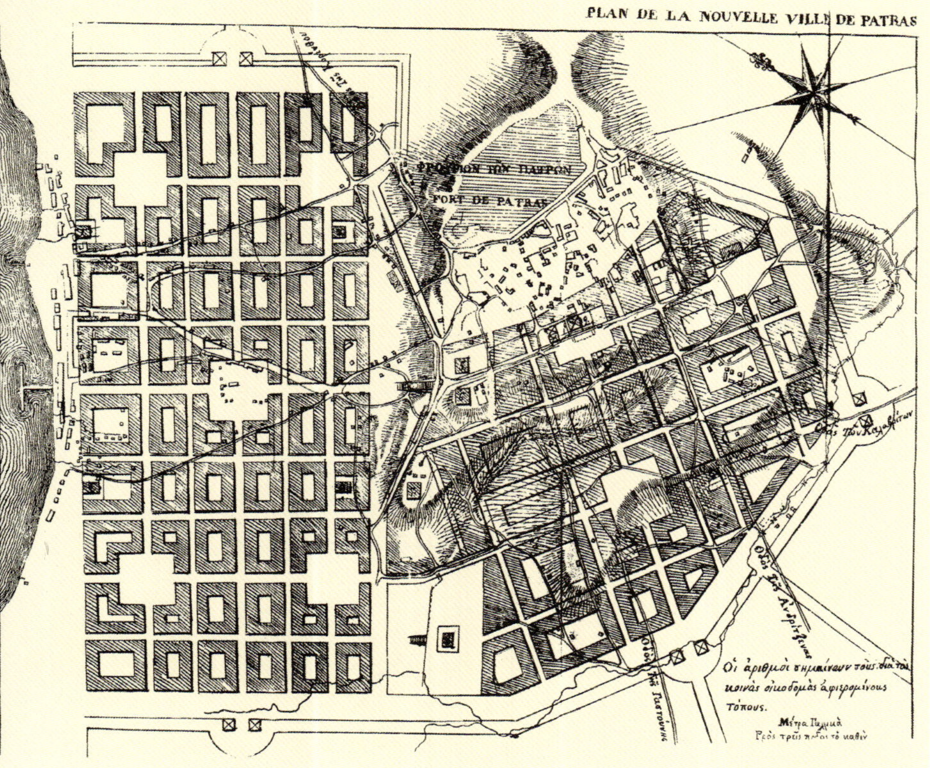

Stamatis Voulgaris designed the modern settlement of Patra, the largest urban centre in the Peloponnese (figs. 126-128, 132-135), in 1829[216] on the traces of the town that had already developed there from ancient times to the Middle Ages and the Ottoman period. In the Ottoman period, the town was concentrated in the south part of the fortress, and from 1829 onwards it began to be built up once more in a disorderly fashion,[217] while there were a few installations on the coast. From the end of the 18th century, however, it was already flourishing (trade and industry).[218] On his own initiative Voulgaris designed a new town that was not confined to the area of the existing settlement around the castle, but extended also to the coastal zone at a lower level (fig. 125). There were two reasons for this: he had (properly) foreseen the later development of the harbour of the town, and at the same time was afraid that if he did not deal with the section on the coast, this would be filled with illegal buildings of makeshift construction – a phenomenon that had already begun at that time.[219] It was envisaged that three areas would remain outside the plan: the zone around the castle which was already built up, the intermediate zone (the slope) between the Upper and Lower Town (which was intended to be a green area) and the coastal zone – where, indeed, Voulgaris placed "a line of trees for strolling, for the creation of which he offered his own salary."[220] The angle between the two parts of the town is 70 degrees. The relationship between the

125. S. Voulgaris, the plan for the new town of Patra (1829), which links the old settlement beneath the Castle (right) with a new, coastal settlement (left).
126. Patra, view of a street with the Court House building at the centre of the town.

PARKING
ΓΙΑ ΤΟ ΚΟΙΝΟ
80m

orientation of the grid proposed by Voulgaris and the grid of the Roman city was of particular importance: in the Upper Town they were completely identical, while in the Lower there was a slight divergence; in any case, for some unknown reason, the Roman grid was not rectangular in the coastal zone.[221] The plan has one inexplicable feature, however: the fortification wall around the entire settlement with four "gates", at a time when this kind of defence work no longer had any meaning.[222] There is another distinctive feature of the plan: the built-up area of city blocks is shown as a band of uniform width: is this merely a simplification, or does it signify something else? Could it indicate a type of layout that was to make its appearance a century later?[223]

Voulgaris sent his plan to Kapodistrias for approval, and quickly received a positive reply, with some reservations. The President saw that the area covered by the plan was too large ("its measurements appear to be longer then necessary"), and its streets were too wide (so that in summer, the sun would shine "heavily and unpleasantly" on the streets and squares). Kapodistrias also undertook to meet half the cost of planting trees near the coast. There is no comment about the perimeter fortification wall.[224]

The plan, of course, was not completely followed as it progressed. Its principles were ignored, its area and the number of squares (figs. 131, 136)

127, 128. Patra, old and new arcades, characteristic features of the street layout in the centre of the Lower Town.

127

128

129

129. Patra, the later church of Ayios Andreas, built to the winning designs in an international competition in 1904.

130. Patra, the church of the Pantanassa, which together with those of the Evangelistria and Ayios Andreas (cf. Fig. 129) are the main churches of the town.

131

were reduced, and all the green areas envisaged were converted into building plots.[225] It also seems that it was not easy to compensate the owners of the Upper Town with plots of land in the Lower Town.[226] Other dangers, too, arose: "We seize this opportunity of communicating a good deed by Mr. Kolettis. The illegal sales of building plots and other spots in Patras by Xepapas Valvis to his close relatives, for about 60,000 drachmas, during the last moments of his ministry, have been revoked by Mr. Kolettis [...]".[227]

A decade later there were further scandals in the distribution of building plots: "Forty buildings have been constructed without the lawful permit. The public building plots lying on the coast, opposite the house of Patrinos, were given to fishermen, supposedly to sell their fish, but they have built little houses and pay a few coins a month in rent to the directorate of sycophants and vultures."[228]

We also have an extensive, if not very flattering, description by a Greek from Odessa (1850): "The town of Patra is the only one [...] that is fortunate enough to have a European character, and a plan which, though small, is rarely found even in the modern towns of Europe; the town of Patra, which occupies first place on account of its extensive trade and lies on an appropriate site [...] occupied by about twenty thousand people, [...] this link, which connects west Europe with Greece, founded from its initial regeneration

131. Patra, the Apollo theatre by E. Ziller (1871-72), on the main square, Vasileos Georgiou I Square. 132, 133. (next page) Patra, characteristic arcades in the centre of the town. 134. (next page) Patra, the old Municipal Hospital in the Upper Town, now a cultural centre. 135. (next page) Patra, view showing the size of typical buildings before the erection of apartment blocks; at the right is the Anglican church of St. Andrew (1872).

132

133

34

by foreign settlers [...] ought to be on a better [...] site. [...] The streets of this fine town of Patra with its wide avenues, are at all times, and particularly at winter, impassable, and more dirty, irregular and ill kept than the Jewish quarters of Turkish towns [...]. The town of Patra, which has an area equal to that of Trieste, [...] is lit at night time by only five lamps [...] but leaving aside matters that refer to the external beautification of a town, which is necessary but entirely material, [...] it is the following that made the worst impression on me [...]. In Patra there are many thousands of foreigners from the nearby Ionian islands [...] these men [...] set up large numbers of tables regularly in all the streets of the town, hold a pack of playing cards in their hands and [...] call upon passers-by [...]."[229]

Twenty years later, the Municipal Theatre designed by E. Ziller (1872) was built on [King] Georgiou Square and the further development of the town followed two familiar methods: embellishment (the creation of the square at Psila Alonia) and technical projects (the designing of the harbour).[230] The enormous importance of its harbour, indeed, which assigned Patra to third place after Piraeus and Hermoupolis in the 19th century,[231] was to be maintained in the future, as is evident from the fact that ocean-going liners en route to America (emigration) put in here before the Second World War[232] and also from the modern sea-links with the Adriatic.

136. Patra, Trion Symmachon Square, between Ayiou Andreou and Othonos - Amalias Streets, at the end of Ayiou Nikolaou Street toward the sea.

1.6

The distinctive character of Kyparissia is that the town derives from the moving of the earlier medieval settlement of Arkadia, built beneath a now ruined fort, which was once more given its ancient name, Kyparissia, thanks to King Otto. It was designed in 1871 as a new settlement in the coastal plains of Messinia,[233] so that it could develop into "a large farm town"[234] 2 km. away from its original site. The difference between the two is impressive. In the eyes of one aware of the virtues of neoclassical towns, historical Arkadia is judged unacceptable from every view point: "[...] although from the outside it appears to be an agreeable town, when one enters one cannot walk in it because of the irregularity of the streets; these are all at oblique angles and are very unpleasant, because not only was no plan provided, but even today anyone builds as he wishes and leaves a pathway where and as he wants, without being prevented by anyone. These streets are overwhelmed by piles of stones from the now demolished ruins, and other rubbish, so that people cannot walk in them [...]".[235]

In contrast with the negative image of the old town, Coastal Kyparissia[236] possesses a regular plan: it has a grid of streets intersecting at right angles and at equal distances from each other, and is sparsely built, with gardens and courtyards. Only one

137. Kyparissia, view of part of the old semi-mountainous settlement (original name: Arkadia, now: Upper Town).

37

138

feature is missing: character. Its boundaries are arbitrary and random, with no relationship to distinct features of the landscape. It is obviously artificially implanted, a man-made structure in the fields (fig. 140). By contrast, Arkadia, despite being administratively downgraded and relatively deserted, continued to exist at the end of the 19th century. Not as a truly neoclassical town, which it could never become, but as a substitute for one. This mixture of ruins and efforts to acquire now coveted features such as squares and neoclassical buildings, now a listed settlement, still gives it a moving interest.

138. Kyparissia, the old settlement, Upper Town, beneath the castle. 139. Kyparissia, the square in the Upper Town with a monument to the fallen in war. 140. Kyparissia, view of a street in the Lower Town, the modern coastal settlement.

139

140

141

The modern settlement of Pylos (figs. 142-144) lies in a region with a particularly rich history, from ancient times to the Greek War of Independence (1821). This is attested, moreover, by the alternative names of the town, borrowed from neighbouring historical place-names (Niokastro, Navarino, and Pylos). According to the plan of 1831,[237] (fig. 141) the settlement evidently developed beneath the castle (Niokastro),[238] following the slope of the terrain and forming an irregular arrangement of closely packed buildings that followed very few straight lines. The plan attempts discreetly to impose order, tracing streets that unify the two hitherto isolated groups of buildings on the corresponding hillsides, at the same time indicating how the settlement might be extended in the future.[239]

I shall close this unit with brief references to Methoni and Petalidi, two distinctive settlements in the Messinia Prefecture.

In Methoni, interest is focused on the combination of the imposing Venetian fortified settlement and the small, modern settlement that developed outside the fortification walls (figs. 147-149). Judging by the Plan des Environs de Modon (fig. 145),[240] the plan drawn up in 1829 ignored the linear arrangement of buildings along the coast road (to Koroni) that had already developed in an unplanned manner, and chose to incorporate the buildings on the hillside at the west, thus distributing the new

141. Pylos (Navarino), plan of the new settlement, 1831.
142. Pylos, view of the settlement from Niokastro in a photograph taken in the 1980s, showing the homogeneous form of houses with neoclassical influences. 143. (next page) Pylos, view of the modern settlement from the harbour.

144. Pylos, typical three-storey neoclassical building outside the dense tissue of the settlement.

settlement either side of the stream, with a large gap in the direction of the castle, which was already planted up. This left a reasonable distance between the fortification walls and the new settlement, as required by the still unclear security regulations of the period. In contrast, Petalidi, with its "fine harbour" acquired a new settlement, in which people from Mani were settled, and for which the Royal Decree of 10.11.1834 made significant areas of land available. Bavarians drew up its plan (fig. 146), with a rectangular street grid, "a rational disposition of functions" and "a spacious square". Building work on it began in 1835 and it had soon acquired a market, a school and commercial activity.[241]

145

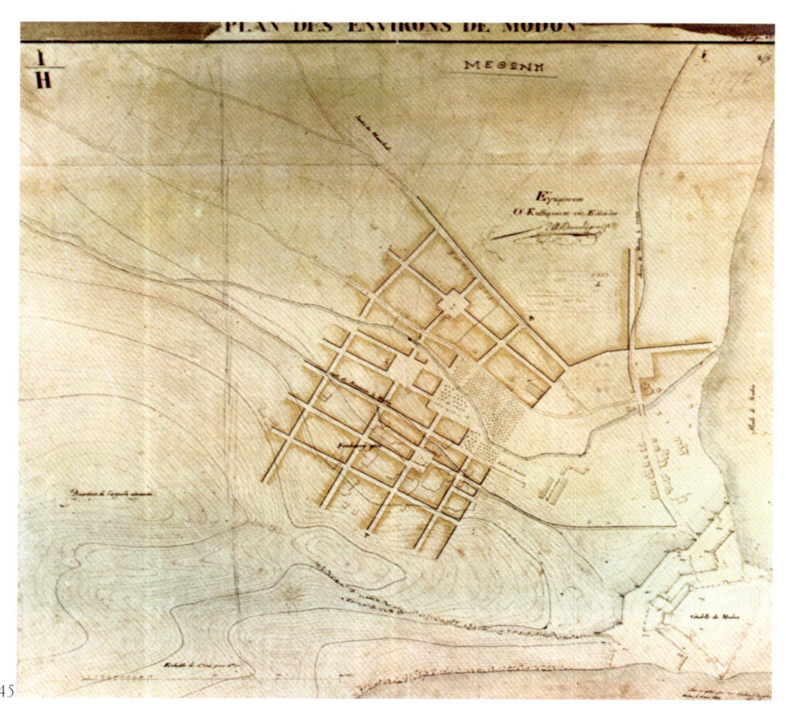

146

145. Methoni, plan of the new settlement, 1829. 146. Petalidi, plan of the new settlement, work on which began in 1835. 147, 148. Methoni, views of the present settlement.

149. Methoni, the relationship between the Venetian fortifications and the new town.

149

150

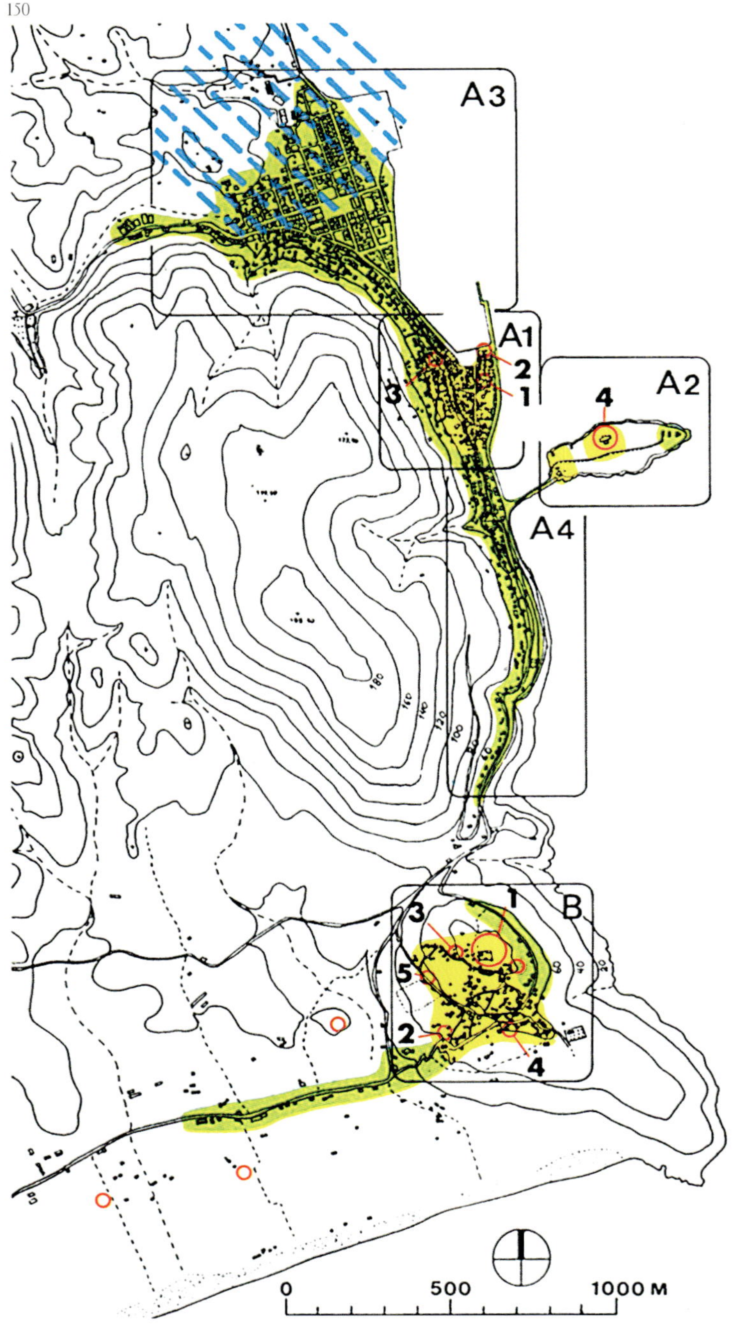

From Gytheio to Nafplio

Even in rebellious Mani, which was in a continuous state of turmoil, there is an example of town planning: Gytheio. On its site, which before the Second World War, at least, was regarded as the "showcase of Lakonia", there was already a settlement dating from the last quarter of the 18th century, which included Marathonisi and Mavrovouni. After the creation of the modern Greek state, the settlement was renamed Gytheio and was given an orthogonal grid plan in 1861,[242] on the basis of which it was extended to the north in the second half of the 19th century, as far as the site of the ancient city there. In the period 1865-70 the old anchorage was filled in to create a public square. Later (1898), the settlement was extended to the south along the road to Mavrovouni (fig. 150).[243] The site of the settlement has a limited area: if one excepts the beautiful coastal avenue with its marble kerbstones (fig. 151), the rest of the settlement has no "spacious squares" nor any straight streets with "seemly houses". The chronological order in which the public buildings were erected at Gytheio is of some interest. The first, in about 1850, was a school, followed in 1886 by a Girls' School, in 1891 the Town Hall, in 1912 the Bishop's Residence, in 1914 a Gymnasium and in 1927 a factory supplying water and electricity.[244] Today it has a good tourist infrastructure.

150. Gytheio, map showing the archaeological site (top) in contact with the modern town, with Marathonisi (Kranai) further to the south and, at the bottom, Mavrovouni (drawn by Yannis Saitas). 151. Gytheio, view of the settlement in a photograph taken in the 1980s.

ROTHMANS

152

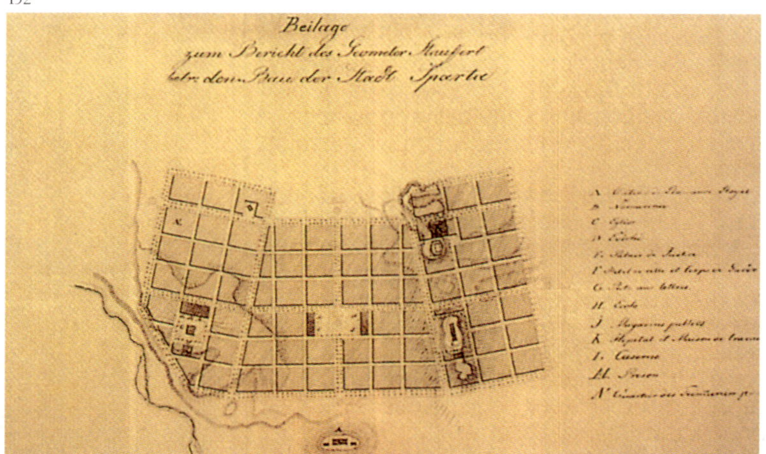

The foundation of Sparti was due to the express desire of King Ludwig of Bavaria to revive the names of the glorious cities of antiquity. The ancient site of Sparta was already known, so a new town had to be designed to the south of it – and not above it, as was to happen in the case of many other settlements. A factor contributing to this decision was the representations made to Otto by merchants from Mystras, the nearest settlement to Sparta, near the Byzantine ruins of the same name, who were being strangulated by the inflated rents they were obliged to pay for the few shops there.[245] The motives were thus mixed, both ideological and commercial. A third factor, initially perhaps unforeseen, was that the site of the new settlement was at the centre of rich farmland, with of a large number of mulberry trees, that had the potential to move its products by sea (ports of Gytheio[246] and Kalamata). This attracted interest in industrial investment (silk factories) and in exports to Europe during the second half of the 19th century.[247] This trend had already emerged earlier, albeit on a small scale: in 1838 we read of K. Feggaras, who "made significant modifications to the local oil-presses and was the first [...] and [...] intends to introduce the European manner", and of the family of N. Louizelis, which set up a "silk-thread" factory.[248]

The Royal Decree founding Sparti on 26.12.1833 provides that the government "should grant

152. Sparti, plan of the new town next to the ancient city, 1834 (source: General State Archives, Ministry of the Interior. File 114). 153, 154. Two views of the metropolitan church of the Evangelistria, built on a hill next to Lykourgou Street.

153

154

155

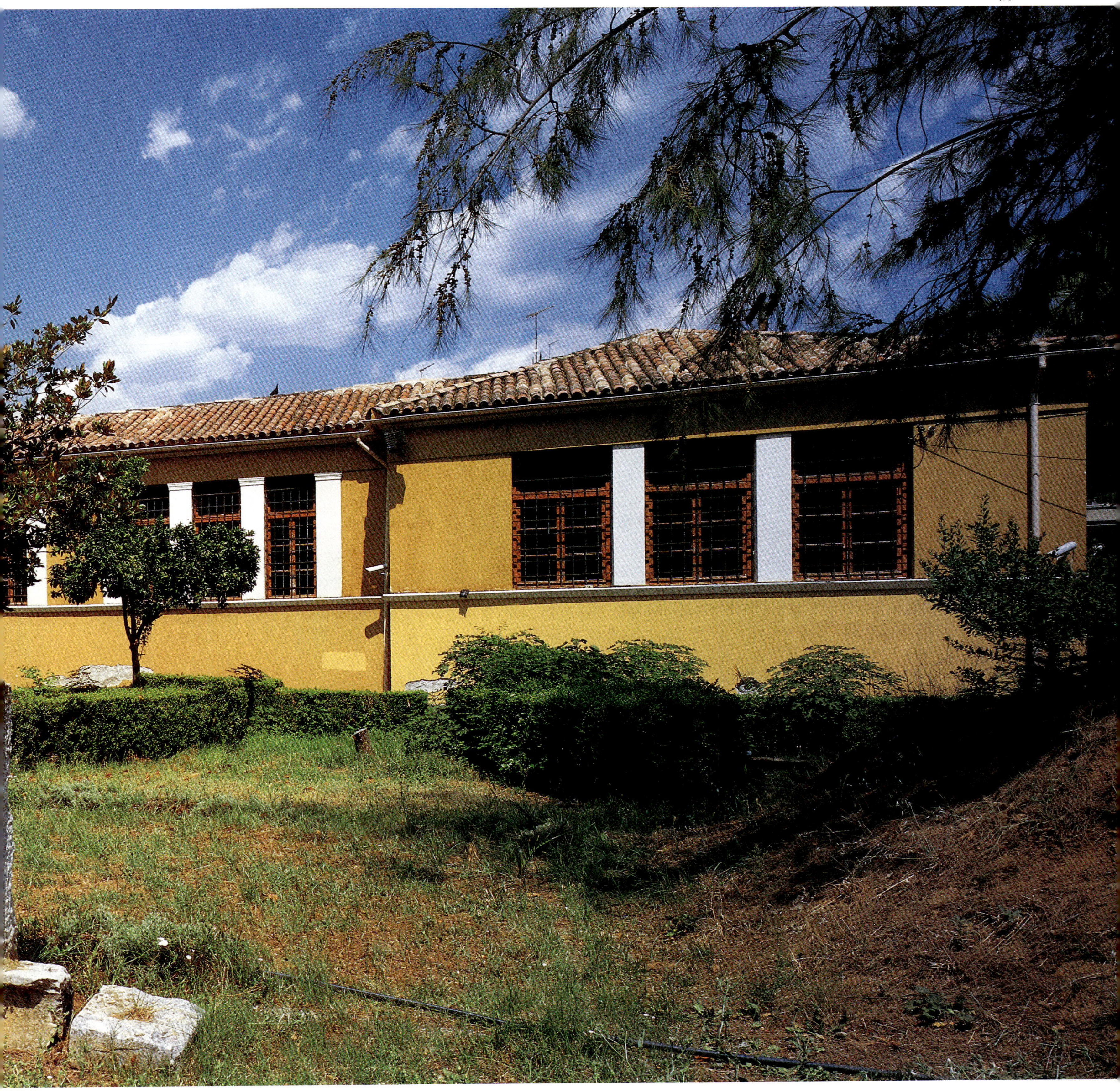

155. Sparti, the Archaeological Museum in Nikonos Street, by Th. Hansen (1875-76).

156, 157. Sparti, neoclassical buildings. At the left, with consoles beneath the eaves and two-storey pilasters. At the right, a two-storey building with a balcony and a pediment on the main axis.

one stremma of land to everyone who settles there, and it should create primary schools and high schools, and it should encourage trade, farming and industry, so that Spartans will see things that they have never known." Moreover, the Royal Decree properly "grants the inhabitants of Mystras, preferentially, the right to choose plots of land for a period of forty days." In practice, however, those interested received plots of land from 500 to 900 cubits.[249] The plan was a simplified version of the plan for Athens, with the two rectangular parts of the town diverging slightly, in order to open up to the archaeological site (fig. 152), with a tributary of the river Evrotas to the south.[250] The main street (K. Palaiologos Street) intersects Othonos - Amalias Street (where the first inhabitants took their stroll, as we shall see below) at right angles.

To enable the new settlement to establish itself, Mystras "was declared an abandoned" town, and it was not even permitted to repair buildings there. This did not prevent local conflicts from breaking out, since there was little enthusiasm amongst the inhabitants to move to Tourkovouni, as the hill of new Sparti was called.[251] In a characteristic episode, the commercial life of Mystras, in the form of the weekly market, was transferred "by very harsh force on the part of the police" to Sparti. In order to overcome the opposition, the government agreed that the market should be held successively at

158. Sparti, characteristic wide streets of the rectangular grid in the centre of the town with neoclassical and modern buildings.

58

the two towns, but when it was the turn of Sparti, the inhabitants complained because they did not find there "the shady trees and the cool waters which we have in Mystras", whereupon they tried to set up the market illegally in Mystras and were driven away by the police.[252]

Despite these difficulties, the first signs of optimism for the future of Sparti emerged in 1835: "I announce to you also that the town of Sparti under erection is making progress, the bishopric is approaching completion, the foundations of ten private houses have been laid, a vast number of building plots have been registered, and many are preparing to build on them. [...] Sparta, 8 December 1835."[253] And the same climate prevailed a year later: "Announcement from Mystras: that the city under erection on the site of old Sparta is making progress as we would wish, thirteen houses are approaching their completion, the foundations of about one hundred have been laid, and those of three or four are being laid daily." There were not enough builders, even though they were being paid high wages.[254] In 1837 an ancient well was found on the building plot of a silk factory,[255] and, more importantly, a road was under construction to link Sparti with Gytheio in order to bolster trade: "In the town being settled, which lies on a conspicuous airy hill in the centre of the province [...]. Forty houses have been built, some of which have the appropriate spaciousness and embellishment."[256]

159. Sparti, typical neoclassical residence restored for a new use.

The problems were overcome albeit temporarily, and gradually "nascent" Sparti acquired a notable industry (advanced oil-press, silk factory),[257] while the "fine plan of the town" and the "unexpected progress in so short a space of time" impressed the members of the royal family who visited it in 1838.[258] A year earlier, the new model of life was being promoted quite strongly: "equality, friendship and harmony are the characteristics of the Spartans. One sees with great pleasure civil servants and private citizens walking together in Othonos and Amalias Street."[259] Conversely, however, the picture was completely negative two years later: there were still no public buildings, the weekly market was in decline, plots of land were no longer offered even for auction, land was not being made available on the periphery of the town for farming, "even if one wished to pay for it".[260]

In 1840 we again read paeans of praise: "The new Sparti being built to a regular plan on the territory of ancient Sparta between two rivers [...] is becoming a beautiful town, magnificent, hygienic, centrally placed, and renowned all over the Province, and consequently the only acceptable and worthy, as in the past, capital of Lakonia."[261] Yet four years later, again a taste of bad news: "The thousands of wrongdoers, night-thieves and others we learn today that they are tearing apart our town [...] it is not only the condition of the capital city that is wretched. The condition of the provinces is even more wretched and unfortunate.

160

160. Sparti, entrance to the courtyard of a neoclassical house lavishly adorned with clay statues.

161

In Sparti eight or ten men circulate and frequent the streets, stripping, killing and terrifying everyone [...]".[262] These sudden fluctuations reflect similar transitions that are to be found at the same period even in the "safe" city of Athens – indeed, reference is made to this in the above article. In a small town, however, the consequences can be even more painful.[263]

At any rate, the town (figs. 156-161) was gradually to acquire its buildings: in 1838 the Court House (which originally functioned as the Administrative Building) was built, in 1840 130 houses had been completed and in 1844 all the authorities moved from Mystras and the church of the Evangelismos was inaugurated (figs. 153-154).[264] Later, the archaeological museum (Th. Hansen, 1875-76, extended in 1908), the pride of the town, was constructed (fig. 155). The "fine street layout" was completed by two large squares, Olgas Square (in which was the Court House) and Georgiou Square, with porticoes all around it.[265] Nearer the beginning of the 20th century, the Gymnasium was finally built (1895), as were the High School (1908-09)[266] and the Town Hall (G. Katsaros, 1909). Amongst the notable modern buildings in the town are the school complex of Kyriakos Panayiotakos (1930s) and the Olive Museum on the site of the old Electric Company factory (Pleias group, 1998-2001 and 2007) in Othonos and Amalias Street.[267]

161. Sparti, row of neoclassical buildings in Agidos Street, next to the church of the Evangelistria.

162

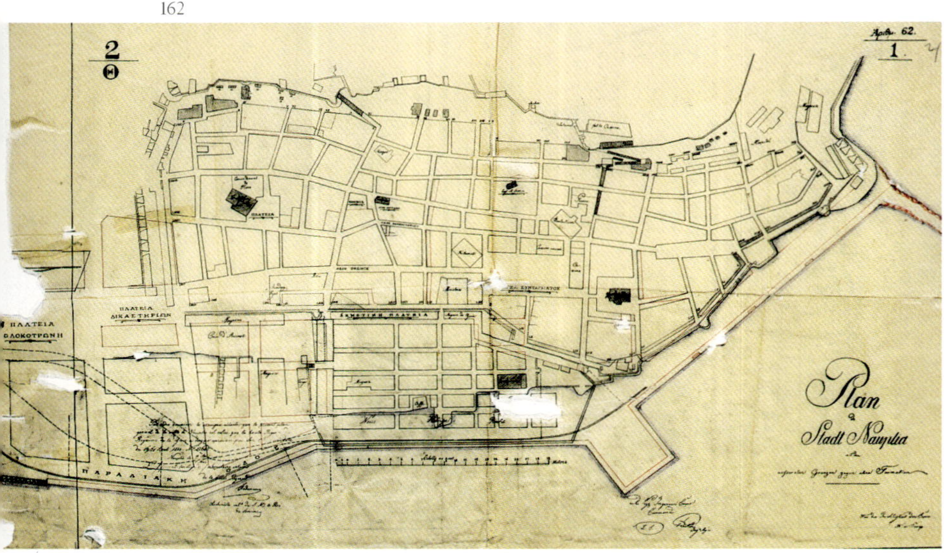

The choice of Nafplio as the original seat of government (1823) and its designation as capital of Greece (Kathedra) (1827), and the arrival of Ioannis Kapodistrias (8.1.1828)[268] signalled an "orgy of architecture", as its "confined space" was filled with "a sample-book of nations of all kinds [...]".[269] The result of this was that the face of town changed yet again: "the [...] fact that the government resided in this town for so long, and the high rents, [...] led to the town being almost completely renewed, its houses being built in the European manner and its streets being laid out in straight lines; so that at first sight, the town of Nauplia today resembles a European town rather than a Turkish one."[270]

The only significant project that survived from the very short – a mere three years – presence of Kapodistrias, who was noted for his town planning ambitions, was the laying of the "Great Street" (now Vasileos Konstantinou street) which leads from the edge of the town to Syntagma Square, with the monumental Venetian Arsenal (now the Archaeological Museum) in the background (fig. 174).[271] The layout of this square was originally the work of the Venetians (second period of Venetian rule), though they were unable to bring it to completion, since it was interrupted by military operations against the Ottomans. When the town was liberated, the long side of the square was bordered by a typical oriental Seraglio, as seen in a watercolour

162. Nafplio, plan of the settlement, 1834. 163. Nafplio (Napoli de Romania), representation of the important Venetian harbour with its fortifications, 1690. 164. Nafplio, view of part of the settlement by L. Lange, showing the area around modern Syntagma Square, with the two mosques that are preserved and with buildings in which elements of Ottoman architecture predominate. 165. (next page) Nafplio, view of the historical centre from Akronafplia.

163

NAPOLI DE ROMANIA.
Castel del Scoio.
A. de Stadt. B. het Casteel. D. het Casteel der Grieken. E. S. Maria del Grotta. F. S. Thodaro. G den Bergh Palamido.
Gasp: Bouttats fecit
ca. 1640
Iac: Peeters. excudit An

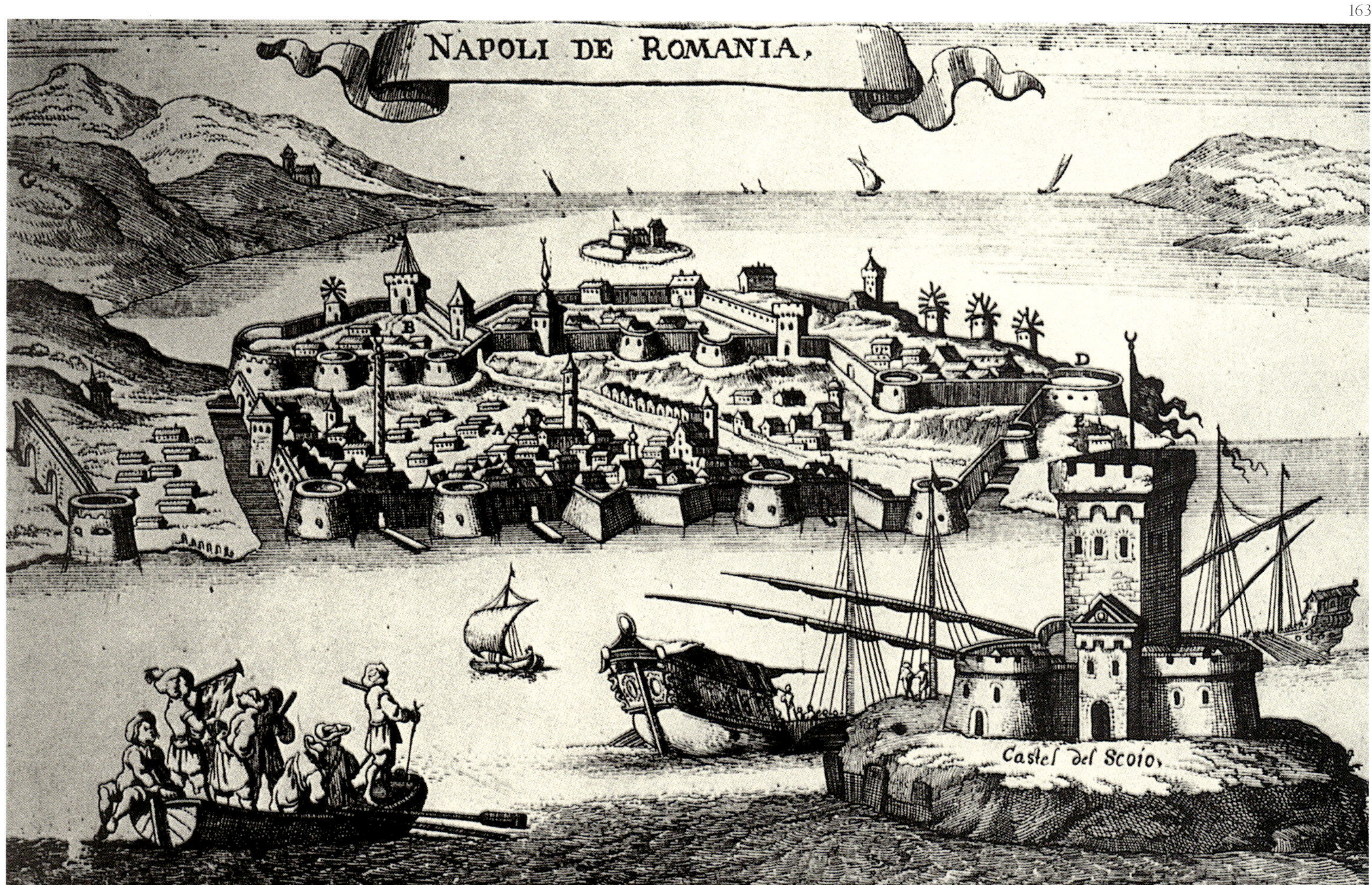

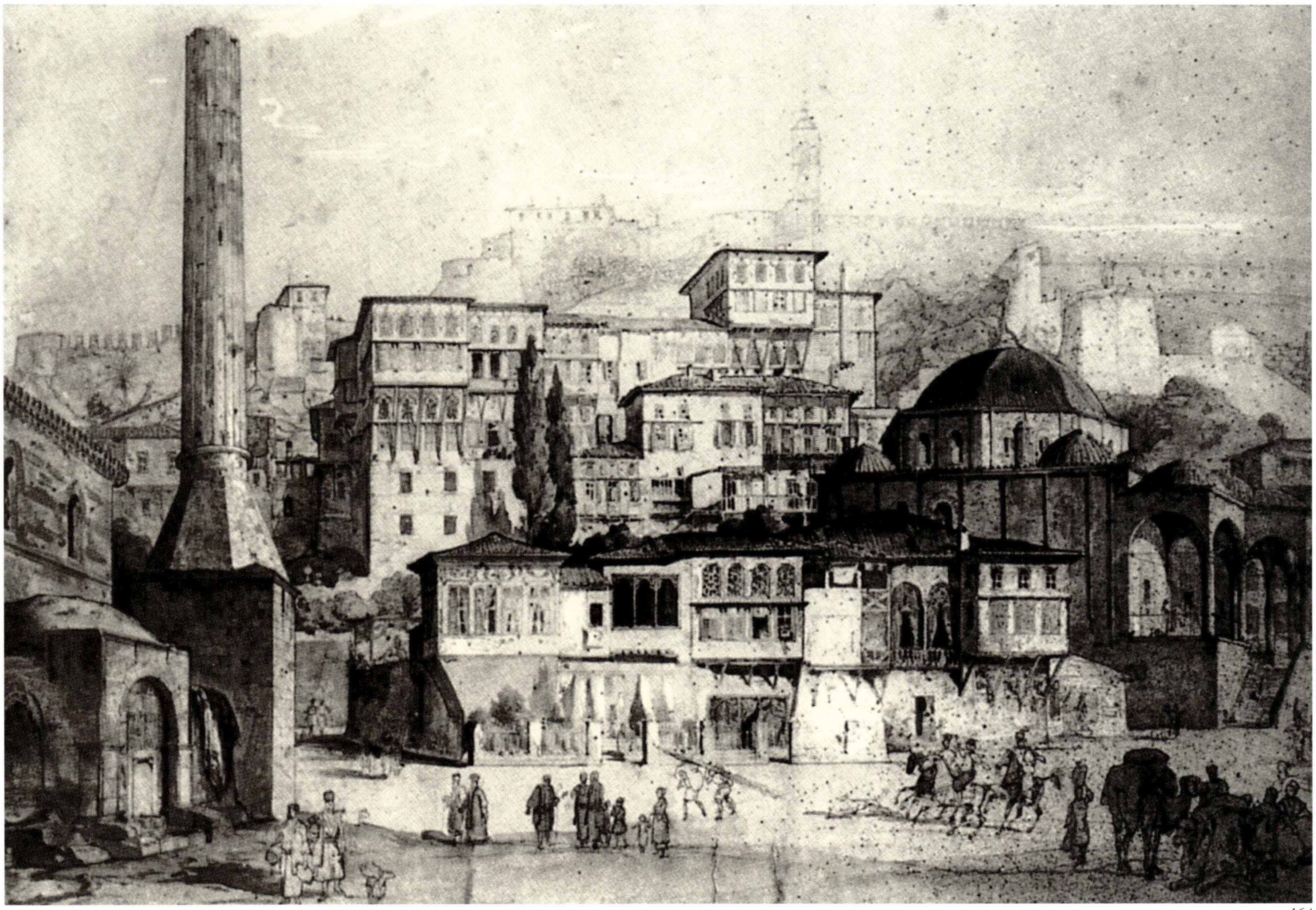

164

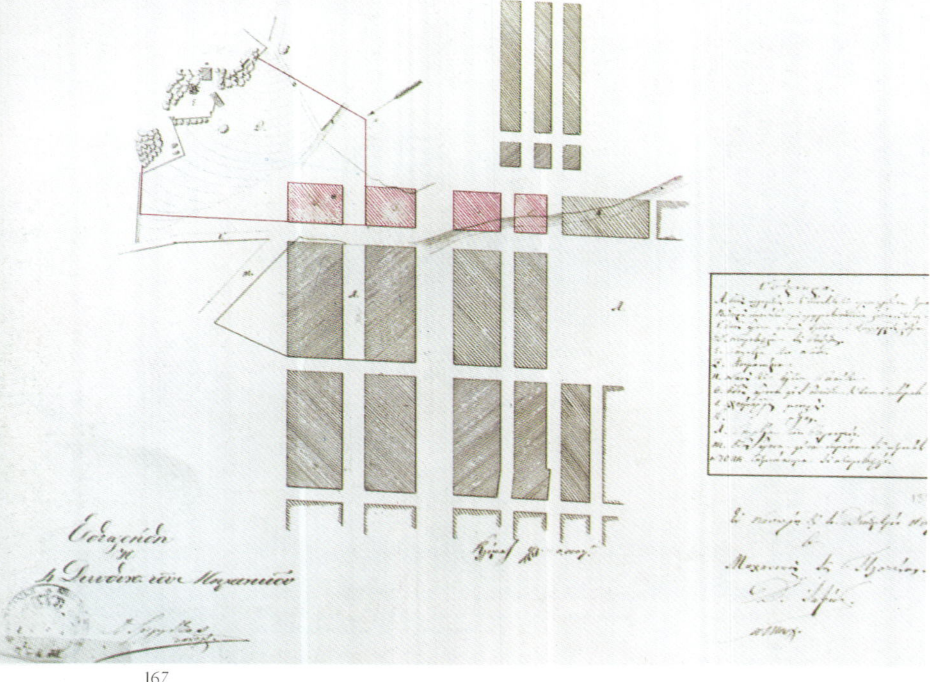

167

by Ludwig Lange (fig. 164).[272] The general image of that town, moreover, with its Ottoman character, even after the interventions of Kapodistrias, can be seen clearly in the background of the painting of the reception given to King Otto (fig. 166). It is only in this way that we can assess the extent of the changes that had to take place to produce the 'neoclassical Nafplio' that we know today, beneath the Akronafplia fortress (figs. 168, 169, 173).

The changes made in the layout of the settlement were perhaps less spectacular, but nonetheless existed. The plan of 1834, attributed to Theothoros Vallianos and Stamatis Voulgaris,[273] records the long, rectangular layout of the old town beneath Akronafplia, as formed during the successive conquests of Napoli de Romania – as it was formerly called – by Venetians and by Ottomans (fig. 163). This can still largely be recognised, apart from the sea walls (now demolished)[274] that enclosed the town on the south and the coastline next to them, which was later largely filled in. To the south of the fortification wall, indeed, an extension of the town based on a regular grid of streets was traced, with perceptibly smaller building blocks then in the old town. In other words, the earlier building blocks not only had an irregular outline but were also inappropriately large for modern construction, which was based on a typical building plot: they could not, that is, be divided into equal plots, as the rule for the neoclassical town dictated.

166. Nafplio, painting of the reception of King Otto, as he arrived by boat in Greece (1833), with the town in the background (source: *Istoria tou Ellinikou Ethnous*, vol. 13). 167. Drawing of part of the 'Suburb of the Town of Nauplia', 1847. 168. Nafplio, view of Philellinon Square. 169. Nafplio, the Venetian Arsenal, now the Archaeological Museum (right) and the mosque in the background, which now belongs to the Archaeological Service.

170-172. Nafplio, characteristic neoclassical buildings in the historical centre, showing forms from the earliest (fig. 170, right and 172, right) to those typical of the late 19th century (170, left and 171), and the latest from the early 20th century (fig. 170, background).

The other innovation of the period of Kapodistrias was the designing of the suburb of Pronoia to the east of Nafplio, where Cretan refugees were settled. The National Assembly met in the square of this suburb in 1832 to welcome King Otto.[275] All of this, however, was abandoned with the final transfer of the capital to Athens: "The Respectable Government left our town a short while ago. The reduction (not to say stagnation) of trade and other exchanges has been so perceptible [...] that people are reasonably shocked at the unexpected decline of the once populous commercial city within the space of a few days."[276] Despite this fact, the city continued to grow (fig. 167).

This marked an abrupt change from an administrative and trade centre to a minor provincial town, though one that enjoyed a certain political and military prestige down to the dethronement of King Otto (1862), and which continued to develop, albeit at a slow rate.[277] The change thereafter helped to preserve 'old' Nafplio intact, now in the form of a neoclassical town, down to the period when it began to be threatened by remorseless tourist exploitation.[278] Thus, the neoclassical character of old Nafplio, originally an example of past glories and decline, ultimately led to a revival of the present town as a service centre, since precisely these characteristics are appreciated as a competitive advantage.

173. Nafplio, the Court House on 25 Martiou Street with the Palamidi in the background. 174. (next page) Nafplio, view of Syntagma Square, with the Archaeological Museum in the background. The modern square was designed by Alexandros and Charis Kalligas, 1983.

173

Café
δωδώνη

noufara • εστιατόριο • καφε

Part III

The Greek Islands

AEGEAN ISLANDS

From Lesvos to Andros

The distinctive character of the three large islands in the Eastern Aegean – Lesvos, Samos and Chios – is due to the considerable degree of industrial development that they underwent during the final phase of the Ottoman occupation (1880-1912), thanks to the implementation of the relevant state policy. Given the nature of the local produce, Lesvos was oriented towards olive growing and the other two islands towards tanning.[279] In the main settlements of these islands it would be easy to identify abundant traces of modernised town planning (street layout, infrastructure networks, harbour installations) which, in combination with the erection of important public buildings, attest to the influence of classicism. It would be preferable, however, to mention the complex of industrial installations created at that time, on the rationale that these perhaps represent more directly the new attitudes that accompanied the dissemination of neoclassicism within the Ottoman Empire. This will in any case make clearer the affinities between the layout of such installations and those of Hermoupolis, which we shall encounter immediately afterwards.

According to Nikos Sifounakis, there is on Lesvos "an impressive dispersal of industrial buildings [...]. They are to be found at the entrances to the settlements, in olive-groves, and also in industrial zones on the island (Perama, Plomari, Dipi

175. (spread) Hermoupolis, buildings on the south side of Miaouli Square. 176. (spread) Hermoupolis, Cyclades Workers Centre (Velissaropoulos Mansion, 1871), detail of the interior decoration.

178

177. Hermoupolis, detail of the side of the church of Ayios Nikolaos (Y. Metaxas, 1848-70) facing on to Babayiotou Street. 178. Hermoupolis, view of the town from the sea, after 1840, showing the main landmarks. 179. (next page) Hermoupolis, view of the east part of the town from the Vaporia district.

and Tabakaria), near the sea, on makeshift anchorages."[280]

Similarly, on Samos "the larger part of this activity was concentrated at Riva in the town of Karlovasi. A special zone of warehouses and industrial buildings was created along the coast, between the Fourniotiko and Kerkiteio streams, a short distance from the harbour." While "the town of Chios and the region of Vrontados are still dominated today by the shells of the imposing tannery-factory buildings."[281]

From the Eastern Aegean we move to the most important urban centre in the entire Aegean in the 19th century, Hermoupolis on Syros Island. When their home islands were devastated during the War of Independence, merchants from Chios and Psara fled to the natural harbour of Syros where they formed the town of Hermoupolis.[282] Amidst the uncertainty of war, the first facilities were built in makeshift fashion on the vacant coast, beneath the gaze of the settlement of (Upper) Syros on the hill nearby, on which the local population, of the Catholic creed, was concentrated.[283] Since the two communities represented conflicting religious creeds, their coexistence was uneasy. In 1841 Alexandros Axiotis, the eparch of Syros, describes the difficulties encountered in the attempt to find a building plot on which to erect the church of the Metamorphosis. The "local Syrians would not give even an inch of land to the settlers, however much money they were prepared to offer, particularly

180. Hermoupolis, Tsiropina Square, with the Cyclades Prefecture building at the centre, in the Vaporia district.

180

181

since the issue in question was the erection of a church of the Eastern Creed."[284] The children's stone-throwing game that developed into a general conflict between the two communities in 1842[285] is indicative of relations between them.

As early as 1828, the population of the town had reached about fourteen thousand, and according to Fr. Thiersch, in 1833 Hermoupolis "[...] numbers 5,000 houses and 17,000 inhabitants. Here one finds a shipyard, inns of all kinds, schools, a literary society, a casino, a museum, a printing press, a theatre [...]", and all of this "without any aid or financial grant from the Government [...]".[286] This was unusual: private initiative was able to work miracles unaided. The lesson is of an active bourgeoisie, of European inspiration, which was just beginning to emerge in Greece. In practice, of course, this was not without precedent: the active merchants of Hermoupolis had a short time earlier been the successful merchants of Chios.

According to Maria Synarelli, this town was the "leading harbour for Greek imports and a great transit warehouse for the Archipelago, [which] purchases and stores European merchandise in order to distribute it later to mainland Greece and the neighbouring islands." In this way it controls "half the volume of Greek imports and more then 80% of the carrying trade." This was the situation down to the 1880s; thereafter the sceptre passed to a combination of Piraeus (eastern distribution network) and Patra (western network).[287] Given

181. Hermoupolis, Cyclades Workers Centre, interior (cf. fig. 176). 182. Hermoupolis, I. Vardakas Square in front of the restored Apollo theatre (by P. Sampo, 1862-64).

182

183

184

the character of Hermoupolis as a predominantly harbour-town, one can immediately appreciate the importance of its harbour installations. In 1832, a preliminary quay was constructed in a makeshift fashion to the north of the harbour (figs. 183-185). This was followed by the involvement of the town in the processes of the Greek state, with the Royal Decree of 1834 "Concerning the construction of quays on Syros", and a later law of 1849,[288] designating the way in which the project should be financed and the individual projects that should be carried out, which were to continue until 1865. Finally, new extensions began in the 1880s in order to modernise the port,[289] despite the fact that the local economy had already taken a different turn. The industrial installations of the town, which were laid out according to the models of the period in an independent coastal zone next to the city, underwent a similar development.[290] As in many other islands before the advent of steam, shipbuilding and repairing occupied an important place in the local economy and also a large area of the harbour (fig. 187). Although the shipyards continued to operate down to the present day – naturally in a modernised form – the other units gradually closed; they are now the object of historical studies, though some of them have recently been restored and function as museums.

In terms of the designing of the town, the basic point of interest here – that is, the circumstances under which Hermoupolis was created – is reflected in the manner in which it developed,

185

183. Hermoupolis, the construction of the mole of the harbour in a drawing of the period (W. von Weiler, 1841) (source: *Istoria tou Ellinikou Ethnous*, vol. 13).
184, 185. Hermoupolis, the Customs House building, by Al. Georgantas (1859-61).

186

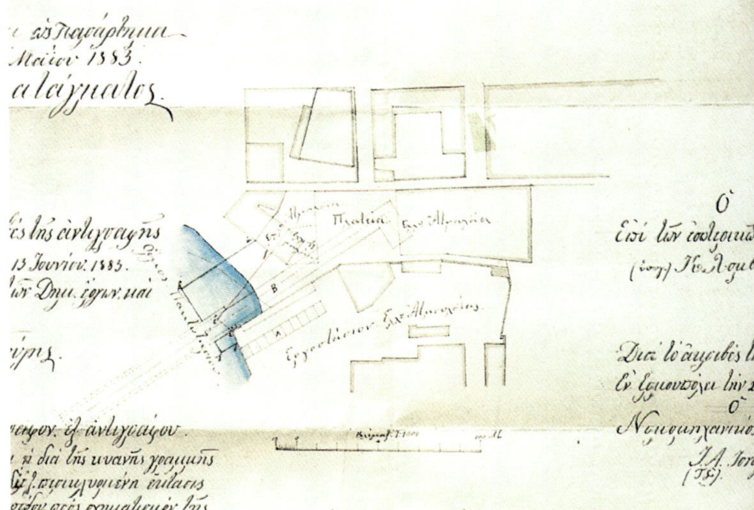

which can be seen clearly in a description of 1833: "All the buildings and streets bear the marks of the disorder and ugliness of the former atmosphere of temporariness and uncertainty; everyone dwells and lives here in order to dwell and live somewhere else, as though they are certain that they will live for a long time, or that they will be as happy as they hope in the promised land; but I would urge them to preach present certainty by living, building, engaging in trade, and working for the common good in Hermoupolis [...]. There should from the very beginning, in the time of the late Governor [Kapodistrias], have been a plan for this town too, so that henceforth buildings could be erected and repaired according to it. [...] There are still places that are not built up, there are also good places covered by huts and little houses, which are being purchased very cheap every day

186. Hermoupolis, decorated ceiling in the central hall of the K. Nikolaidis mansion. 187. Hermoupolis, plan for the extension of the shipyard facilities (1883) (source: archive of the Municipality of Hermoupolis, Industrial Companies and Houses file).

in order to be demolished; the Government should [...] from the outset have bought from the locals all the property needed that lies in the area of the port and the town, in order to plan properly and increase the town."[291]

Despite all its deficiencies, the town was to change in a very short space of time, as we have already noted, with the aid of its plan and the basic infrastructure works.[292] This contributed from an early point in time to the creation of a shared feeling of exultation amongst the inhabitants (1837): "The inhabitants of Hermoupolis are the only inhabitants of whom Greece could be proud today."[293] This, however, does not mean that the problems known elsewhere did not continue to exist. In 1839, the accusation is levelled that the implementation of the approved plan for Hermoupolis "will serve as a stone of scandal amongst our fellow citizens [...]. Partly because of the distorted implementation of it by the Mayor [...] and partly because of the illegal sale of plots of land, which will remain empty when access streets and alleys are blocked [...]."[294]

A decade later (1846) we encounter an unembroidered description of life in Hermoupolis by a certain Andreas Kolezis: "Since my house is very low at the back, I cannot open its door, because the pigs that are at large in the street, in contravention of police orders, immediately enter. Boats are piled up in front of my storerooms, and pots in which they boil tar and the like, and a vast amount of rubbish. A slaughterhouse has been

188. Hermoupolis, view of the town towards the end of the 19th century (source: M. Eleftheriou, *Enthymion Syrou*, 1993). 189. Hermoupolis, the highest part of the settlement with Ano Syros on top of the hill. 190. (next page) Hermoupolis, view of the town from on high looking towards the Customs House.

191

built in Hermoupolis, but where are the animals slaughtered? In the market, outside the warehouses, and by the sea. [...] Our town is full of rubbish; one cannot pass by the coastal area because of the mud, the water-carriers gallop on horseback and strike people [...]. I live in a neighbourhood of prostitutes, though there is a place designated for them [...]."[295]

These episodes, however, did not change the general image of the town. Its face changed in the 1840s thanks to the "almost general reworking" of the plan by the municipal authorities, and to the zeal of its inhabitants for education and progress: "Several important buildings were erected a short time ago and continue to be erected, the streets of the town are being laid out, and, in a short while, the town is becoming a European-class town." The

191. Drawing of the coast of Hermoupolis, with tanners processing hides, and with the Lazaretto under construction in the background (designed by W. von Weiler) (source: Benaki Museum). 192. Hermoupolis, modern view of the town with the ruined building of the Lazaretto in the background.

192

193

193

Mayor built schools, extended the hospital, which became the best in Greece, and built a third church. "In a word, one sees in Hermoupolis what one does not find either in Nauplia or in Patra, or in Kalamai, or in Tripolitsa, and not even in the capital of Greece itself [...]." Despite all its problems, as early as 1840 "it is a desirable town, and everyone takes pleasure in living in it," because, in addition to material goods "they also find several moral goods."[296] This rare quality makes Hermoupolis unique amongst 19th-century Greek towns. For, as we have seen, many of them boasted of the achievements of the progress that they had attained, but none is so convincing as Hermoupolis. One ingredient in this rare "recipe for success" was the large number of public buildings that were erected, combining collective functions and cultural services in such a way as to produce an "order" typical of the European cities of the period. To cite two examples: in 1840 the creation is recorded of two "national establishments" in Hermoupolis: "the warehouses of the carrying trade (*transito*) and the new lazaretto"[297] (figs. 191, 192). While in 1841 it was proudly announced that "the paving and regularisation of the streets of our market is proceeding admirably [...]. On them a notable slaughter house is being erected at the outer coast of the town, [...]."[298]

Naturally enough, the central area of the town attracted the greatest interest, its reference point being Ermou Street, running at right angles to

193-195. Hermoupolis, the church of Ayios Nikolaos, details of side view and facade.

the coast (now E. Venizelou Street), and the area around the important Othonos Square (now Miaouli Square) (figs. 175, 198, 199), where the imposing Town Hall was later built (E. Ziller, 1875-98) (figs. 196, 197). The present image of this particular zone is due, then, to the coordinated efforts made from an early point in time to give it a neoclassical form, which proved possible thanks to its level ground. The decree "of reform" of plots of land in "Ermou Street, which has just been laid out" (1843) is characteristic: "1. We permit, according to the plan submitted to and approved by us: the creation of a new street in the form of a portico on the left side of Ermou Street [...] for two building blocks, and the erection of commercial and industrial establishments on either side of these streets; similarly, the creation of a new street on the right side of Ermou Street [...]."[299]

This "new street" on the right (Babayiotou Street) was to be the main link between the centre and the most important landmarks in the part of the town on the sloping hillside. These included the Apollo Theatre (P. Sampó, 1862-64), the Vaporia neighbourhood, occupied by wealthy merchants and shipowners – the only area today uniformly neoclassical – and the terraced, trapezium-shaped square with a Monument to the Fallen in front of the imposing church of Ayios Nikolaos (Yerasimos Metaxas, 1848-70).[300]

The importance of Miaouli Square as the centre of the life of the town and the measure of comparison with its great rival, Athens, may be

196. Hermoupolis, the Town Hall building in Miaouli Square, by E. Ziller (1875-98). 197. (next page) Hermoupolis, interior of the Town Hall: the glass roof of one of the two symmetrical atriums of the building.

196

ALPHA BANK

198

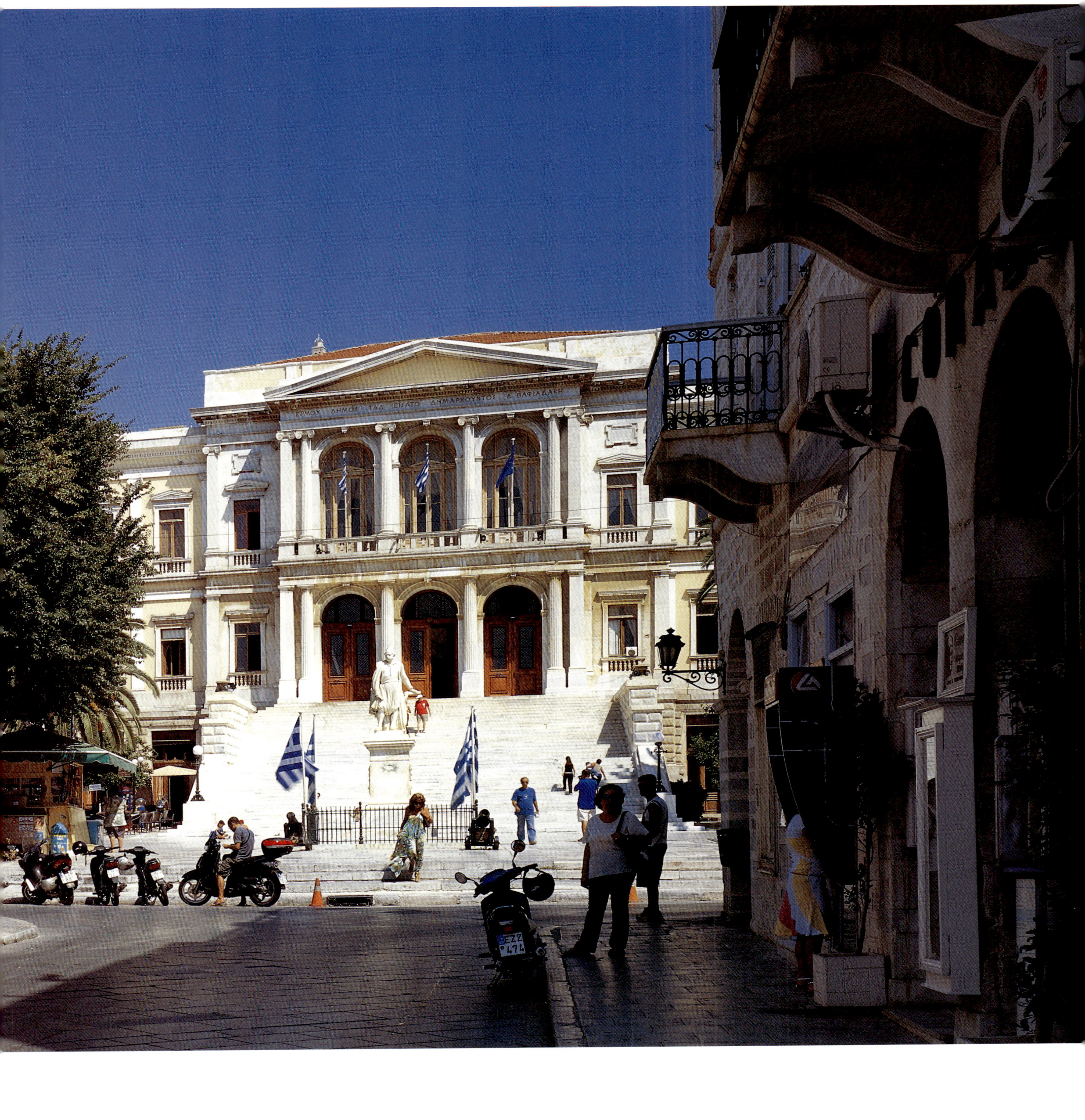

198. Hermoupolis, view of Miaouli Square, with the statue of the admiral flanked by Greek flags.

seen from references in the local Press. The first evidence is cited in a report of 1855: "The fine square of Hermoupolis, which is very spacious, obviously needs another row of trees at the south, in the interest of good taste and of the stroll commonly taken in it by families [...]."[301] Similarly, a flattering description of the town is recorded on the occasion of the laying of the foundations of the Municipal Market in Othonos Square (1857): "Over these last months, Hermoupolis is daily undergoing change through the efforts of the administrative and municipal Authorities. Everywhere in the town sewers are being laid, [...] streets are being paved again, the construction of a carriage road from Hermoupolis to Poseidonia is expected to begin soon, the works on the quay are progressing admirably, and it is hoped to create a perfect custom-house [...]. This progress is notable, and of the Greek towns, only Hermoupolis is providing an example of it."[302]

Hermoupolis, we are told in 1859, did not cease "to make every effort for its own embellishment. What is curious is that whereas the city of Athens, planned on open ground, is being distorted and, as it proceeds, departs from the order of the civilized cities of Europe and tends to take a form that is completely Turkish, the municipal authorities of Syros, through great sacrifice, destroy the buildings that were erected out of need during the days of Hermoupolis' misfortunes, to lay streets and to give their town a European form, though this is very difficult. [...] The unique [...]

199. Hermoupolis, the side of Miaouli Square opposite the Town Hall (cf. fig 175). 200-202. (next page) Hermoupolis, three views of streets with contiguous neoclassical buildings.

201

202

203

Municipal authority of Syros [...] has created two large squares at great expense, one in the name of our King Otto and the other in the name of our Queen Amalia, the former of which is already nearly adorned with rows of trees and various buildings." Moreover the owners of property around the square were required to incorporate porticoes in their buildings, which had already been done on the south side, while on the west it was planned to erect two porticoes with a food market. The relevant plan was sent to Athens for approval, was held up for two years, and then vanished.[303]

The element that is naturally missing from Hermoupolis today is a taste of the former life of this genteel coastal city. A description dating 1856 suffices: "Here the market throngs with people of all kinds, all of them workers, and all of them industrious; the mason's wedge and the shipbuilder's axe sound perpetually, hand-drawn carts move through the paved streets transporting merchandise everywhere from the market: in a word, everywhere there is movement and life, nowhere idleness."[304] Even in 1884, when the signs of decline were now apparent, the town did not give up: "We now come to the trade of Syros, which has something essentially different from other commercial centres in Greece. Whereas, that is, lack of movement and inactivity is generally speaking to be found at this time in many of the highly commercial centres of Greece, the market of Syros, because of the varied nature of its activities

203, 204. **Hermoupolis, characteristic stepped streets paved with a combination of stone and marble.**

and the fact that it is not confined to financial and brokerage enterprises, invariably finds new havens and new resources amidst similar *storms* [...]."[305]

The present summer tourism, with its attendant congestion (fig. 206) – a familiar hallmark of many historical summer resorts in Greece – is but an imperfect substitute for that vigour.

The old glory of Hermoupolis, in any event, is attested not only by the resplendent remains of neoclassical architecture on the island (figs. 176, 177, 180-182, 186, 190, 193-195, 200-202),[306] but also by the design of its open spaces, both in the level area of the town, which has already been mentioned, and in the slopes that are characteristic of the rest of its urban tissue. From this perspective, as we now move within the town searching for traces of its neoclassical design, we cannot fail to admire the continuous, effortless endeavour to lay out a system of amphitheatrical staircases, all of them straight and with no distortion of their outlines, which direct movement from the upper zones of the town to the coastal zone. It is mainly these axes that attest to the neoclassical foundations of the plan of Hermoupolis (figs. 203, 204).

In addition to the two-dimensional tracing of the public staircases on the plan or the map, the three-dimensional projection of them on the ground is registered emphatically in the eyes of the stroller. This experience, which is characteristic of other island settlements, as we shall see, cannot be fortuitous or have escaped the attention of the

204

designers of the town. In fact, these wide staircases frequently offer distant prospects that make it easy for anyone moving parallel with the contours to get their bearings. In this way, the general impression of space is preserved, despite the fact that the city has very few open spaces. In other words, the most important stepped streets of Hermoupolis correspond with the monumental axes of the typical neoclassical towns that are laid out on relatively flat ground. If the neoclassical character of the latter is identified by locating, *inter alia*, a rectangular grid, the emphasis in the natural amphitheatre of Hermoupolis is shifted to the existence of these theatre 'wedges'.

In order to illustrate this feature, I cite a few examples. A significant nucleus, with individual open spaces, was to be formed around the church of the Metamorphosis (1824), which was mentioned above. Here, the approach on the west side is by way of an imposing stepped street leading down to the courtyards with their pebbled floors (dated 1859 and 1862), while correspondingly, on the east side, there is a fan-shaped composition of three discrete elements with staircases. The first, with obliquely traced steps, forms an entrance to the church forecourt, the second is a stepped expanse like an amphitheatre, and the third, with steps parallel to the previous one, is Levendopoulou Street, which ascends to the upper part of the town.

Although it is probably marred by later amendments made to improve the circulation

205. Hermoupolis, amphitheatrically arranged staircases outside the courtyard of the church of the Metamorphosis and next to Levendopoulou Street (right).

of motorcars in Babayiotou Street, the square in front of the church of Ayios Nikolaos intensifies (inevitably on a miniature scale, due to the lack of space) the neoclassical organisation of the main axis of the church. This axis extends beyond the monumental staircase at the church entrance to include the Monument for the Fallen in the War of Independence of 1821 at the centre of the tree-covered area. Lesser, but equally imposing, open spaces include Tsiropina Square, in Kalomenopoulou Street, which is dominated by the building of the Prefecture of the Cyclades, and I. Vardakas Square in front of the renovated Apollo theatre.

From the large port of the Cyclades that dominated the Aegean, we now travel to a much smaller one nearby, the port of Andros, to see how the neoclassical spirit penetrated here. It is an established fact that Andros – the entire island and not simply the capital, Chora – turned to the adoption of neoclassicism in architecture since the local economy was dominated by shipping from a very early point in time,[307] and this made the local society receptive to innovations from outside the island. This change of direction was accompanied by a break with the previous architectural forms typical of the Aegean islands (tightly grouped volumes with flat roofs covered with earth). The new model involved a single, roughly cubic, volume covered with tiles and with neoclassical formal elements (at least on the facade), which predominated from about the middle of the 19th century.

206. Hermoupolis, view from the quay towards the interior of the settlement.

AGENCY
Blue Star Ferries
HIGHSPEED
AMSTEL

The modernisation of Andros was not confined to architecture. Following the general trend of establishing industries in the Cyclades in the 19th century, Andros acquired a large-scale flourmill owned by Al. Embeirikos (in the village of Stenies, 1870?), though the early attempts to acquire a regular harbour met with failure,[308] and in 1884 the inhabitants were still petitioning for the founding of a High School.[309]

After the liberation of Greece, the settlement of Chora, in particular, rapidly extended outside the bounds of the fortified medieval castle at the end of the peninsula (fig. 207), where cramped houses were built on small irregular plots on either side of an oblique central spine (Epam. K. Embirikos Street, fig. 212). The new settlement followed a similar street pattern, based on an extension to the castle's central spine. This new axis (Georgios K. Embeirikos Street), designed as a typical urban street, completely straight and with the appropriate width, formed the backbone of the modern settlement from the outset. From the middle of the 19th century, monumental neoclassical facades were set along its sides (figs. 208-211, 215), and the large V. I. Goulandris Square was created, with the Embeirikeion Old People's Home and Hospital. At the same time, neoclassicism penetrated the very dense tissue of the castle, modifying the earlier facades

207. Chora on Andros, part of the modern settlement from Paraporti of the Kastro (Castle) (left) to the church of the Koimesis Theotokou (top right) and the ruined Xenia Hotel, by A. Konstantinidis, 1957 (bottom right) in the Plakoures district.

208 

209 

(fig. 213) and adding balconies (a neoclassical innovation) where possible. In this way, the older and newer zones of Chora were united and still coexist today. This unity is symbolised by the procession of the icon of the Virgin Theoskepastos,[310] which is carried every year from the metropolitan church of Ayios Georgios tou Kastrou to the main square, in which the Town Hall is located.

This continuous route, which is now paved[311] and links the earlier settlement with its later extension by way of a monumental axis, symbolises the complex ways in which a now open island-society a new, powerful model, neoclassicism. The 19th-century settlement never acquired a fully developed plan, which was in any case impossible in a place which had such a strongly sloping terrain.[312] As soon as one departs from the monumental axis, one finds oneself in narrow, irregular little streets with large numbers of intermediate staircases, all typical of a traditional settlement. Despite this, a number of the transverse staircases have monumental dimensions and a regular tracing (fig. 213). Thus, all the other elements of neoclassical design are present here: a central straight axis with staircases at right angles to it, a rectangular main square, and monumental facades. Chora is a neoclassical island town based on the model of the much larger town of Hermoupolis, which undoubtedly influenced the manner in which the main settlements on the Cycladic islands developed.

208. Chora on Andros, view of Georgiou K. Embeirikou Street, looking west (early 20th century postcard). 209. The same view as in fig. 208 in a modern photograph. 210. Chora on Andros, view from Georgiou K. Embeirikou Street, looking towards the Kastro (Castle) (postcard of the early 20th century). 211. The same view as in fig. 210 in a modern photograph.

210

211

212

213

212. Chora on Andros, view of Epam. K. Embeirikou Street in the Kastro (Castle) as seen from Paraporti. 213. Chora on Andros, detail of old residences with loggias (covered colonnaded balconies) in the Kastro (Castle). At the left, a house dating from 1859 and at the right one dating from 1889. 214. Chora on Andros, the stepped E. Poumboura Street, at right angles to Georgiou K. Embeirikou Street, leading to the square with the bus station. 215. Chora on Andros, the High School (1926) in Georgiou K. Embeirikou Street.

214

215

From Symi to Chania

The Dodecanese islands have mixed features, borrowed from the Eastern Aegean islands, Crete, and to a lesser extent from the Cyclades. Their proximity to the rich coast of Asia Minor, combined with the favourable policy pursued by the Ottoman Empire (the Tanzimat reforms), allowed them to develop close commercial and cultural ties with the coast opposite and the hinterland, which were strengthened by a considerable current of seasonal migration. A similar current was directed to Crete. These relations where interrupted by the Italian occupation (1912-47) and those islands that had no farmland suffered a considerable contraction of population and a decline in activity. The impressive, albeit brief, development on a number of small barren islands (Symi, Chalki, Kalymnos and Kastellorizo) represents a special case in the Dodecanese. It was due to sponge fishing, which began to exploit the rich coasts of North Africa for the first time, in response to the great demand from the European industry of the day.[313] The flourishing of these islands coincided with the general abandonment of the earlier defensive settlements in the Aegean and the creation of new coastal settlements, which expanded spectacularly throughout the 19th century. The Italian occupation abruptly interrupted this development, particularly on the islands named above. The population of Symi, for example, fell from 22,500 inhabitants in 1912 to 7,300 in 1917.[314]

216. Symi, view of Yialos from the castle.

217

During the time of their economic prosperity, which climaxed at the end of the 19th century, the Dodecanese were subjected to strong neoclassical influences from the large urban centres of the Ottoman Empire, in a process similar to that at work in North Greece, as we shall see below. Less cosmopolitan than that which originated in the Ottoman capital, Constantinople, the architecture that prevailed here had a provincial character and greater homogeneity. Town planning interventions in a neoclassical style are less evident, though this is due rather to the geomorphology of the settlements on the small barren islands than to a lack of knowledge. On Rhodes or Kos, for example, the Ottoman Empire left easily recognisable examples of modernising town planning as known in other parts of mainland Greece. Again, these interventions were of necessity only sparse, and took the form of the redesigning of open spaces around new monumental public buildings, as in the medieval tissue of the Old Town of Rhodes (e.g. in contact with the Palace of the Grand Masters in Panaitiou Street – a building complex that consists of an Ottoman school on the ruins of the Hospitaller church of Ayios Ioannis in the Collachium, the Early Byzantine fortification wall, and the Suleiman mosque). Also, at least in the case of Rhodes, modern settlement extensions are to be encountered outside the fortification walls, called 'Marasia',[315] which lack any distinctive character, and where the large-scale Italian embellishments were later added on the north coast of the town.

217. Symi, view of Chorio from the windmills.
218. (next page) Symi, view of houses at Mourayio at Yialos.

Κατοί
PHARMACY
KALODOUKAS
YACHTING
ΑΓ. ΝΙΚΟΛΑΟΣ ΝΡ147

Crete is one of those special cases in which foreign occupation over long periods of time gave rise to the creation of settlements with distinctive features. It was on these features that the neoclassical town was based, bringing with it its own innovations. On the eve of the liberation of Crete (1913), the three fortified harbour-towns on the north coast of the island (Heraklion, Rethymnon, and Chania) presented a mixed character, the product of successive periods of Venetian and Ottoman rule. While the former introduced Italian Renaissance models unmodified – before the appearance of neoclassicism, of course – the latter imitated them, adding its own versions and variations. This smooth transition was augmented from about the middle of the 19th century by interventions in planning and architecture, made by the Ottoman administration and directly influenced by European neoclassicism. In other words, Crete found itself in a position similar to that of north Greece, as we shall see below. The change of guard, even in the transitional period of the High Commission (1898-1913), did not bring about any perceptible break with the past, but simply helped to secure a smooth adjustment to the new circumstances of the Greek state.

On Symi we encounter one – and perhaps the most extreme – case of the abrupt change of fortune in the Dodecanese mentioned above. As on the island of Kalymnos, the greatest development of the settlement dates from the period of the gradual shift of the centre of gravity

219. Symi, part of Yialos around the Naval Museum (centre).

219

220

221

from Chorio – the earlier settlement, which extended to the west of the Castle and the Byzantine fort – to the harbour (fig. 217). This led to the creation of Yialos, the modern settlement nucleus with public buildings on the sea, as an extension of Chorio (figs. 216, 218, 219). The change coincided with radical changes in the economy of the island: sponge fishing abandoned the exhausted beds nearby and ventured further afield to the rich African coast, while the production and trading of sponges was at the same time reorganised on a new footing. This led to the formation of a rapidly developing commercial centre, with pronounced urban features, based on the sponge-fishing economy. In contrast with the abandoned old settlement on Kalymnos, Chorio on Symi, built on the site of the ancient city, continued to be inhabited by the larger part of the population down to 1930,[316] who were "men of toil",[317] in contrast with Yialos, where the merchants dwelt. Today these distinctions are blurred and the local population is distributed evenly between Chorio and Yialos.

There is an astonishing affinity between the small sponge-fishing towns that flourished in this way in the Dodecanese. They have roughly the same features: a splendour that recalls the much larger town of Hermoupolis on Syros, combined with a spatial scale inappropriate to the size of the island to which they belong. The neoclassical character of Yialos is thus not due simply to the impressive homogeneity of the neoclassical forms

220. Symi, the small square at the end of Kali Strata as it was in 1985. 221-223. Symi, details of the staircases of Kali Strata.

in its buildings. It also includes, as we have seen in many examples so far, the way in which the public space is organised. The amphitheatrical arrangement of the modern settlement in the hollow of a strongly sloping hillside precluded from the start the application of any regular street layout. On the contrary, it dictated the frequent use of stepped streets. The main street, the marble-paved Kali Strata (figs. 221-223, 232, 233), forms the backbone of the settlement and links Chorio with Yialos, starting from the square-shaped, similar to a theatrical scene, square of Skala (fig. 220) and ending about five hundred paces away at a second square, with an ingenious design, on the fringes of Chorio, thus to some extent penetrating its labyrinthine tissue. Kali Strata, with its considerable width and the geometric features of its tracing, is the closest analogy to the monumental axis designed in other settlements that were found on more level ground. Its affinity with the stepped, stone-paved streets of Hermoupolis is obvious.

Similarly, the tracing of stepped streets in the tissue of Symi because of the strongly sloping terrain frequently creates the impression that provision has been made to secure views of particular parts of Yialos (fig. 234). This impression becomes stronger as one moves along the axis of Kali Strata: as one ascends, one sees at intervals on the left visual 'fissures' looking towards the sea, with similar prospects on the right towards higher points of the settlement. In other words, the

222

223

224. (next page) Symi, steps in Kali Strata near Chorio (photographed in 1985), painted for Easter. 225. (next page) Symi, painted steps and rocks in a street.

design of the street network on Symi, and possibly in other similar settlements, has a much more complicated three-dimensional system of reference than that found in the familiar grid of neoclassical town plans. The investigation of this hypothesis – which is now technically possible – would probably reveal the small extent to which 'chance' was involved in these strategic interventions in the 19th-century urban landscape.

The importance to the inhabitants of these carefully designed public paved spaces in which they moved and rested, was evident, at least until a few decades ago, in the way that the joints in the paving stones were meticulously picked out with blue paint at Easter (fig. 224). Even today, when the practice of this impressive embellishment is in decline, traces of it remain here and there, though usually uncoordinated and using different colours (fig. 225).

An additional feature in the public space of Symi is the number of open level areas, again with a terraced arrangement, designed so as to resemble tiny theatres. These spaces, which encourage social intercourse amongst the inhabitants, are the nearest thing to neoclassical squares that Symi has to offer. This kind of feature was originally missing from the typically labyrinthine tissue of (traditional) Chorio, with its very narrow streets and the frequent interposition of covered passageways. The creation of modern Yialos, however, also led to changes in Chorio, and not only in its architecture (conversion of buildings with flat roofs into

226

227

228

229

230

231

226, 227. Symi, entrance to the forecourt of the metropolitan church of Ayios Ioannis, with the bell tower (1838), from a street in Yialos, and the corresponding view towards the entrance from inside the forecourt. 228. Symi, the narrow passageway to the church of Ayios Ioannis next to the staircase. 229. Symi, the pebbled floor of the church courtyard. 230. Symi, the side of the church of Ais Yiannis, which is continued in visual terms by the facade of the Petrideion Didaskaleion (School). 231. The Petrideion Didaskaleion (1886).

232

neoclassical buildings with pitched roofs), but also in the treatment of public space: this can be seen in the individual scattered, scenic clearings between groups of houses and around churches – for example at the church of Ayios Athanasios. In these the organic or random development found in typical traditional settlements ceases to apply, yielding to an organising spirit that exudes a design intention of neoclassical character. In other words, as happens on a larger scale in both mainland and island settlements, modernising design elements insinuate themselves into the earlier tissue, where this is possible. This creates mixed spaces, perhaps richer than those that would have emerged in purely neoclassical town planning compositions.

A wonderful example of this is still preserved intact, in contact with a zone that has deteriorated in many respects – where once there were old ship sheds and giant eucalyptus trees shading the ship's carpenters at their work[318] – behind the little bridge at the head of the coast of Yialos. This is a triple complex consisting of a) the metropolitan church of Ayios Ioannis (1838) with its pebbled courtyard, b) a long, paved forecourt with a bell tower and a symbolic mast, and c) the Petridion Didaskalion (1886) (figs. 226-231).

The proportions of the individual areas, the slight curve in the main circulation axis, and the gradual unfolding of the building volumes, as, leaving the street behind, one ascends a few steps and passes through the gate to enter the forecourt,

232, 233. Symi, houses on Kali Strata. 234. Symi, view of the sea through a gap between houses.

together form a highly enchanting example of 19th-century designed public space in Greece. In comparison, the old clock tower at the end of the wharf (1880) and the typical Government House of the Italian Occupation next to it, the product of the conversion of an older building,[319] have very limited value, despite being distinctive landmarks of Symi.

Symi, with its population decimated, and isolated in communications terms, was preserved as a fossil after the Second World War and was 'rediscovered' about two decades ago,[320] when it began to come to life again through the restoration of old building shells. The most radical change it suffered, however, was the invasion of the motorcar, which now, using a newly laid road to the west of Yialos, ascends as far as Chorio and continues along branch roads to the hinterland of the island. The present improvement of sea communications with Rhodes and the Turkish coastline, the presence of vehicles, which has dictated the widening of the wharf, and the development of a continuous string of tourist shops, together with the lively investment in renovated properties, have all led to fateful deterioration in this unique jewel of Aegean urban design. The listed island of Symi does not seem able to escape the fate of similar cases of coastal settlements with a neoclassical flavour in Greece, which have survived precisely because they have been converted into modern summer holiday resorts.

233

234

Of the settlements on Crete, we have singled out Chania for closer inspection for two reasons: Chania retains clear traces of the previous phases of its planning development, and the suburb of Chalepa (once a village outside the fortification walls) was the headquarters of the High Commission. The town thus acquired a purely cosmopolitan air, which did not disappear when Crete was united with Greece. These modifications and changes are imprinted in the distinctive manner in which Chania developed down to 1920.[321]

Beginning with the late Ottoman period, there is abundant evidence for intensive activity on the part of the Ottoman administration in the erection of important public buildings and interventions in the public spaces of the town. These reflect the direct influence of European neoclassicism, as implemented in the Ottoman Empire. Thus, after the middle of the 19th century, the Seraglio was built in about 1860 (later the V Division, and now a facility of the University of Crete), and "the Harbour Mosque (Yiale Çamisi), fountains, *tekedes*, pavilions and other buildings".[322] Modern E. Venizelou Street (fig. 235) was also constructed to link the town with Chalepa, and as a place to "stroll outside the fortification walls [...] to the present garden, where an enormous fig tree stands in a sandy area, around which people take their Sunday walk." In 1870, indeed, in the interests of this 'walk', the Municipal Garden was laid out "on European models", the first 'social welfare' project outside the fortification walls, to which

235. Chania, view of the old town from El. Venizelou Street on the coast.

236

a performance hall was added in 1889.[323] Relatively soon after this (1893-94) work began on the construction of the important Military Hospital (now the Courthouse and Administrative Building), which was completed in 1900, and a new town was founded at Almyroupoli, which quickly acquired forty houses.[324] In 1900-01, an official street plan was drawn up for the town to a scale of 1:500, the main elements in which were the demolition of parts of the fortification walls and the erection of "a special large market" at the Piatta Forma (the main bastion), which was approved in August 1901.[325] There followed breaches of the fortification walls and improvements to the tissue of the old town, as well as the creation of the central axes of the new town, which were planted with trees, and finally the erection of the indoor Market (1910-13) (fig. 239). Work on the water supply and lighting proceeded at the same time.[326] Alongside these public works, mention should be made of the overt turn towards neoclassicism in the residences and neighbourhoods outside the fortification walls, many examples of which are still preserved (figs. 238, 240). The 'return' to the Old Town and its values took place much later, transforming it in the period after the Second World War into a listed historical complex and an attraction for tourism and recreation.

From the above notable planning activity, we may single out three architectural projects: the Courthouse-Administrative Building, the Municipal Garden and the Market. In addition to the

236, 237. **Chania, the Administrative Building – Court House on Dikastirion Square (1900), built by the Ottoman authorities as a Military Hospital.**

distinctive features of the imposing Administrative Building, great importance is attached to the observation that "[...] through its forms it exercised a great influence on the articulation of the first plan for the new town and the tracing of some of the basic street axes, as well as on the creation of Dikastirion Square."[327] This is confirmation of the view expressed in the introduction concerning the relationship between architecture and town planning. In the Garden, again, we encounter all the features of the modern way of life: "the paths [...] laid out according to European garden models [...] are covered with vines at many points. Inside the Garden, two statues and a Hermes derived from ancient Kydonia were erected. Twice a week, martial music is performed there."[328] The cruciform indoor Market contained seventy-eight shops that functioned and were supplied impeccably, so that "the lamentable spectacle of people and animals jostling in the rain or sun is now at an end [...]".[329]

The above accounts convincingly for the cosmopolitan character of Chania, at least down to 1913, when the foundations were laid for the development of the modern town. There were many leading players at this critical phase: Turkish administrators and European and Greek engineers, several of whom indeed had either undertaken similar projects in Athens (foreigners) or had studied there (Greeks). Neoclassicism served as a means for the mixed population of the town to achieve progress, gradually acquiring and assimilating the goods of modernism.

238

239

238. Chania, Elenas Venizelou Square in the Chalepa district, with Venizelos's house at the extreme left and the National Centre for Research Studies on the right. 239. Chania, the Municipal Market (1910-13), a cross-shaped building erected at the boundary between the old and the new town, on the demolished fortifications that can be seen in the foreground. 240. (next page) Chania, characteristic houses in Andrea Papandreou Street with neoclassical features.

IONIAN ISLANDS

From Corfu to Zakynthos

As we noted at the outset, the character and form of the settlements on the Ionian islands differ from those in the rest of Greece. Thanks to the long period of Venetian rule (1204-1214 and 1386-1797), these settlements were directly influenced by the Venetian models contemporary with them. In some cases famous Italian engineers of the day intervened in their design, mainly in defence works. The Ionian islands differ also from Crete, another Venetian possession down to 1669, when it was conquered by the Ottoman Turks. A second point of difference is that the Venetians were succeeded in the Ionian islands by the French, Russians (for a short period), and finally the British, until the unification of the islands with Greece in 1864. Neoclassical architecture, which is directly of interest to us here, was the result of this last foreign presence in the 19th century.

Neoclassical architecture in these islands was normally integrated into a structure, urban and architectural, that had already been formed in accordance with earlier design principles and values and had been preserved at the period under examination without suffering any damage. Accordingly, when we attempt to describe the neoclassical phase in the settlements of the Ionian islands, we are referring essentially to their earlier built environment, to which important public buildings with neoclassical features were added.

241. Corfu Town, view from the Old Fort. In the foreground is the open area•of the Spianada (formerly a defensive moat) and a row of buildings in the Liston.

242

243

We shall examine the cases of Corfu, the most important fortified settlement of the group, and Zakynthos, one of the settlements that was never enclosed within defence walls.

The layout of Corfu Town is defined by the main features of the local topography and by the defensive requirements of a fortified town of the period. The citadel formed the first defensive nucleus, the Old Fort, while the town, the 'Burgo' or 'Xopoli', developed outside this fortress. Since it was not originally walled (fig. 242) it was given a double defensive line of fortifications, which included a second fort, in the late 16th century. For defensive reasons, an extensive open area known as the Spianada, was formed between the Old Fort and the town. For the same reasons, the first row of building blocks beyond the Spianada was composed of identical squares arranged radially.[330] This was the only part of the town, along with the main network of streets, that was linked with the four gates of the fortifications, which seem to have been designed.[331] The rest of Corfu Town consists of a labyrinthine tissue of narrow streets and multi-storey buildings – typical of a fortified settlement – which seems, indeed, to have been created by a process of accretion.[332] Thus, the form of the settlement "encompasses two very different features: geometric tracing and dynamic development".[333]

The built area of this settlement, which had no plan, and which is today enclosed between the

242. Corfu Town, drawing by Braun (1575) with the moat separating the citadel (left) from the still unfortified town (right) (source: Gennadius Library).
243. Paintings showing the circular monument of the first High Commissioner of the Ionian islands, Thomas Maitland, on the Spianada (cf. fig. 241) and the Yiallinas mansion (right) (source: British Embassy Collection).
244. Corfu Town, the continuous facade of buildings on the Liston.

Spianada and the west fortification walls of the town, is bounded by three hills (Kambielo at the north, Ayioi Pateres and Ayios Athanasios at the south). Between them pass the two main streets of the town, which start from the Spianada: N. Theotoki Street, which runs from the Spilia gate to the harbour, and E. Voulgareos Street, which formerly ended at the now demolished Royal Gate. These main streets are of some interest: "[...] the changing proportions of the width and height of the buildings that flank them, the uniform character of these buildings in themselves, and above all the arches on their ground floors [...] create a harmonious whole which, with its various articulations, breaks the monotony of constant repetition."[334] The rest of the streets, the narrow alleys (*kantounia*), which are 1-3m. wide, sometimes pass beneath arches that have houses above them. In these alleys, "the prevailing element is the instinctive, a spontaneity, a flexibility and possibly some confusion, [...]" while their adaptation to the topography produces a "picturesque form of enchanting variety."[335]

The manner in which the individual neighbourhoods of the town are organised follows the model of the city of Venice, with its scattered open spaces (*campi*). Similarly, on Corfu there are small irregular openings here and there, normally in front of a church, which serve as central points of reference for the neighbourhoods (fig. 252): the only difference is that, whereas in Venice these are designed, in Corfu they are the result of a

245

246

245, 246. Corfu Town, two views of the Spianada.

247

248

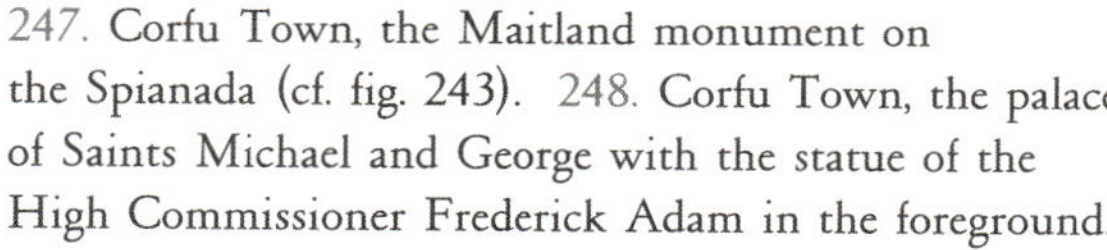

247. Corfu Town, the Maitland monument on the Spianada (cf. fig. 243). 248. Corfu Town, the palace of Saints Michael and George with the statue of the High Commissioner Frederick Adam in the foreground.

KOPEA
μέσα από τα τοπία της
OREA
through its landscapes

249

249, 250. Corfu Town, arcades in the streets of the town. At the left, Nikiphorou Theotoki Street and at the right, Evgeniou Voulgareos Street.

process of accretion.[336] The most important square in the town – with the Catholic church and the (now demolished) residence of the Venetian *Bailo* (Consul) - is in front of the modern Town Hall (formerly the *Loggia Nobilei*, the Club of the Noblemen) at the intersection of two main streets, Theotoki and Voulgareos Streets (figs. 254, 255).[337]

Another distinctive feature of the commercial streets of Corfu is the sequence of arcades (*voltes*) at their sides (figs. 249-251, 253). Again, this is not due to the imposition of any overall town-planning measure, but to the initiative of the owners.[338] This accounts for the fact that they do not exist everywhere and in some cases were added afterwards.

The period of British rule (1814-64) is characterised mainly by the construction of public works[339] and by a series of educational measures, the most important being the foundation of the Ionian Academy, whose building stands in the south part of the Spianada. Apart from new defence works and the demolition of sections of the fortification walls to facilitate the extension of the town to the west,[340] and also a number of cases where corners were rounded at the intersection of streets[341] or projecting staircases were removed in the narrow alleys *(kantounia)*,[342] there appear to have been no other interventions in the tissue of the town. The buildings of this period "in the neoclassical spirit and indeed by Greek architects, bind harmoniously with the town as a whole" as "a smooth continuation of the previous forms".[343]

250

251. (next page) Corfu Town, characteristic multi-storey building with an arcade on the ground floor in Evgeniou Voulgareos Street. 252. (next page) Corfu Town, square with a well in front of the church of Panayia Kremasti. 253. (next page) Corfu Town, view of Evgeniou Voulgareos Street.

251

The British, after carrying out demolition work, erected the neoclassical church of Ayios Georgios on the south side of the Old Fort.[344] The French had previously built the Liston on the west side of the Spianada, with a highly characteristic arcade in imitation of similar examples in Paris,[345] while in 1819, the Palace of Saints Michael and George (now the Museum of Asian Art) was built at its north end, with arched gates at either side. The open area of the Spianada was divided between a park at the south (Pano Plateia), with the circular monument to the High Commissioner Maitland (figs. 243, 247), and a northern part (Kato Plateia) which includes, among other things, a cricket ground.[346] Finally, Mon Repos, the residence of the British High Commissioner and later of the Greek royal family, was built in the area of Palaiopoli to the south of the town, beyond Garitsa bay.[347]

252

254

254. Corfu Town, Dimarcheiou Square. At the left is the Town Hall and at the right the Catholic church of St. James. 255. Corfu Town, Dimarcheiou Square with typical buildings of the town in the background.

Buondi
ΦΑΡΜΑΚΕΙΟ
Α. ΜΠΑΜΙΧΑ – Σ. ΠΟΛΕΝΤΑ Ο.Ε.

256

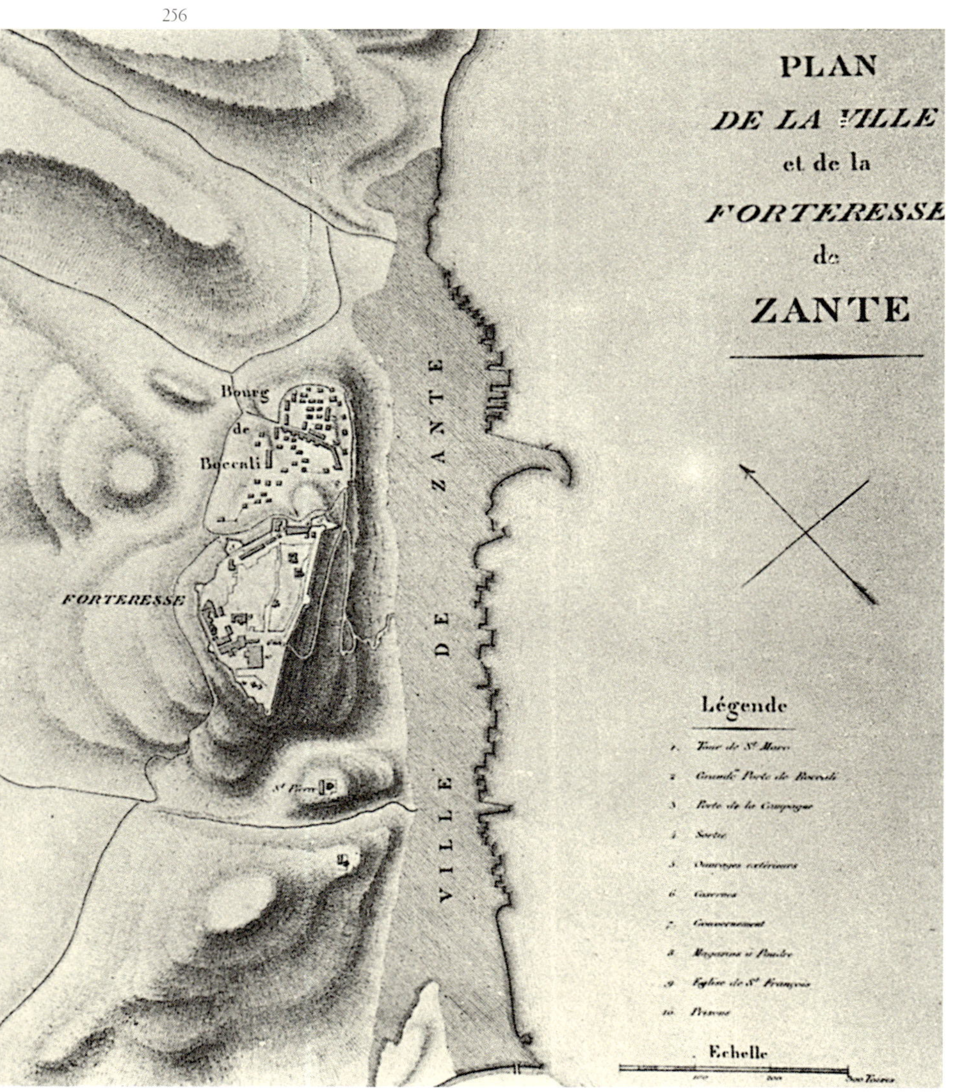

As noted above, Zakynthos (figs. 256, 257) is one of the non-fortified towns of the Ionian islands, which developed freely without having to resort to high-rise buildings, as on Corfu. Moreover, when one reads descriptions of Zakynthos Town before the earthquake of 1953, one has the impression that on Zakynthos, as indeed on the Ionian islands in general, the town planning interventions dating from the period of neoclassicism, that is to say, the 19th century, either continue the earlier historical tradition of the Ionian islands, from the Venetian period to the period of British rule, or function in a different manner, closer to the practice of mainland Greece – though again not with the same quality. Here, then, the basic structureof the settlement already existed, and what happened later did not affect its basic core but related to a constantly shifting coastal zone:

"[...] the history of the urban-design development of Zakynthos is the history of constant landfills, [...] (fig. 258). The history of landfills continued throughout the entire Venetian period, the British Protectorate, and even the period after unification down to the last decades of the 19th century. The expansion was not, of course uniform throughout its entire length [...] so that the line of the coast is irregular and uneven. [...] The areas of D. Solomou and Ammou Squares were the last to be filled and incorporated into the town. Finally, the coastal avenue began to be constructed in 1872 [...]".[348]

256. Zakynthos Town, map of the castle and the settlement (B. de S. Vincent, 1823), before the town was transferred to its present site on the coast. 257. Zakynthos Town (M. Lountzis, 1820). 258. Zakynthos Town, plan of the area of the Customs House in the harbour (G. Trichas, 1862).

257

Proprietà del governo
C. Macri
Nuova Dogana proposta
Luogo appartenente al Governo proveniente dall'
Imbonimento
Dogana attuale

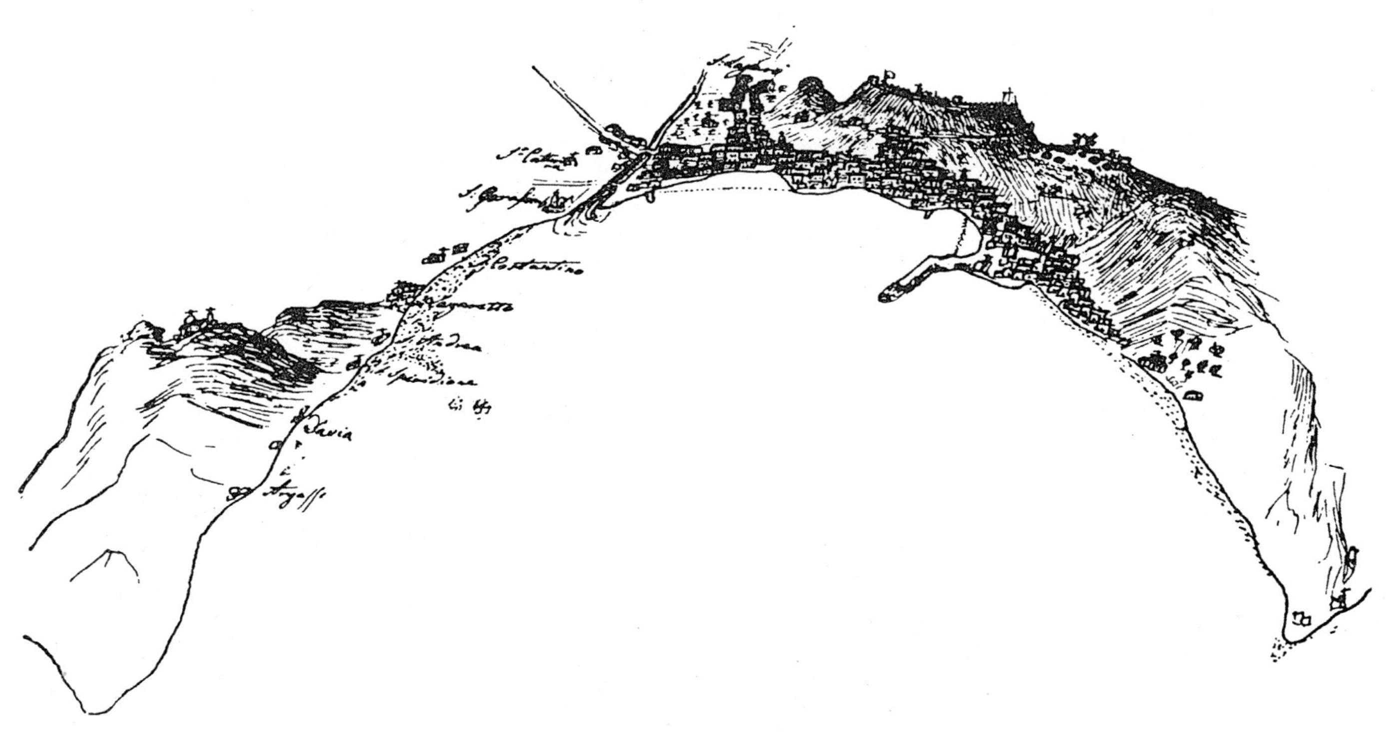

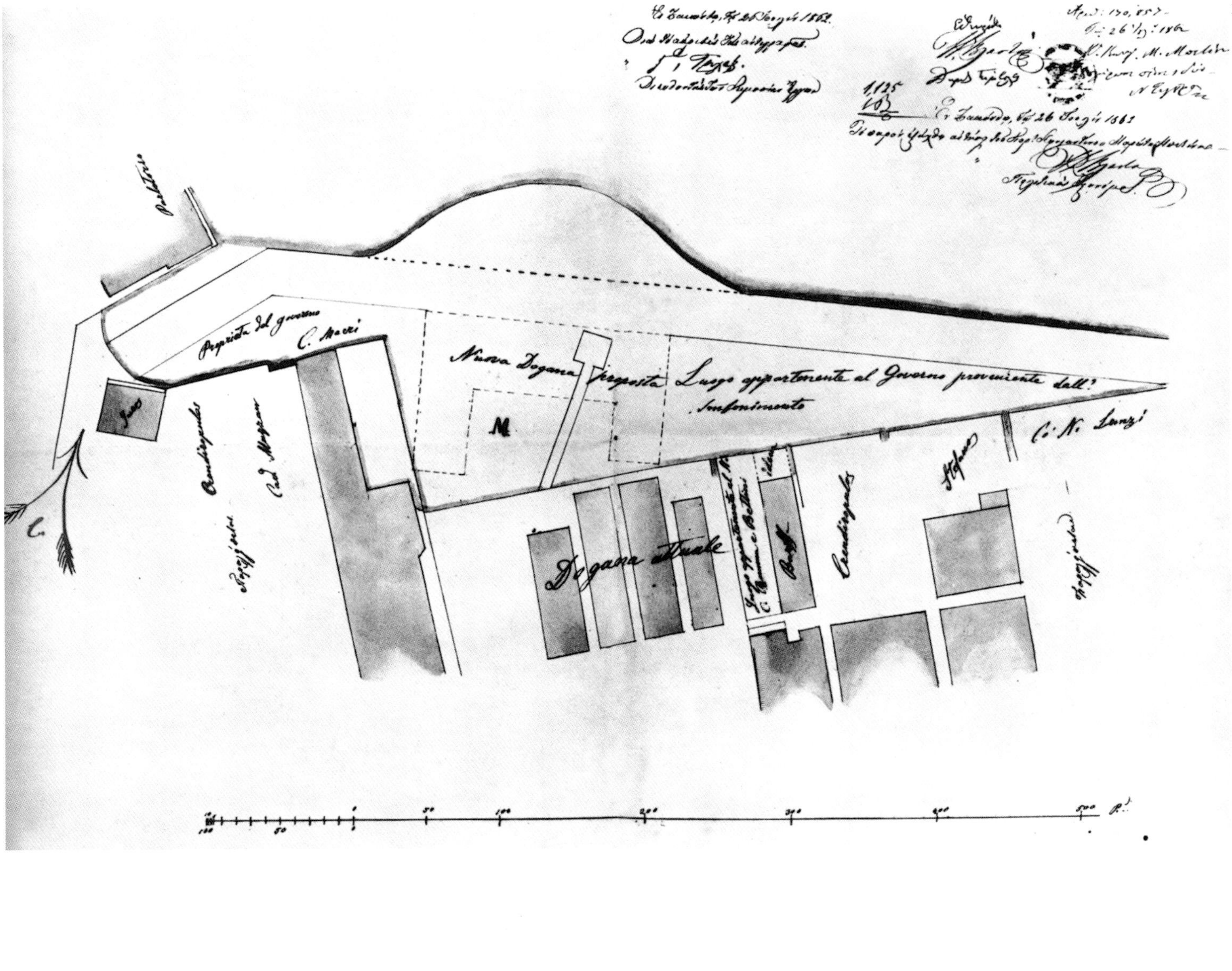

258

259

As the town has an elongated form, the corresponding axes acquire particular significance, the most important being Platia Rouga ('wide street'), which serves as its backbone and the (later in terms of landfills) Strata Marina by the coast.[349] The former is important for three reasons: its slightly zigzag course, the buildings that flank it, and the porticoes that accompany it (figs. 259, 260).[350] There are also porticoes at other points in the town, though these are simpler in form.[351] Thus, this highly definitive element of the tissue already existed and was to be transferred to the new towns that developed on the opposite coast of the Peloponnese. On the Ionian islands, the portico is a 'Venetian' element, in Patra it becomes a 'neoclassical' one.

Similarly, the squares of Zakynthos Town are also not typically neoclassical. The two (old) main squares of the town, Ayiou Markou and Phaneromenis Squares, are triangular in shape and have about the same area. In the former "the spectator has the impression that he is standing before a stage set, but a stage set with real dimensions, with a real perspective and side entrances. Indeed, when the theatrical dialogues ('omilies') of the popular theatrical companies are performed there [...] the urban tissue and architectural space are transformed into an unusual theatre." In the latter "the space [...] becomes [...] ritualistic, a veritable centre of social and spiritual life."[352] This distinctive character is due to the complete integration of the two squares into the urban tissue.

259, 260. Zakynthos Town, row of buildings in Ammou Square, with arcades on the ground floor, before the 1953 earthquake. 261, 262. Zakynthos Town, two old triangular squares in the urban tissue: at the left, Ayiou Markou Square and at the right, Phaneromenis Square.

260

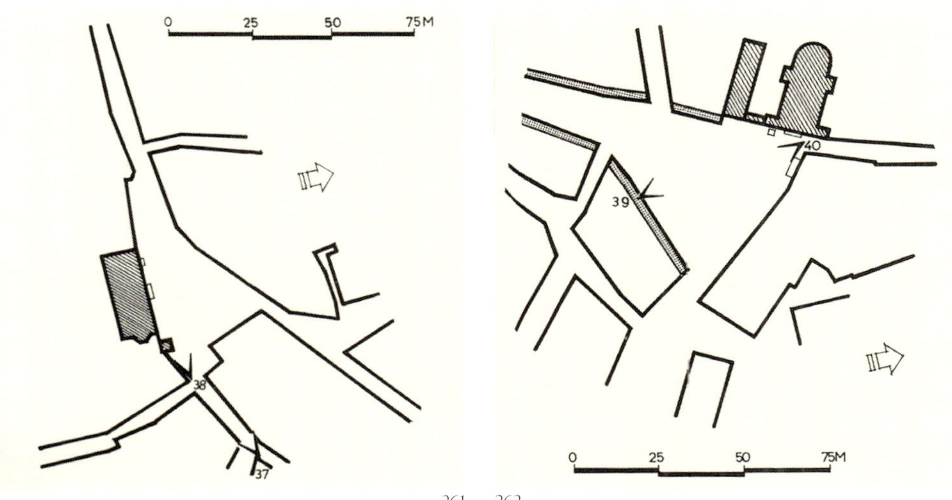

261 262

FLAME of DANCE
ΣΧΟΛΕΣ ΧΟΡΟΥ
POWER

Part IV

Thessaly & Nothern Greece

265

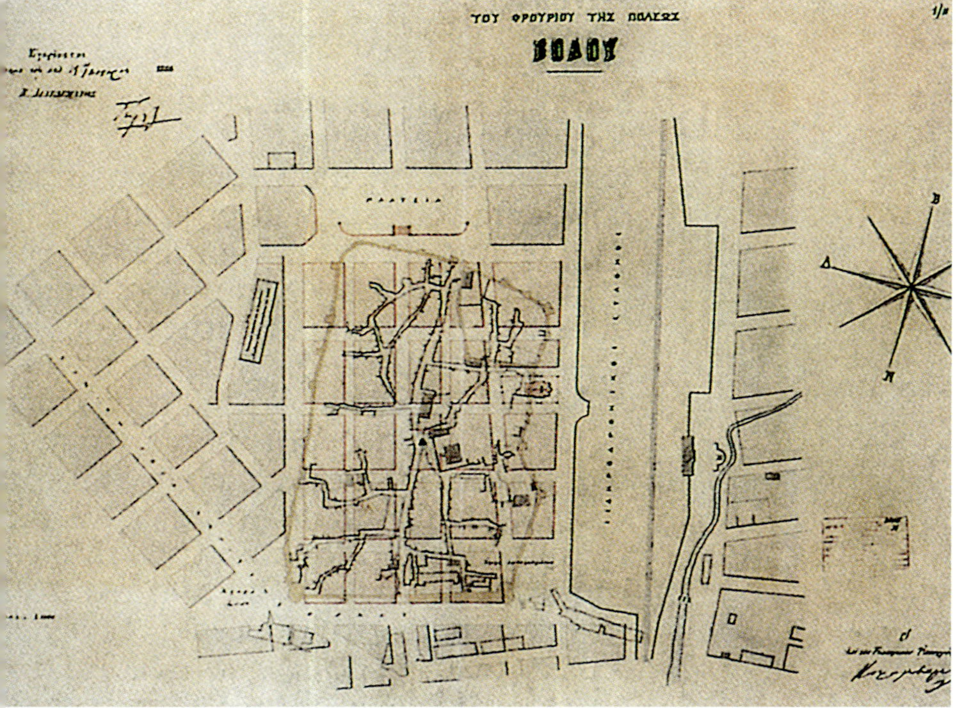

266

THESSALY
From Volos to Pilion

With the liberation of Thessaly in 1881, a variety of different areas were annexed to Greece, ranging from the plain of Larisa (of great value for its farming output), to the outlying mountain areas, and also a large number of settlements (Trikala, Karditsa, etc.), as well as areas like the flourishing communities of Mount Pilion, which enjoyed a special form of local autonomy. The Muslim population was dominant in the larger settlements in the plains, while Pilion was the focus for Greeks, who maintained commercial relations with the Mediterranean. The Greek population of Pilion, which flourished economically from as early as the 18th century, contributed to the introduction of innovations that were imprinted on the settlements of that area. In the rest of Thessaly, the only similar case was the harbour of Volos, which, thanks to its position, had begun to develop before Liberation, expanding outside the fortification walls of the old Fort.

In Thessaly, as in North Greece, as we shall see below, the Ottoman empire set in train a process of building modernisation the main feature of which was its fragmentary character. Through this process, Larisa acquired a plan in 1882 and Karditsa in 1890. The interventions in these cases, however, were of lesser importance than those recorded in Volos, and we shall therefore pay particular attention to this last town. Despite the fact that Pilion was not a suitable area for

263 (spread) Thessaloniki, Aristotelous Square. 264. (spread) Volos, detail of the railway station building. 265. Volos, amendment of the street plan of the Frourio (fort), integrating it into the urban tissue of the town (1888). 266. View of Makrinitsa (top) from Volos. 267. Distant view of Volos from Makrinitsa, showing clearly the rectangular street grid.

modernisation on a similar scale, it was influenced by the current of neoclassicism, which now radiated not only from the large urban centres of the eastern Mediterranean, but also from Athens. The adaptation of Pilion to neoclassicism is of commensurate interest.

Chronologically speaking, Volos (fig. 267) took the lead in the whole of Thessaly and North Greece, with projects to modernise the urban design as early as 1833. The reason for this was the asphyxiating conditions that prevailed in the small Fort,[353] in which only Ottomans resided. The Greek merchants of the town kept their families in the villages of Pilion and visited them at the weekend – a custom that was to last, as we shall see, down to 1863. Originally, all that existed outside the Fort was a complex of "wretched buildings", warehouses and privately owned shops, belonging to an Ottoman Turk, a "powerful local figure", towards the sea in the area now called Palia.[354] Encouraged by the provisions of the Tanzimat, the Greeks sought permission in 1841 to found a new settlement: permission was granted, and an engineer was dispatched to draw up the relevant plan "worthy of a European town". There was at once a flurry of sales of building plots in the area of the town inside the plan, houses were constructed, as was a school and a church, but in 1856 building was abruptly prohibited. The most probable cause was that the interests of the Ottoman landowners

268. Volos, view of buildings of Thessaly University in the harbour.

268

269

269. Volos, the restored Spirer warehouse, now an exhibition and conference hall. 270. Volos, the restored Tsalapatas brick-factory, now a multi-functional centre (2007).

270

271

271. Volos, view of the seafront. 272. Volos, Argonafton Street, the western part of the wide pedestrian way that runs along the coast of the town.

273

274

were affected, and, on the other hand, a rapidly growing (Greek) town would constitute a threat to the Fort, since the Greek claims to Thessaly were well known.[355]

The ban was lifted in 1863, after a way had been discovered to involve Ottoman Turks in land speculation schemes. The population increased in leaps and bounds thereafter, reaching 5,000 in 1881, and just before they departed, the Ottomans entered into a contract with their Greek fellow-townsmen, granting them rights in the coastal zone, with permission to fill in a strip 50m. wide, before the Greek state could stop them (figs. 278, 279).[356]

Liberation gave the signal for development at a more rapid rate. In June 1882, the town plan for Volos was ready, drawn up by an engineer, who unified the extension at the east with the area around the Fort, "in a simple rectangular grid with identical building blocks". The Fort itself was not affected in any way, since it was the place where the Ottoman population lived.[357] A similar grid was applied to the new quay.[358] It was not until 1889 that the fortification walls of the Fort were demolished, in order to "apply the new street layout which would obliterate the 'filth' and also the oriental aspects of the town."[359] A few years earlier, in 1886, the quay was widened by ten metres, and after 1910 it was embellished "with a pavement and lighting" (fig. 280).[360]

The author Zacharias Papantoniou commented in 1937 that Volos had "large streets running

273. Volos, the eastern part of the pedestrian way on the coast (see fig. 272), flanked by a park.
274. Volos, view of the coastal park before the church of Ayios Konstantinos. 275. Volos, the Archaeological Museum on the western part of the town.

1909
ΑΘΑΝΑΣΑΚΕΙΟΝ : ΜΟΥΣΕΙΟΝ

longitudinally, but no great avenues towards the mountains which [...] would allow the emerald of Pilion to spill down to the harbour."[361] And he compares the town with Thessaloniki: "When the whole of Thessaloniki, laid out by Hébrard [...] was condemned, despite such an exceptional fortune, to be confined to a thrice-accursed strip of coastline, how can one not consider the quay of Volos to be an outstanding Greek phenomenon. [...] A blessed work, a true monument of municipal foresight. Only Volos in Greece was bold enough for such a coastal avenue. This is its square – there are no squares in the town – this is the place for its stroll, its meeting place and its theatre box."[362] This is true: what the new town could boast of was arranged along the two kilometres of its coast (figs. 268, 273, 274). Behind it there were only endless, identical building blocks, all built up. Not only were there no squares, but not even sites allocated for major communal buildings, which resulted in the emergence of a curious group of social welfare foundations at the east end of the settlement.[363]

The liberation of Volos, however, contributed not only to the growth of a new town, but also to its transformation from "a commercial town dependent on its hinterland" into "a field for intense industrial activity, with the result that at the end of the century it had become the second industrial town after Piraeus."[364] The new

277

276, 277. Volos, single-storey buildings with courtyards, characteristic of the area of Palia.

278

279

character of Volos however, did not "disrupt the urban tissue with uni-functional zones, degenerated working-class districts, a congested historical centre, and pronounced breaks or rapid extensions."[365] The industrial units were dispersed within the urban tissue, the largest, naturally, being near the harbour and the railway station (figs. 264, 269, 270). In comparison with Larisa, indeed, the administrative centre of the region, Volos developed at a more rapid rate and acquired greater density.[366]

The public and private architecture that completed the urban form of Volos was to be neoclassical and eclectic, faithfully following the predominant models of Greece, and with a spirit similar to the one that we shall encounter later on Pilion. If on Pilion, which had a rich architectural tradition, adaptation was necessary, in Volos the assimilation of neoclassicism was uniform and sweeping (fig. 275). No one, of course, considered transferring to the new town the earlier neighbouring models. When this did happen, after the Second World War, with the erection of the (neo-traditional) Town Hall to designs by Dimitris Pikionis, and the Museum of Folk Art by Kitsos Makris, perceptions had already begun to change – though again, there were to be no imitators. Three separate churches built between the two World Wars by Aristotelis Zachos, who believed that the regeneration of Greek architecture would take the form of a continuation of Byzantine architecture, also remained unique.

280

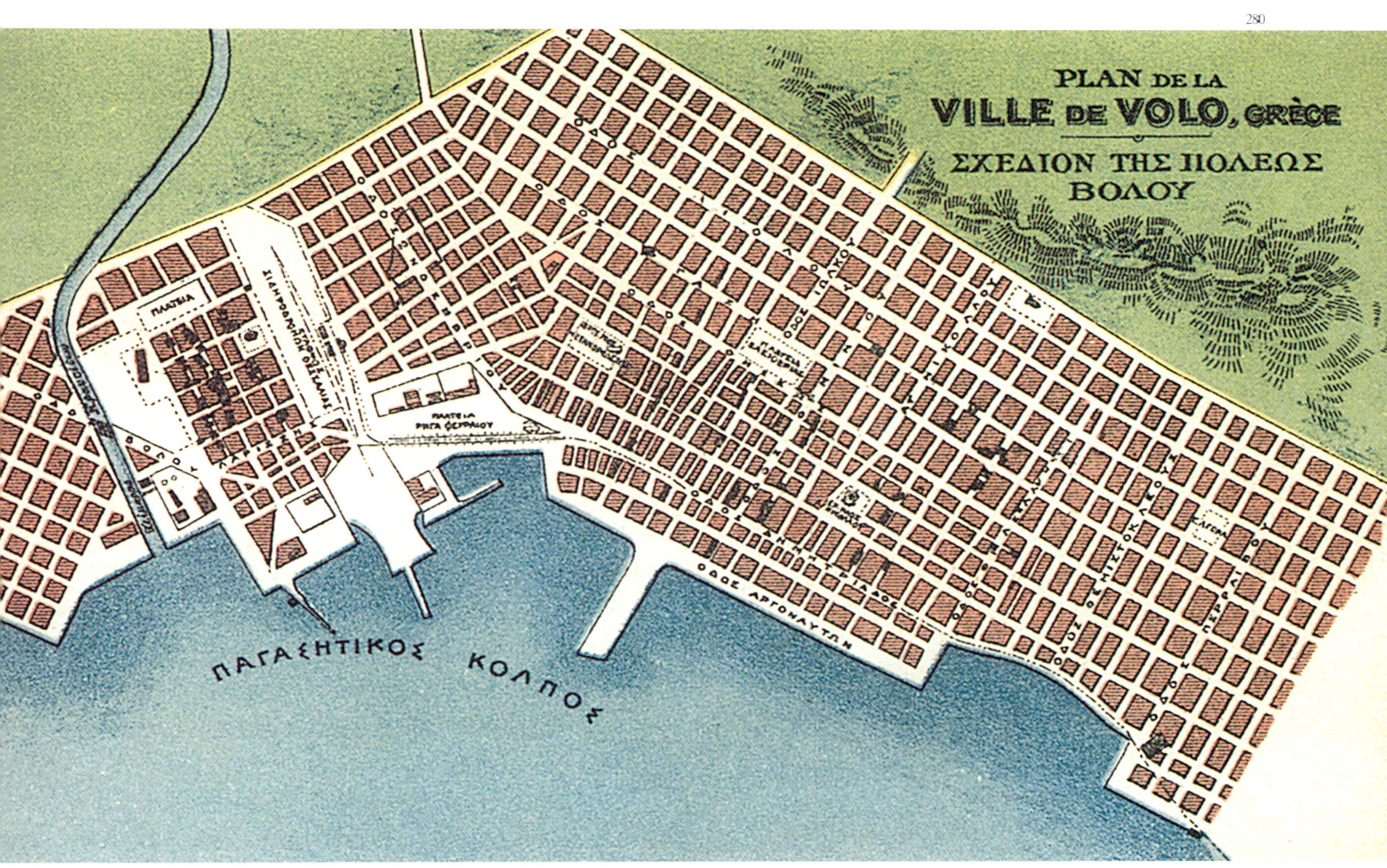

278. Volos, the Frourio (fort) and its extension at Palia, as shown on a map of 1882 (cf. fig. 279) (redrawn by V. Chastaoglou). 279. Volos, the town plan of 1882, showing the extent of the city's growth at the time (redrawn by V. Chastaoglou). 280. Volos Town Plan (1904), showing the outline of the seafront (St. Batoudakis collection).

The transition from tradition to neoclassicism in the architecture and public space of Pilion is described very vividly by Yannis Kizis: "The abandonment of some of the old buildings, the radical renovation of others with new neoclassical interventions, and the building of new 'extrovert' *archontika* [...] was detrimental to the relationship between the volumes, and changed the scale [...]. The relationship between private property and public space changed, together with the features that bounded the courtyard and the cobbled street (*kalderimi*): the high enclosure walls became lower and were topped by iron railings, and the roofed wooden courtyard gates were replaced by iron gates of neoclassical type. The private outdoor space was perforated, in an attempt to expose to common view the innovative [...] elements that adorned the late traditional mansions (*archontika*) or their newer historicist equivalents [...]. Finally, interventions were even stronger in the design of squares and church enclosures. Marketplaces (*pazaria*) were paved with schist slabs in regular patterns (*kapakia*) and were made completely level, approaching the model of the squares in towns. Their boundaries were defined more clearly by the erection of municipally owned coffeehouses, which gave a new dimension to the recreational role of the square. Neoclassical forms were imposed through donations: fountains with learned inscriptions, bell-towers, clock-towers, and entire churches replaced the earlier traditional structures."[367]

281. Makrinitsa, view of the area of the sloping main street of the settlement, where Ph. Tsikriktsis designed a monumental staircase flanked with cypress trees, as an alternative route to the church of Ayios Athanasios at the centre of the picture.

282

283

Makrinitsa, and nearby Portaria, are an important pair of neighbouring traditional settlements of Pilion, on account of their size and position (they lie on the hillside above Volos, a short distance from the town). At the same time they differ from each other in terms of their urban design. The general shape of Makrinitsa is long and narrow, with a distinct difference in level between the upper and lower part of it, which reaches almost to the outskirts of Volos. Portaria, in contrast, is a more solid settlement with a virtually square shape. The two settlements also differ in the manner in which they adopted 19th-century neoclassicism, a circumstance that is due only up to a point to geographical factors. I shall refer to only three features of the settlements: the formation of the central (secular) square in comparison with the enclosure of the main church, the incorporation of geometric tracings in the urban tissue, and the architectural forms selected. In its present form, the main square of Makrinitsa, which is impressive for the wide view it offers (figs. 286, 287), was created by the Municipality, probably at the beginning of the 20th century,[368] and was later embellished through a private donation in 1930[369] and more recently (1972) by the addition of new buildings at the back of the settlement.[370] Although the fountain and the church of the Timios Prodromos next to it show that there was previously a central clearing here,[371] the bold projection

284

282-284. Makrinitsa, details of the work of Ph. Tsikriktsis. At top left is the beginning of the staircase emphasised by a fountain. At bottom left is a view below, with the axis slightly changing direction. At the right, a view below, with the beginning of the staircase in the background.

285

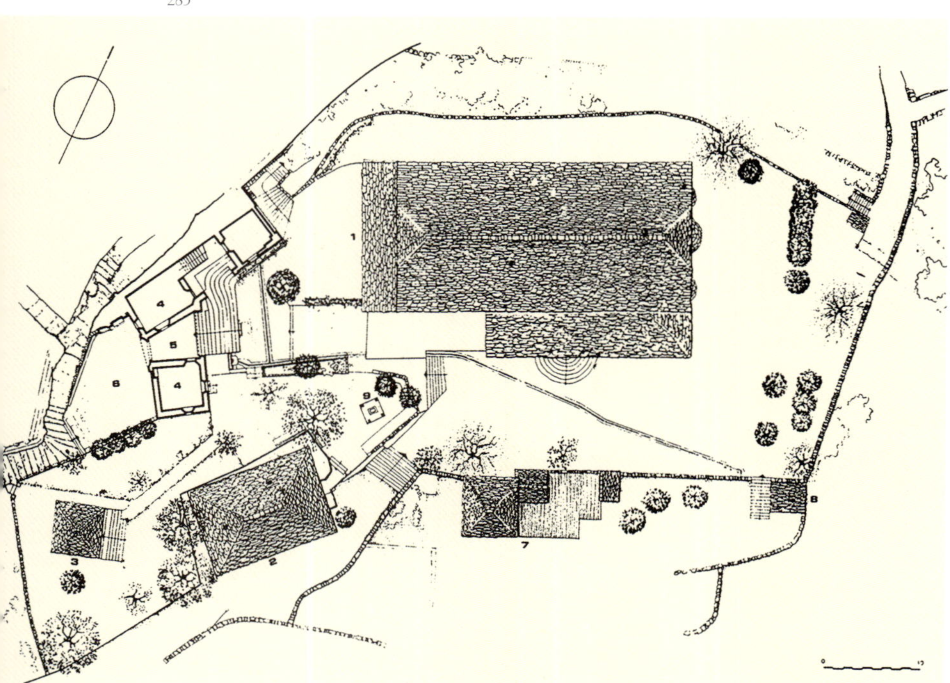

286

of the completely level square, as we know it today, gives expression to the collective desire for the recognisable central reference point provided by a typical town square. In this way, Makrinitsa automatically acquired the basic ingredient of every neoclassical settlement – the square – transforming the original shape of the clearing and overturning the traditional way in which a formation of this kind is integrated into the strongly sloping terrain characteristic of the settlement as a whole. The resulting square, formed like a 'balcony', has no traditional features: without detracting from the earlier, familiar symbols in the background (church and fountain), an almost rectangular level surface is formed that seems to hang in space.

To make the difference clearer, it is enough to compare this square with the superb sequence of varying levels encircling the main church of the Panayia (Koimesis), above the present car park of the settlement (figs. 285, 288). The subtle gradations in the 'landings', interconnected by sets of stairs, and the larger, slightly sloping paved areas, the integration of built forms into the slope, and the carefully studied perspectives, create an exceptionally fine composition of buildings and open spaces.[372]

The second distinctive ingredient of Makrinitsa is the linear form of a staircase of monumental scale, with 81 'strides', which ends at the forecourt

285. Makrinitsa, the gradation of finely articulated open spaces around the church of the Panayia (Koimesis) of 1767, with the official entrance at the left, passing under the building of the Bishopric (source: Rea Stylianou). 286. Makrinitsa, the fountain known as Athanato Nero ('Immortal Water') (1809) at the back of the main square of the settlement. At the back of it there was once a level area where the dignitaries of the local community used to congregate. 287. Makrinitsa, the main square with the coffee-house. 288. Makrinitsa, view of the south part of the open spaces around the church of the Panayia (Koimesis) (cf. fig. 285).

287

288

289

290

of another church, that of Ayios Athanasios (figs. 282-284).[373] This staircase – exclusively for humans –, flanked by imposing cypress trees, reduces the distance between two points of the central spine of the settlement, which twists and turns up the hill in the traditional form of a cobbled alley. The project, which is attributed to the "popular urban designer" Philippos Tsikriktsis,[374] is unique in the settlement and its monumental character betrays an expediency that is not related solely to function. It is a work of pure embellishment, the jewel of the settlement, as too are many of the public fountains that adorn the same central axis. Apart from these two public works, the square and the staircase, the adaptation of neoclassical forms in the settlement of Makrinitsa is very limited – especially when compared with Portaria.

In contrast with the situation at Makrinitsa, Portaria had the misfortune to be split in two by the modern thoroughfare, which destroyed part of its central nucleus. What has survived, as an adjacent public open space, which was once adorned (as at Makrinitsa) with abundant running water, but which is now dry, is a row of terraced open spaces with plane trees, which form a peaceful square for pedestrians (fig. 290). Here, however, we do not have the large level surface with a regular outline of Makrinitsa that hovers in space. Nor does it have a historical character, or a fine view.

289. Portaria, forecourt of the church of Ayios Nikolaos (1856). 290. Portaria, Melina Merkouri Square, with plain trees and formerly with running water.

This space does not seem as though it could ever form the central reference point for the settlement as a proper neoclassical square, either in formal or in functional terms. It would in any case be difficult to imagine the old atmosphere of this area.[375] The form of the enclosure of the main church of Ayios Nikolaos, however, remains unchanged; the church follows traditional models (fig. 289), though it is less imposing than the Panayia of Makrinitsa. Although there is no recognisable trace of neoclassicism in the public spaces of Portaria, the architecture of the buildings, in contrast, does express a very strong neoclassical presence, with abundant examples ranging in date from the middle of the 19th century to about 1920 (figs. 291, 292).[376] This is due to the economic flowering of Portaria during this period, as a result of the investment in new houses by Greeks of the diaspora, in which the forms were imported from abroad, and at the same time to the conversion of the settlement into a popular summer holiday resort. Makrinitsa, in contrast, entered upon a comparative decline. Strangely enough, 'retrogressive' Makrinitsa used neoclassicism in the public domain (the square) while 'innovative' Portaria expressed it in the private domain (the houses): it is no coincidence that the Theoxenia, the first hotel on Mount Pilion – which is now slowly being restored – was built in the latter, and, indeed, in the main square.

291

292

291. Portaria, the Kantartzis Mansion. 292. Portaria, the Athanasakeion Nursery School (K. Argyris, 1903).

293

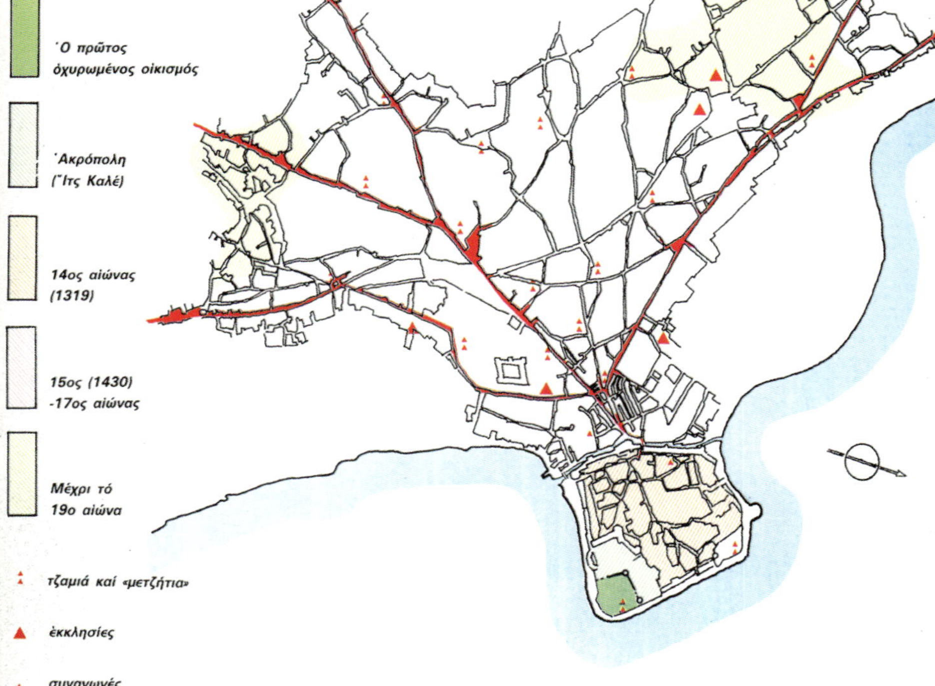

294

NORTHERN GREECE ('NEW LANDS')

From Ioannina to Kavala

The special feature of Northern Greece, in terms of its adoption of the procedures for drawing up town plans and implementing them in the period under examination here, derives from two main factors: the delayed – after the Balkan Wars – liberation and incorporation of these regions (as 'New Lands') into the Greek state, and concomitantly, the opportunity that was afforded the Ottoman authorities to move in a similar direction, planning and implementing a variety of works to improve the urban fabric and modernise the towns. The time lag in Greek intervention in the settlements of Northern Greece had two consequences: that it was the continuation of a policy that had already been inaugurated by the previous regime and that it adopted more updated methodological tools for physical planning that came from Europe.

Given this situation, a number of points of clarification are required before the settlements of Northern Greece are included amongst those that reveal neoclassical influence in their town planning and architecture. In fact, the neoclassicism of 'Old Greece' was not only earlier, but also came directly from Europe, through foreign architects and engineers who visited the country or settled in it as soon as the Greek state was founded. Its development thus followed a different course from that of Northern Greek neoclassicism, which was subjected to similar, direct influences both from

293. Ioannina, view of the Castle (engraving).
294. Ioannina, map of the evolution of the urban tissue (late 19th century) (redrawn by Dimitra Rogoti).
295. Ioannina, view of the town from Litharitsa Square.

296

central Europe and from the capital of the Ottoman Empire, Constantinople. These two currents were related and shared a common aim: modernisation through Europeanisation. But whereas this affinity manifested itself in free Greece as a promotional tool for nationalism, in the territories that were still under foreign rule, the same innovations were regarded simply as a modernisation of the (Ottoman) state machine. The latter had no reason to intervene and change the existing social structure, which was interwoven with the multinational identity of the geographical regions of Northern Greece. The Greek side, for its part, however, was forced to clear away the now inappropriate "mosaic" of ethnic and religious communities in order to assert the presence of the Greek state.

To summarise, the two state machines interpreted similar methods and ulterior motives of physical planning differently. The Greek authorities inherited an Ottoman infrastructure, which might have distinctive features but was nonetheless familiar, since it had been known for about three quarters of a century in the rest of the country. Therefore, the discussion on Greek neoclassical towns may legitimately be extended to include Northern Greece. At the same time, it may be noted that there was actually no significant time lag recorded in the northern regions, since the relevant interventions in the south only slightly preceded those in the north.[377] The reforms of Ottoman society as a result of the Tanzimat, which were accompanied by corresponding

296. Ioannina, Market. Passageway between shops, at right angles to the commercial street. 297. Ioannina, Market. Shops along the street.

297

298

299

town-planning reforms, had been set in train as early as 1839, and were subsequently imposed with increasing effectiveness – with further legislation in 1856, 1869 and later.[378]

On the other hand, if we assess the end product of the town planning interventions in Northern Greece down to 1920, two aspects may be cited. On the one hand, "the experimental use of new planning methods" in these towns[379] is signified by the very coining of the term physical planning (*'poleodomia'*) in modern Greece; [380] and on the other an awareness of the exemplary character of the interventions in the north – either contemporary or later than the period under examination here.[381] This explains the comment in an Athenian newspaper of 1917: "The rebuilding of Thessaloniki in a more European manner has aroused a lively debate about a similar reform in Athens."[382] The examples of town planning in Northern Greece are thus not simply dependent on, or "a poor relation" of, what was happening in the south, but represent a development of it and a link with the present day; and, indeed, in certain cases, such as Thessaloniki, they form an outstanding example, as we shall see below.

Ioannina (figs. 293, 294) is one of a group of important centres in Northern Greece that received town planning interventions intended to modernise it at virtually the same time and in the same spirit as all the others. As we have noted, these changes followed the reforms set in train in the Ottoman Empire largely from the middle of the 19th century

298. Ioannina, Market, reuse of an old passageway with new commercial and recreational facilities.
299. Ioannina, Market, the Liabeis Arcade in Anexartisias Street.

onwards. Ioannina, of course, could not match Thessaloniki: in addition to the difference in size there was a difference in method and objective. In Ioannina the objective was the modernisation of the commercial market, while in Thessaloniki it was the creation of an infrastructure to link up with the European rail network.[383] More specifically, in Ioannina the reform took place after a fire and involved "the provision of a street network".[384] The fire, which was an act of the 'progressive' Prefect ('*Vali*') of Ioannina, Ahmed Rasim (1869), destroyed the market and the area around it. In accordance with the plans that were drawn up within two months, the market was extended to the northwest, along Anexartisias Street (figs. 296-299, 302). Although this change was not drastic in town planning terms, "it made an important contribution to the renewal of the structure of the shopping centre."[385] According to the minutes of Ahmed Rasim's report for 1869 "[...] that the Polytechnic and orphanage are being erected in Ioannina; that the market of Ioannina is being built in stone, and is regularly divided by broad streets [...]."[386] Thirty years later, an Italian visitor was to describe this market: "The bazaar of Ioannina is not in enclosed, roofed arcades as is the case in many oriental cities, but in three broad, spacious streets, at the side of which are low buildings in which the shops are established, with large openings through which one can see from the street everything that is happening in the shops, which are at the same time shops for selling and workshops."[387]

300

301

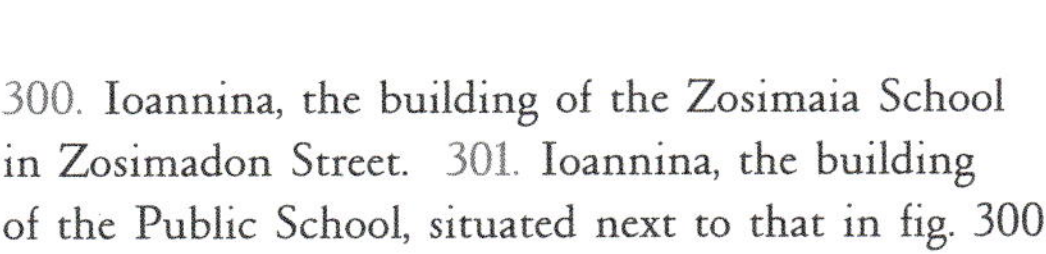
300. Ioannina, the building of the Zosimaia School in Zosimadon Street. 301. Ioannina, the building of the Public School, situated next to that in fig. 300.

The later vicissitudes of the Ioannina plan illustrate the great difficulties in carrying out town planning modernisation during the transitional period from the Ottoman to the Greek administration: "The first to see to the drawing up of a comprehensive plan for the town was Chairis Patsandas, who was mayor during the Ottoman period. He assigned the execution of this plan to Italian engineers, the brothers Bernasconi, who drew up a topographical map of the town in 1900. After this had been drawn up, the then Vali of Epiros, Osman Pasha, formed a committee to study and execute the plan for the street layout. The original [...] was lost [...] in 1912-1913 [...] and only a copy is preserved on which the street layout study was based. In 1913, the then general director sent an engineer employed by the Municipality to Switzerland, who gave an expert Swiss engineer the details with which to draw up a new street plan, which was approved in 1916 and implemented. Then the famous engineer Hébrard was summoned, and the drawing up of a new plan was assigned to him. This plan, however, was not put into use, as being difficult to implement."[388]

The urban tissue at the centre of the town today has undergone many additional interventions, such as the laying of streets and the formation of large squares (Litharitsa) (fig. 295), but the market has retained the image it acquired in the late 19th century. The local architecture constantly harked back to Classical and Byzantine memories (figs. 300, 301).

302. Ioannina, Market, old shop fronts.

ΕΥΑ·5172

303

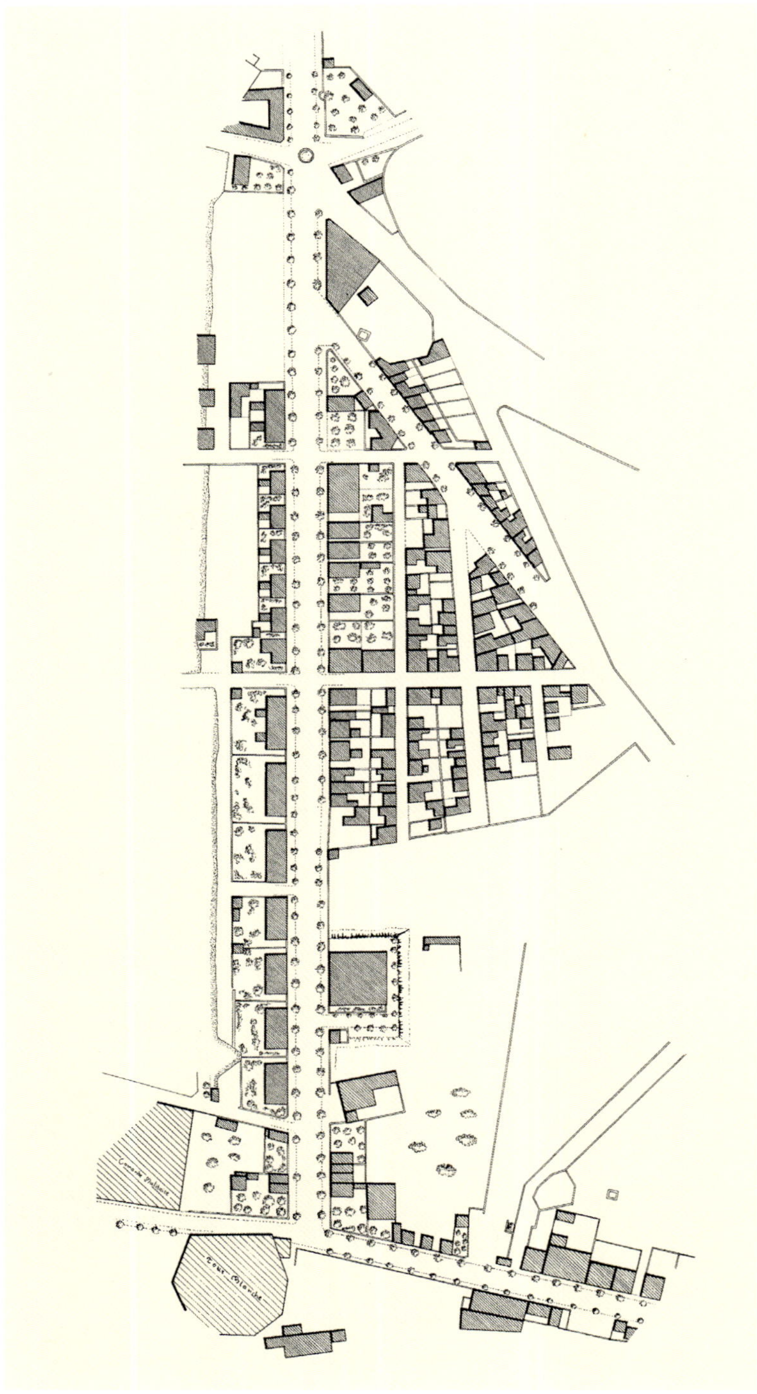

Thessaloniki is a unique example from any point of view, as we have already noted, and is an unsurpassable achievement of urban design in Greece. The redesigning of the city immediately after the fire that destroyed its centre (1917) (fig. 309) had all the features for it to be considered a model and also "the greatest town planning achievement ever carried out in Greece."[389]

Before vindicating this judgement however, we have to go back in time to the interventions that had taken place in the city from the middle of the 19th century onwards, in the context, as we have seen, of the reforms implemented by the Ottoman state. In 1858, the sultan Abdul Metzid visited Thessaloniki, a circumstance that supplied the spark for changes in the town. The first substantial intervention came eight years later with the demolition of the sea wall and the creation at the same time of a quay and a coast road, as well as with the later laying out or straightening of a series of streets, the unification of functional zones, and improvements, especially in the harbour (figs. 306, 307).[390] These projects continued until 1902 and had direct consequences for the expansion of the town market. At the same period, the infrastructure networks were modernised and many public buildings were erected.[391] In 1886, Thessaloniki began to extend outside the fortification walls, a trend that accelerated from 1890 onwards (fig. 303), while in the same year, the existence of two "large suburbs" is already

303. Thessaloniki, plan of Chamidié Avenue with the new extensions, traced outside the fortifications on the eastern side of the city in 1899. 304. Thessaloniki, the New City Plan designed by a committee headed by E. Hébrard (1918).

ΒΑΣΙΛΕΙΟΝ ΕΛΛΑΔΟΣ
ΘΕΣΣΑΛΟΝΙΚΗ
ΣΧΕΔΙΟΝ ΡΥΜΟΤΟΜΙΑΣ
ΣΤΑΘΜΟΣ
ΟΔΟΣ ΕΓΝΑΤΙΑ
ΤΟΥ ΛΙΜΕΝΟΣ
ΥΠΑΡΧΩΝ ΛΙΜΗΝ
ΑΝΑΠΤΥΞΙΣ
ΣΧΕΔΙΟΝ ΕΚΠΟΝΗΘΕΝ ΠΑΡΑ ΤΗΣ ΕΠΙΤΡΟΠΗΣ ΕΠ ΤΗΣ ΜΕΛΕΤΗΣ ΤΗΣ ΝΕΑΣ
ΡΥΜΟΤΟΜΙΑΣ ΤΗΣ ΠΟΛΕΩΣ ΘΕΣΣΑΛΟΝΙΚΗΣ ΥΠΟ ΤΗΝ ΔΙΕΥΘΥΝΣΙΝ
ΤΟΥ Κ. ERNEST HEBRARD
ΥΠΟΓΡΑΦΟΝΤΑ ΜΕΛΗ ΤΗΣ ΕΠΙΤΡΟΠΗΣ
E.HEBRARD E.MAWSON A.ΖΑΧΟΣ Κ.ΚΙΤΣΙΚΗΣ Α.ΓΚΙΝΗΣ J.PLEYBER
Κ. ΑΓΓΕΛΑΚΗΣ
TH. MAWSON
'Ο
Ἐπὶ τῆς Συγκοινωνίας Ὑπουργός

attested. These extensions, indeed, led the authorities to draw up a street-plan in order to control the urban development.[392]

These interventions and the modernisation measures implemented in the town demonstrate that its population was also rapidly increasing. In fact, "for various reasons, as a result of urbanisation and urban renewal, the city was growing larger. Indeed, the "ethnic element" that is said to have benefited most from this, and which possessed "the most qualities for progress," were the Greeks.[393]

The above flurry of planning and architectural activity in Thessaloniki was the result of the application of new legislation ("Regulations concerning streets and buildings", 1864: "Law concerning buildings", 1883-1891). The law of 1891, in particular, which delineated the boundaries between public and private space,[394] was implemented directly in the form of a redistribution of urban land in the central area of the town, which had been destroyed by fire in this same year.[395] This town planning mechanism, which abolished existing property boundaries and distributed building plots to those entitled on the basis of an entirely new street-plan, was not to make its appearance in Greek law until 1914.[396] A redistribution of urban land was carried out in Serres after the destruction of the town, again by fire, in 1913.[397]

This, in general terms, was the institutional and practical groundwork that formed the basis for the important redesigning of the burnt city of

305. Thessaloniki, the seafront of the town (Nikis Street). 306. (next page) Thessaloniki Port, Passenger Terminal.

ΕΠΙΒΑΤΙΚΟΣ ΣΤΑΘ

PASSENGER TERMINAL
planet
seaways
ATHOS
Ν.Θ. 736

307

Thessaloniki in 1917. At this point we may insert the image of the town before the fire: "The separate communities remained faithful to their place of origin [...] and the town assumed a cosmopolitan aspect. [...] At the same time [...] the harbour was widened and received a large number of sail and steamships, the city was embellished, more Byzantine fortification walls were demolished, streets were laid out or widened, avenues were created, and Thessaloniki began to acquire the regular appearance and order of a European city."[398] It is very gratifying to encounter in a text written in 1930 a vocabulary identical to that used a century earlier in Greek settlements that had been given a town plan.

In addition to previous experience, a factor completely essential to the implementation of any town planning intervention was political will. This was set in train in two ways: through commitments entered into by the far-sighted prime-minister Eleftherios Venizelos, and decisive action by the Greek state machine. The former took advantage of every opportunity he had to claim to have been the inspiration behind the idea of designing the town from scratch. The British town-planner Thomas Mawson, a member of the Plan Committee, summarised Venizelos's tactic in a single sentence in 1917: "one's task became simple enough by considering Thessaloniki a piece of blank paper."[399]

During the critical first period after the fire the state, for its part, moved with unaccustomed

307. Thessaloniki, plan of the walled city by the Municipal Engineer A. Wernieski (1880).
308. Thessaloniki, the archaeological site of the Roman Agora on the axis of Aristotelous Street.

309

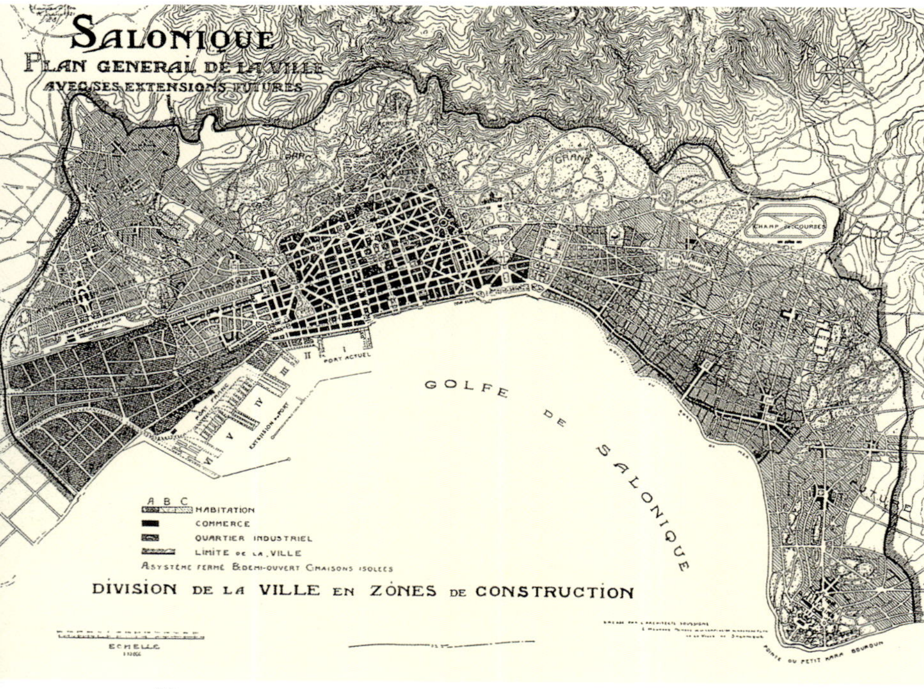

310

rapidity to take the necessary decisions and organise the business of redesigning the town. A mere six days after the fire, the necessary strategy was drawn up at a meeting organised by the minister of Communications, Alexandros Papanastasiou. The newspapers wrote: "It is proposed to expropriate the burnt area and dispose of the building plots formed after the new street-plan is produced, with preference given to the owners of the old plots." And one day later, the announcement was published in greater detail: "It has been decided to purchase the burnt area compulsorily. The owners of plots will be given bonds that can be transferred."[400]

Behind this concern lay specific political expediency: the Greek state wished to make its presence directly felt, as has already been emphasised, and moreover desired to impose a modernising town plan bearing a Greek seal. Thessaloniki had to acquire a Greek character immediately. In an attempt to investigate the motives of the Greek government in this intervention, Aleka Karadimou-Yerolympou wonders: was the objective "to obliterate the traces of the old occupation of the town? [...] To adapt it [...] to the role [...] of a 'Hellenised' economic and administrative centre for a wider hinterland? Or simply to make [the state's] presence felt by linking itself with an ambitious far-reaching project?"[401]

Much more was at stake here than in the Greek settlements after the War of Independence which

309. Thessaloniki, the area burnt in the fire of 1917. 310. Thessaloniki, master plan, 1918.
311, 312. Thessaloniki, archaeological sites on Navarinou Street (top) and in Diikitiriou Square (bottom).

311

312

had to be transformed immediately from 'Turkish villages' into European towns. In the case of Thessaloniki, embellishment was not enough, since the Ottoman state had already implemented a policy of modernisation. Something more was needed, corresponding of course with the ethnic diversity characteristic of the population of the town, and also with the political developments and strong nationalist claims of the period.[402]

The Plan Committee, headed by the French town-planner Ernest Hébrard[403] at once set to work and delivered the first final plans in May 1919 (figs. 303, 310, 313-319).[404]

I borrow a few phrases from the Committee's report: "We imagine Thessaloniki as a very beautiful town, with its modern monuments inspired by the fine examples that it already encloses. There is no need to stress, of course, that we do not mean faithful copies of these, but architectural compositions of the modern period that should be influenced not by any other foreign influence but by the local character, which will make it possible to achieve a homogenous harmonious complex without any sacrifice of the demands of the modern age."[405] And in an additional reference to a relevant publication by Mawson in 1918, he argues that "the city will attract visitors, since all its monuments will be found now in a far better environment, with wide streets and ample open spaces around them, thus promoting the beauty of their proportions and the details of their construction."[406]

313. Thessaloniki, view of Aristotelous Square.

314

315

The main features of the plan proposed by the Committee are listed by Nikos Kalogirou and include four design principles: "The adoption of a geometric system of tracings [...]. Giving prominence to the monuments and at the same time isolating them from the urban space. [...] The creation of new monumental complexes and prospects with 'neoclassical' principles of planning. [...] The adoption of unified principles [...] on the basis [...] of the obligatory facades and the combination of 'modern' and 'historical' design elements."[407] These definitions describe the design course followed by the Committee according to "the level of development of town planning at the beginning of the century".[408] Karadimou-Yerolympou also noted three consequences of the design: the obliterating of "the spatial organisation based on ethnic-religious groupings", "the securing and strengthening of land values" through the "modernisation of the infrastructure" and "the connection with the natural environment".[409]

The result, which is what is mainly of interest to us here, was described as follows about two years later: "Creating a modern, beautiful town, pleasant for its inhabitants and for visitors, preserving its historical character: to protect and exploit the ancient, Byzantine and Muslim monuments [...]" (figs. 308, 311, 312).[410]

At virtually the same time, in 1930, we encounter a similar description of the town: "In the interior,

316

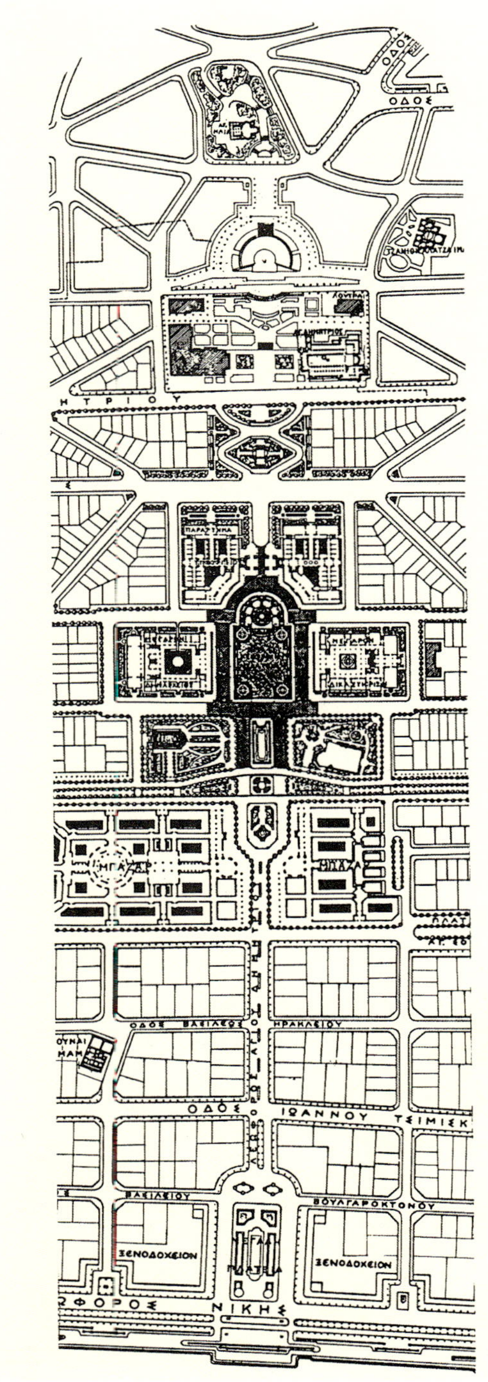

314, 315. Thessaloniki, views of Aristotelous Square.
316. Thessaloniki, proposal for the Cultural Centre along Ayiou Dimitriou Avenue (now Aristotelous Street), with public buildings and markets (E. Hébrard).

317

318

this town has the image of a genuinely oriental town, and this picturesque character has not completely vanished even today. [...] Immediately after liberation, however, the aspect of the town began to change and today one can see this old oriental colour only in very remote districts. The town very rapidly acquired a truly Greek character, despite the variety of the foreign inhabitants. The exceptional architectural design applied after the great fire of 1917, and the building of new large structures will shortly make Thessaloniki one of the finest towns in the eastern Mediterranean basin."[411]

In closing our reference to this very fine plan, I cite three conclusions from Karadimou-Yerolympou's study: it was a "utopian vision by bourgeois-reformers" for "social harmony": it was a genuine innovation, since the inhabitants and the government "grasped the singular nature of the historical moment and introduced a new form of organisation and function of the urban space in Thessaloniki"; finally, this town came to be described as "the 'exemplary' modern Greek town".[412]

I shall not deal with the later fortunes of the Thessaloniki plan; in closing I refer simply to two recent examples that are directly connected with this subject: the proposal by Anargyros Dimitrakopoulos (1939) for the Administrative Centre of Thessaloniki[413] and the recantations regarding Aristotelous Square – from the

317, 318. **Thessaloniki, perspective drawings of the Cultural Centre, along Ayiou Dimitriou Avenue (now Aristotelous Street) (E. Hébrard).** 319. **Thessaloniki, view of the lower part of Aristotelous Square.**

international competition in 1997 to the proposals by the Municipality in 2006.[414]

The development of Kavala (fig. 320) during the period under examination was influenced in some ways by the fact that it was the birthplace of Mehmet Ali, the founder of the Egyptian Dynasty at the end of the 18th century. In 1817 he created the Imaret, a seminary that functioned until 1902 and thereafter became a charity foundation. The repair of the impressive aqueduct of the town in 1816 (fig. 322) was also his work. He was also the benefactor of the inhabitants, paying their tribute from the income from Thasos island, which he had purchased earlier. One of his descendants, moreover, purchased the town fort in order to create an industrial and craft-industrial school, though the Bulgarian invasion in 1912 prevented the realisation of this project.[415] By the time of its liberation, then, the town of Kavala had received some financial exemptions and had modernised part of its infrastructure. On the other hand, it had not acquired a nucleus of technical education, that was so useful at the period, nor had it succeeded, for the same reasons, in constructing the most important installation for a coastal town, a modern harbour.[416]

It was the Greek merchants who exercised the pressure that led to the beginning of the relevant work – we shall see them later in this role of renewal.

About the middle of the 19th century, the town of Kavala itself retained the characteristic features

320. Kavala, view of the settlement. In the background is the Aqueduct (see fig. 322) and the area of the Panayia beneath the Castle (see fig. 321).

SAOS FERRIES

of a typical Ottoman Balkan town. It was confined within the narrow bounds of the Panayia area (fig. 321), apart from an extension with the market (*'Tsarsi'*) to the north. The market was reduced to ashes by a fire in 1862, and within two years the Greek inhabitants, encouraged by the reforms being promoted by the state itself, attempted once more to put forward their demand that the city be extended outside the fortification walls in the direction of the coast. Up to this time the Ottoman Turks had rejected this demand since they were afraid that this would lead to their losing the high rents that they charged for sites inside the town: "[...] we are seeking a place to live outside the fort, a place of building plots, which is rocky, steep and sandy and cannot provide even grass for raising animals, nor can it be used for anything other than houses," with the promise, indeed, that "the town will be increased, will be embellished, and the Government will benefit from selling plots of land in places that are now useless, the output of tobacco will be multiplied [...] and the customs duties will increase one hundredfold."[417]

The request was ultimately granted and the extension of the town was then laid out on the basis of a plan that is unknown to us, with "regular and identical building plots".[418] The result of this approval was a conflux of Greek merchants on the area of the extension. Four years later the prospects of the town seemed very optimistic, and twenty years later (1892) the local

321. **Kavala, view of part of the Panayia district.**

metropolitan bishop describes the extension as "a very beautiful, newly built neighbourhood of the town" and "a very fine suburb".[419] By the end of the century, all the administrative services and consulates had been transferred there.[420]

The coastal site now had advantages. The merchants could build – sometimes directly on the sea –, large, multi-storey tobacco warehouses (fig. 323) with their characteristic forms and houses. The architecture of the new town was neoclassical with an admixture of eclecticism, and also purely eclectic, and was frequently designed by European architects.[421] Finally, the development of Kavala did not relent in the period between the two World Wars as a result of political and social vicissitudes, and only slowed after 1940, when the international demand for eastern tobacco declined.[422]

322. Kavala, the old Aqueduct. 323. Kavala, tobacco warehouses with eclectic features.

322

323

THE END OF THE SECOND UPRISING

Although it originally stood on glass legs, the modern Greek state, as we have seen, immediately and dynamically promoted the modernising institution of the neoclassical town throughout the entire kingdom, as it then was. At precisely this first period, the as yet indestructible vision of the neoclassical town gave grounds for hopes of a new social contract in Greece. The institution was so innovative that it has reasonably been reckoned to have assumed utopian dimensions. So, with its decantation into regenerated Greece, the 'European' institution of the neoclassical town acquired a new, and enriched content. For this reason, by analogy with the Greek Uprising of 1821, this innovation may reasonably be regarded as the second uprising after the War of Independence, this time against the despotism of the 'barbaric' Turkish town and all it represented.

Although there was a similar effort at reform in the town-planning sector during the final period of Ottoman administration, which looked forward to Europeanisation just as much as the Greek administration did, this was passed over in silence for ideological reasons. When the Ottomans left, however, they left behind them incontrovertible testimony to their turn to neoclassicism, in the form of infrastructure works and public buildings, everywhere from Thessaly and Northern Greece to the islands of the eastern Aegean, the Dodecanese, and Crete. Neoclassicism was ultimately an international movement in which anyone who sought progress and modernisation had the right to participate, even as a superficial fashion. It was only in Greece that neoclassicism assumed 'national' dimensions. In the same way that neoclassical architecture symbolised the Greek presence in the unredeemed territories, so neoclassical urban design set its seal on the 'Greekness' of the corresponding towns. If we go back to the first years of the Greek kingdom, the innocence of the initial enthusiasm was followed by a period of realism, some traces of which had been apparent from the very first. The heaven-sent 'Plan' was subverted by the turn to land speculation and was replaced by procedural mechanisms, which may have recalled it superficially but were free of any kind of ideological expediency. In this way, Europeanisation through neoclassicism was adapted to local circumstances, securing the satisfaction of the interests of society.

After so much disillusionment and disappointment, both political and social, recourse was had, not surprisingly, to a distinctive form of imperialism, the Megali Idea (Great Idea). Similarly, after all the adventures of the plan in practice, it was not surprising that emphasis shifted to grandiose 'visions' and 'miracle-plans', that is to the metaphysical dimension of the neoclassical town.

This despairing flight from the present in some ways prepared the ground for the abrupt return to reality with the collapse of modern Greek expansionism, which was accompanied by the major wave of refugees of 1922. Circumstances now, however, were not the same as those of 1830, when the country had also been inundated with a wave of wretched refugees. On that occasion solutions had been sought in groundbreaking 'new settlements' and 'suburbs'; now, with few exceptions, only makeshift measures were taken to regularise the situation. Today we can distinguish on the various topographical plans of settlements those irregular extensions of the orthogonal fabric of the neoclassical town that were designed hastily to house refugees, and which were even described on the maps as 'refugee areas'. This historical event marks the well-defined end of the neoclassical town and signals the beginning of a new period. In Greece, in particular, it was not the arrival of the town of the modern movement that put an end to the neoclassical town, but the creation of these refugee settlements.

If the retreat from the fierce hopes engendered by the original reception given to the neoclassical town was everywhere visible after the Second World War, the erosion of it had been accomplished much earlier, as we have seen: when the essence of the plan was dissolved by a coalition of uncontrolled forces, which we can still see active around us with such terrifyingly accurate marksmanship.

From the very first, however, the idealistic town plan existed alongside the poorer, practical tool of the street plan. This was properly applied in rudimentary small settlements and townships, but its use eventually spread everywhere. Stripped of any intensions of embellishment, this tool – which now had little relationship with the ideological substructure of the neoclassical town – was the cynical conclusion, the practical transfer of physical planning to Greek reality. The street plan corresponded to the level of development of the country in general, and to what are called "private interests", in particular,[423] and has therefore survived without change down to the present day, as the official expression of state planning.

If the above is an albeit summary outline of the course followed by neoclassical town-planning in the mainland section of the kingdom of Otto, this general picture is subject to variation, with varying degrees of divergence, thanks to local distinctive features and particular historical circumstances. Thessaly, Northern Greece, the islands of the eastern Aegean, and Crete – since they were liberated later – were subjected to similar interventions of a neoclassical nature by the Ottoman state itself. The Cyclades and the Dodecanese – which already had a very strong architectural tradition – and the Ionian islands, with similar timeless profound western influences – adopted a different version of neoclassicism. In many cases, the urban-design aspect of neoclassicism penetrated fragmentarily and as a 'corrective' into what already existed. This was true after Liberation of many already active settlements in mainland Greece. In some cases, the penetration was so discreet that it is difficult to recognise its presence today.

However, it is this highly variegated mixture of earlier and later elements, which sometimes happens to be composed in unique landscapes, that perhaps has the greatest interest, since it expresses a perfect 'fit' between three types of landscape: the historical, the built and the natural. Future research should perhaps turn its attention in this direction while there is time: to constellations of formerly flourishing communities in mainland Greece that are favoured by fortune, and to island complexes in the Aegean and the Ionian sea, which have survived the maelstrom of development after the Second World War.

NOTES

1. Mention may be made here of the brief reference by A. Papageorgiou-Venetas (Ministry of Culture and Sciences, *Έτος ευρωπαϊκής αρχιτεκτονικής κληρονομιάς. Εισαγωγική έκθεσις της Ελληνικής Επιτροπής*, 1975, p. 28). He suggests, perhaps for the first time, a tripartite classification of the historical settlements of Greece: medieval; those with vernacular architecture; and neoclassical towns or districts of the 19th century.
2. In the first fifty years, organisation proceeded as follows: 1833: economic and administrative organisation; 1834-35: Judiciary and Council of State; 1836: taxes, professions and stamp duty; 1841: foundation of the Bank of Greece and Provincial Councils; 1845-47: taxation on buildings, organisation of Bishoprics, the Cadet School; 1855: buildings on national land; 1880: taxation of landed property.
3. These were surveyors. See, e.g. the approval of "the arrangement of the market" by the geometer Naoum ("Decree concerning the planning of the town of Livadia") *Athina*, 953/23.9.1842).
4. A. Kokkou, "Η πολεοδομική ανασυγκρότηση στην περίοδο 1828-1843. Κρατική πολιτική και πραγματικότητα", *Νεοελληνική πόλη. Οθωμανικές κληρονομιές και ελληνικό κράτος*, Proceedings of an International History Conference (Athens – Hermoupolis 1984), 1985, p. 360.
5. See M. Kardamitsi-Adami, "Κορυφαίος αλλά αγνοημένος", *I Kathimerini*, 23.7.1995 and A. Angelopoulos, "Το σπίτι του Σταμάτη Βούλγαρι", *To Vima*, 3.9.1995.
6. These were preceded by a catalogue of the Technical Chamber of Greece: P. Kyriazis (ed.), *Πρώτοι Έλληνες Τεχνικοί Επιστήμονες Περιόδου Απελευθέρωσης*, 1976 (hereafter PETE catalogue). It will be followed by another, based on the archives of the Ministry of Environment, Planning and Public Works "Έκθεση σχεδίων ελληνικών πόλεων 1828-1900", 1984. In any case, the important event that gave a major impulse to our knowledge of the phenomenon was the exhibition "Athens, A European Matter" held in the Zappeion Hall (1985; curated by G. Tsiomis), as part of the events celebrating "Athens, European Capital". Its importance is incalculable, because neoclassicism was presented as an international cultural phenomenon for the first time since it had begun to be discussed in Greece (that is, since 1930).
7. A start was made by J. Travlos (*Πολεοδομική εξέλιξις των Αθηνών*, 1960) and K. Biris (*Αι Αθήναι από του 19ου εις τον 20όν αιώνα*, 1966), who were followed by many younger writers.
8. This was published in the PETE catalogue and included in V. Dorovinis, I. Sotiriou, P. Tsakopoulos (eds.), *Έκθεση Σχεδίων Ελληνικών Πόλεων 1828-1900*, 1984 (hereafter ESEP catalogue).
9. A. S. Arvanitopoulos, "The changes of names in the new lands" (series of articles), *Athinai*, 27.3.1913; Archaeological Society, committee for baptising the "freed villages" (*Athinai*, 3.3.1913); G. V. Tsokopoulos, "Names", *Athinai*, 4.3.1913.
10. E. P. Dimitriadis, "Η παραγωγή του αστικού χώρου και ο αρχιτεκτονικός κλασικισμός στους οικισμούς της Θράκης κατά το δεύτερο μισό του 19ου αι.", *Νεοκλασική πόλη & αρχιτεκτονική*, Proceedings of a Panhellenic Conference (Thessaloniki 2-4.12.1983), [1984], p. 184.
11. Attempts to connect economic activity with the development of 19th-century settlements had been made as early as the 1880s, with the systematic study of Hermoupolis. See related papers in *Νεοελληνική πόλη. Οθωμανικές κληρονομιές και ελληνικό κράτος, op. cit.*
12. Originally dispersed in the provinces, industries gradually began to be concentrated on the large centres (P. Kalogri and V. Tsokopoulos, "Βιομηχανία και πόλεις στην Ελλάδα το β΄ ήμισυ του 19ου αι.", *Νεοελληνική Πόλη. Οθωμανικές κληρονομιές και ελληνικό κράτος, op. cit., p.* 431.
13. Although there are a number of individual studies (e.g. V. Theodorou, *Το εργοστάσιο εμαγιέ στην Κέα*, 1994), the full extent of the phenomenon is only just starting to be studied ("Ιστορικά μεταλλεία στο Αιγαίο 19ος-20ός αι.", Athens Technical University research programme, 2000-05, led by N. Belavilas, study forthcoming).
14. The first carriage road was laid from Pylos to Methoni before 1832 (T. Demodos, "Ο πρώτος δημόσιος δρόμος στην Ελλάδα", PETE catalogue, *op. cit.*, pp. 227-234), and a cart was seen for the first time in Athens in 1831 (K. Biris, *Τα πρώτα σχέδια των Αθηνών*, 1933, p. 38). Cf. M. Synarelli, *Δρόμοι και λιμάνια στην Ελλάδα 1830-1880*, 1989, pp. 24-25.
15. As far as I know, this question has not been studied, as it has, for example, in the case of the Arabic-Islamic towns (B. S. Hakim, *Arabic-Islamic Cities. Building and Planning Principles*, 1986).
16. A. Karadimou-Yerolympou, "Εκσυγχρονισμός και πολεοδομία στη Θεσσαλονίκη του 19ου αιώνα", *Νεοκλασική πόλη & αρχιτεκτονική, op. cit.*, p. 65.
17. *Geniki Ephemeris tis Ellados*, 46/20.6.1831.
18. *Athina*, 374/30.9.1836.
19. Decree "Περί της διαιρέσεως του Βασιλείου και της διοικήσεώς του", *Athina*, 102/12.4.1833. This was followed by the abolition of prefectures and the creation of a new Regulation (1836) with 30 'dioceses' and 14 'subdioceses'. The new, different distributions created chaos. In 1842 the 'dioceses' had been reduced in number to 24, and even this was thought to be inappropriate for so small a country – compared, e.g., with France (*Athina*, 925/13.6.1842). Within a few months, six transfers of municipalities were recorded (*Athina*, 960/17.10.1842) and we now have a first, perhaps sober assessment of the original decrees ("Provincial Councils", *Athina*, 976/12.12.1842). The question came to the fore again seven years later: the 10 'dioceses' (prefectures) are 'incompetent' for the administration of the state (*Athina*, 1598/29.5.1849), and it became even sharper five years after this, when it was noted that the division into 10 prefectures and 48 provinces led to bureaucracy ('*polygraphia*') (*Athina*, 2145/13.8.1854).
20. This mixed character was the rule for the period: cf. the official dress of the members of the government, who one year "wore Frankish dress, were Europeanised and adorned with gold from top to bottom" and the next were called upon "to cease to be Franks and turn Greeks into primitive mountaineers" (*Athina*, 233/20.4.1835).
21. For example, the fierce criticism levelled against the (exotic and expensive) "dress of civil servants" (Decree: *Athina*, 119/7.6.1833).
22. *Athina*, 149/3.6.1834 and 150/6.6.1834. The importance acquired by industry (by the standards of the time) was, as we shall see, a factor in the modernisation of the structure of the 19th-century urban centres, through the organisation of "industrial zones".
23. *Athina*, 2145/13.8.1854. What had not changed were the forest fires that created areas of land for pasturage (*Athina*, 2674/18.6.1858, Cf. a related draft parliamentary bill, *Athina*, 3004/12.8.1861, and the later attempt to deal with the "forest issue", at least down to 1884).
24. *Athina*, 2770/20.5.1859.
25. *Athina*, 3006/19.8.1861.
26. *Aion*, 2374/2.9.1868. The problem became even more acute twelve years later when 'place-seeking' was identified as a major wound that could be healed only by industrial development (*Aion*, 3359/23.10.1880).
27. *Athina*, 3187/21.10.1863.
28. *Aion*, 2718/30.9.1871. I. Latris is also said to have encouraged the creation of the new settlement of Voion in Lakonia.
29. The inhabitants of Adamantia were given half a *stremma* (0.05 hectares) of land to build on, one and a half *stremmata* (0.15 hectares) for farming, and an interest-free loan for building (*Athina*, 560/17.9.1838). In general, about 800 Cretan families were distributed amongst seven provinces (*Athina*, 1092/5.2.1844). A later reference to Cretan refugees raises the number to 60-65,000, whom Kapodistrias tried to settle at Minoa and in the area of Nafplio and Argos. In the reign of King Otto, 855 families settled at Minoa and another 15,000 people remained dispersed throughout Greece (*Athina*, 1315/16.5.1846, Cf. *Athina*, 1564/27.1.1849). In the period 1848-50, the Press frequently reported the issue of the settlement of Cretans. We read, characteristically that on Milos and at Minoa, if available land could not be found, it would be taken from the monasteries, and everyone entitled would have a little house, an ox, and tools (*Athina*, 1532/30.9.1848).
30. *Athina*, 1323/13.6.1846.
31. *Athina*, 1331/14.7.1846 and a long series of articles in the following three years on these problems of the settlement.
32. Γ. Saitas, "Μάνη", *Ελληνική Παραδοσιακή Αρχιτεκτονική* (hereafter *EPA)*, vol. 5, 1988, p. 191.
33. Submission of a bill to Parliament on this (*Athina*, 1829/31.12.1851) and the granting of 60-120 *stremmata* (6-12 hectares) of land free of charge to every 'leader' (*Athina*, 1830/5.1.1852).
34. "On the settlement of Thracians-Bulgarians and Serbs", *Athina*, 1340/15.8.1846. Creation of a German colony at Corinth (*Athina*, 1424/26.6.1847).
35. Pamphlet by Lieutenant-Colonel Emm. Manitakis (in French) on the progress made in Greece (*Aion*, 2187/21.11.1866).
36. Euth., "On settlements", *Aion*, 2748/10.1.1872.
37. *Athina*, 1564/27.1.1849.
38. *Aion*, 3157/12.8.1875.
39. *Aion*, 4490/2.6.1884.
40. See Decree banning the sale of "national lands", especially in towns (*Athina*, 89/22.2.1833), provision for the "administration of national lands" by "special economic Authorities" (*Athina*, 102/12.4.1833), debate on "Turkish lands" (*Athina*, 135/2.8 and 138/12.8.1833), debate on the later bill "concerning those who had built on national lands down to 1853" (*Athina*, 2225/21.2.1855 and 2226/23.2.1855).

41. Euthyphron, "On the new town of Voion", *Athina*, 780/1.1.1841.

42. "What is the most pressing need of Greece?", *Athina*, 3127/7.3.1863.

43. See below for conflicts in Hermoupolis and Sparti.

44. *Athina*, 1195/18.2.1845. Cf. the criticism of "the constant making of amendments", *Athina*, 2665/17.5.1858.

45. "You can knock as long as you like at the deaf man's door", *Athina*, 256/10.7.1835.

46. *Athina*, 477/9.10.1837. The towns of the Ottoman empire were generally thought to belong to the barbarous past that was to be rejected.

47. *Athina*, 725/19.6.1840. Cf. Part 3.

48. *Athina*, 730/6.7.1840.

49. K., "General panorama of Athens", *Nea Pandora*, 67/1.1.1853.

50. *Avgi*, 846/22.5.1861.

51. Reference by G. Simaiophoridis to the view of M. de Sola Morales on the extensions of Mediterranean towns in the 19th century ("Αθήνα: μια πόλη πρωτεύουσα του 19ου αιώνα", *Νεοκλασική πόλη & αρχιτεκτονική*, *op. cit.*, p. 105).

52. K. Fatourou-Isychaki, "Δρόμοι του ευρωπαϊκού νεοκλασικισμού προς την Ελλάδα και αντιστρόφως", *Νεοκλασική πόλη & αρχιτεκτονική*, *op. cit.*, p. 23.

53. D. Pikionis, "Η θεωρία του αρχιτέκτονος Κ. Α. Δοξιάδη για τη διαμόρφωση του χώρου εις την αρχαία αρχιτεκτονική", *The 3rd Eye*, issue 7-12/1937.

54. See the foundation of the embellishment committee in Athens (*Aion*, 3192/12.12.1875).

55. *Athina*, 1890/19.7.1852.

56. See the large number of articles on this from 1857 to 1869, when it was inaugurated by King George.

57. Despite this, the publication of various views in 1856 did not lead to a practical result similar to that of the railway. In 1880, visitors to Syntagma Square were still troubled by the "stench" from the sewers there (*Aion*, 3345/7.10.1880). The only solution was to "block" their grates in summer (*Aion*, 3439/16.1.1881).

58. The relevant decisions of Athens Municipal Council (*Aion*, 2564/18.5.1870) provided the spark for a large number of "public works" and the formulation of theoretical "views" and "proposals" down to 1884 (A. Christomanos, 'The water of the Athens aqueduct again", *Aion*, 4448/14.4.1884).

59. *Athina*, 2971/15.4.1861.

60. *Aion*, 4230/1.8.1883.

61. See *Elpis*, 854/26.5.1856, 882/21.12.1856 and 885/12.1.1857.

62. Mishaud, letter, translated into Greek, *Athina*, 134/29.7.1833.

63. A. Karadimou-Yerolympou gives a different content to the symbolism of the Plan: that it reinforced the concept of national identity and indirectly the identification with "ancient Greek models" of town planning ("Σχεδιασμός και ανάκτηση του χώρου της πόλης", *Νεοελληνική πόλη. Οθωμανικές κληρονομιές και ελληνικό κράτος*, *op. cit.*, p. 381).

64. *Athina*, 177/8.9.1834.

65. *Athina*, 156/27.6.1834 and 158/4.7.1834. More on the foundation of a Club in Athens, *Athina*, 1802/27.9.1851.

66. See the protests against the Municipal Council for a typical example of the delay in approving an extension "beyond the military Hospital" (*Aion*, 3564/10.6.1881)

67. *Athinai*, 11.7.1922.

68. *Aion*, 4386/31.1.1884. This trend had, of course, appeared much earlier: "we desire to beautify the language every day" (*Athina*, 98/25.3.1833); Dikaiarchos, "The resurrection of the old place names of Greece" (*Athina*, 106/26.4.1833) and Euthyphron, "Place names" (*Athina*, 312/19.2.1836). "The naming of streets" *Athinai*, 3.2.-8.2.1906. The British town planner Thomas Mawson later fought against the "unchecked changing of the names of Macedonian villages" that had just been liberated in the Balkan wars (*Athinaiki*, 5.2. and 7.2.1919).

69. *Aion*, 4375/18.1.1884.

70. *Athina*, 2698/10.9.1858.

71. G. Tsiomis, "Νεοκλασικισμός: τεχνολογία του χώρου", *Νεοκλασική πόλη & αρχιτεκτονική*, *op. cit.*, p. 233; Cf. *idem*, *Athènes à soi-même étrangère. Eléments de formation et de reception du modèle néo-classique urbain en Europe et en Grèce, au XIXe siècle*, unpublished doctoral dissertation, Paris 1983; *idem* (ed.), *Αθήνα Ευρωπαϊκή Πρωτεύουσα* (exhibition catalogue, Zappeion 1985).

72. "Things and miracles" *To Asty*, 246/8.8.1891.

73. *Athina*, 100/1.4.1833. Cf. the decree of 1835: Concerning the hygienic building of towns and villages (A. Karadimou-Yerolympou, "Σχεδιασμός και ανάκτηση του χώρου της πόλης", *op. cit.*, p. 384).

74. *Athina*, 220/13.2.1835.

75. *Athina*, 339/27.5.1836.

76. *Athina*, 740/10.8.1840.

77. *Athina*, 1520/16.8.1848, *Aion*, 3637/2.9.1881.

78. K., "General panorama of Athens", *op. cit.*, pp. 440-445.

79. By extension, the same intent may be observed in the organisation of a new, mandatory institution, the cemetery (See, e.g., "The second cemetery", *Athinai*, 3473/18.5.1912), or the regulation concerning the 'proper' way to walk on busy pavements ("Walk on the right", *Athinaiki*, 18/21.2.1919).

80. "You can knock as long as you like at the deaf man's door", *op. cit.* Cf. A. Karadimou-Yerolympou, "Σχεδιασμός και ανάκτηση του χώρου της πόλης", *op. cit.*, p. 386.

81. *Athina*, 2677/2.7.1858.

82. Th. Vellianitis, "Syntagma Square", *Athinai*, 29.11.1913. *Idem*, "The French School", *Athinai*, 25.9.1916.

83. Cf. the great concern with public health in the period 1881-83, occasioned by epidemics, hygiene measures, etc., which culminated in the disbanding of the committee "for health and embellishment" (*Aion*, 4231/2.8.1883). Cf. also the condemnation of the stench from the rubbish dump on the hill of Plato's Academy (*Aion*, 4222/22.7.1883).

84. *Alitheia*, 3163/4.8.1878; *Proia*, 81/30.5.1879; *Aion*, 3637/2.9.1881 and 3667/7.10.1881. Even when urinals were being constructed in Syntagma Square, a disagreeable smell could not be avoided (*Neologos Athinon*, 309/6.7.1877).

85. See the statement by Th. Vellianitis that the proper interior design of a house had only just begun to concern architects in 1916 ("Buildings and people", *Athinai*, 5.10.1916).

86. *Athina*, 2685/26.7.1858.

87. "It has been finally decided to lay out and regularise Ermou and Aiolou Streets in Athens", (*Athina*, 232/17.4.1835). Cf. *Athina*, 239/11.5.1835.

88. G. V. Tsokopoulos, "The little megalopolis", *Athinai*, 19.3.1913. The name is copied from a similar project in Nafplio by Kapodistrias.

89. E. About, *La Grèce contemporaine*, 1855; transl. by A. Spilios, *Η Ελλάδα του Όθωνος*, no date, pp. 161-162.

90. "The Greek capital", *Alitheia*, 3174/21.8.1878.

91. E. About, *op. cit.*, p. 159.

92. A. Papageorgiou-Venetas, *Εδουάρδος Σάουμπερτ 1804-1860*, *op. cit.*, p. 14.

93. *Ibidem*.

94. *Ibidem*, p. 15.

95. K. Biris, *Τα πρώτα σχέδια των Αθηνών*, *op. cit.*

96. K. Biris, "Το υπόμνημα Κλεάνθους και Σάουμπερτ για το Σχέδιον των Αθηνών", *Αθηναϊκαί Μελέται*, volume one, I, 1938.

97. K. Biris, "Το υπόμνημα Κλεάνθους και Σάουμπερτ για το Σχέδιον των Αθηνών", *Αθηναϊκαί Μελέται*, volume one, II, 1938, p. 15.

98. A. Papageorgiou-Venetas, *op. cit.*, p. 16.

99. *Aion*, 48/15.3.1839. Cf. *Aion*, 53/9.4.1839.

100. Th. Vellianitis, "The new Athens", *Athinai*, 9.11.1914.

101. According to the budget drawn up by Kleanthis with Misios (member of the Council of Ministers), the total sum (expropriation and demolition) came to 1,563,000 drachmas, which, though "paltry and inadequate" compensation, was at the same time "an enormous sum for the strength of the state purse" (K. Biris, *Τα πρώτα σχέδια των Αθηνών*, *op. cit.*, p. 13).

102. J. Travlos and A. Kokkou, "Πολεοδομία και αρχιτεκτονική", *Ιστορία του Ελληνικού Έθνους*, vol. XIII, 1977, p. 517.

103. "Plan der neuen Stadt Athen [...]", 1834 (Athens National Historical Museum), included in ESEP, 1984.

104. See descriptions: Th. Vellianitis, "The new Athens", *op. cit.*, και *idem*, *Acropolis*, 18.10.1921 (at greater length).

105. Cf. various later articles promoting Byzantine monuments ("Concerning the Byzantine monuments in Athens", *Athina*, 1417/31.5.1847 and "Byzantine churches of Athens", *Nea Pandora*, 54/15.6.1852).

106. Decree "Concerning ecclesiastical estates", *Athina*, 341/3.6.1836.

107. *Athina*, 2581/24.7.1857.

108. *Athina*, 581/31.12.1838. Cf. the question whether architects had made provision for squares in the new Athens Plan (*Athina*, 2537/14.3.1857).

109. *Alitheia*, 3099/20.4.1878.

110. "A second [article on] Lykavittos for the Athenians", *Neologos Athinon*, 107/17.12.1876.

111. ESEP, 1984, included four later maps of Athens (1849, 1860, 1875 and Kaupert 1881), three of which are kept in French archives.
112. *Athina*, 1734/25.1.1851. Cf. the extensive description by E. About (*op. cit.*, pp. 268-269) of the musical accompaniment to a stroll in Syntagma Square.
113. *Proia*, 165/22.8.1879.
114. *Athina*, 2507/21.12.1856.
115. *Alitheia*, 3209/16.10.1878.
116. *Alitheia*, 3226/15.11.1878.
117. "The antiquities and our indifference", *Aion*, 4115/18.3.1883.
118. K. Romaidis, "Concerning the rescuing of antiquities", *Chronos Athinon*, 68/18.5.1885.
119. "The Athens of the future", *Acropolis*, 26.4.1896. The title seems to have had a magnetic effect on the imagination: twenty years later we find reference to an interim date (13.7.1903) in an article by G. N. Philaretos (*Athinai*, 22.2.1918).
120. P. Vakkas, letter, *To Asty*, 7.11.1896. The same thing happened with the Athens Metro a century later.
121. D. Gr. Kambouroglou, "The new Athens", *Athinai*, 25.2.1918 (reply to the article by G. N. Philaretos cited in note 119).
122. Graf, "Palia Athina", *Athinaiki*, 230/29.9.1919.
123. "Byzantine decoration", *Athinai*, 7.3.1920.
124. "Athens is making progress. Its intensity and extent. City-Countryside City-Dream. Water, mayor, engineers", *Acropolis*, 20.10.1898.
125. "New beauty in the Capital", *Acropolis*, 24.9.1899.
126. A. Tanagras, "The Athens of the Future", *Acropolis*, 7.7.1902.
127. "The Court House building", *Acropolis*, 6.2.1901 and a later series of articles down to 23.2.1901.
128. Ch., "Public Buildings", *Athinai*, 3.12.1903.
129. Th. Vellianitis, "In the unknown Athens", *Athinai*, 5.7.1904. *Idem*, "Rizokastro and Anaphiotika", *Athinai*, 6.7.1904. Cf. a series of articles by Stam. Stam. "The Athens that is not Athens", *Acropolis*, 26.1 to 23.2.1908.
130. "How the Athens of the future was designed" *Athinai*, 3186/5.8.1911 and 3187/6.8.1911. A. Mylonas, "The necessary expropriations", *Athinai*, 3190/9.8.1911.
131. *Athinai*, 28.5.1912.
132. *Athinai*, 28.1.1915.
133. *Athinaiki*, 3.2. and 5.2.1919.
134. "The Technical Council", *Athinai*, 6-7-8.4.1920. A. Typaldos Basias, "The Technical Council", *Athinai*, 20.4.1920 and "The plan of Athens", *Athinai*, 20.1.1921.
135. O Anofelis, "Excessive abundance", *Athinaiki*, 181/10.8.1919.
136. *Athinai*, 6.2.1921.
137. *Athinai*, 16.4.1921.
138. "The borders of the two municipalities", *Athinai*, 15.10.1914.
139. *Athina*, 9.1.1835.
140. See the extensive and thorough investigation of the various versions of the plan by A. Papageorgiou-Venetas, *Εδουάρδος Σάουμπερτ...*, *op. cit.*, pp. 126-141.
141. See a later condemnation of the damage to the Long Walls of Piraeus (Ang. Tanagras, "Vandalism", *Athinai*, 12.6.1915).
142. M. G. Malikouti, "Η εξέλιξη του αστικού Πειραιά 1834-1922", in G. A. Steinhauer, M. G. Malikouti, B. Tsokopoulos (eds.), *Πειραιάς, κέντρο ναυτιλίας και πολιτισμού*, no date, pp. 139-140.
143. *Athina*, 254/3.7.1835.
144. *Athina*, 255/6.7.1835.
145. *Athina*, 264-5/10.8.1835. The problem continued to exist later, however (*Athina*, 1740/23.2.1851).
146. *Athina*, 339/27.5.1836.
147. L. Ross, *Erinnerungen und Mittheilungen aus Griechenland*, 1863; Greek transl. by A. Σπήλιος, 1976, p. 280.
148. *Athina*, 342/6.6.1836. See the later practical implementation of the measure (*Athina*, 2770/20.5.1859).
149. *Athina*, 386/11.11.1836.
150. *Athina*, 369/12.9.1836.
151. Euthyphron, "Concerning the Harbour of Kantharos", *Athina*, 329/22.4.1836.
152. See a later reference, *Athina*, 963/28.10.1842.
153. *Athina*, 476/6.10.1837.
154. *Athina*, 532/10.6.1838.
155. *Athina*, 616/17.5.1839.
156. *Athina*, 640/12.8.1839. Cf. "The Mayor of Piraeus, Mr. Skylitzis Omiridis", *Athina*, 892/14.2.1842.
157. *Athina*, 963/28.10.1842.
158. M. G. Malikouti, *op. cit.*, pp. 144-152. This may, however, have been due to the "Government's diffidence", which possibly feared that the development of Piraeus would harm Athens (the view of the French consul, De Varieux, cited in M. Synarelli, *op. cit.*, p. 167).
159. M. Synarelli, *op. cit.*, p. 167.
160. *Ibidem*, pp. 172 και 176.
161. "To the Ministry of Interior", *Athina*, 1744/8.3.1851.
162. "Squares here and in Piraeus", *Nea Ephemeris*, 82/23.3.1893.
163. *Athina*, 1879/23.6.1852.
164. K. "General panorama of Athens", *op. cit.*
165. "The town of Piraeus", *Alitheia*, 3128/10.6.1878.
166. M. G. Malikouti, *op. cit.*, pp. 178-180.
167. *Aion*, 3292/7.8.1880.
168. M. G. Malikouti, *op. cit.*, pp. 180-196.
169. "The progress of Piraeus", *Athinai*, 5.1.1903 (catalogue with 479 enterprises).
170. V. Ganiatsas, "Archaeological park at the gates of Piraeus", digital journal *Monumenta* 01/2007, www. monumenta.org.
171. N. Belavilas and Chr. Tsitsimbikou, "Η βιομηχανική πόλη του Λαυρίου από τον 19ο αιώνα έως σήμερα", in G. Polyzos and V. Panayiotopoulos (eds.), *Ιστορικός βιομηχανικός εξοπλισμός στην Ελλάδα*, 1998, p. 97.
172. The town began to be formed after the foundation of the first mining company by I. Serpieris (1864), which led to a great influx of population – workers and employees of the companies (D. M. Papayiannopoulos, entry "Λαύριον", *Μεγάλη Ελληνική Εγκυκλοπαίδεια (MEE)*, vol. XV, p. 853). N. Belavilas and Chr. Tsitsimbikou, *op. cit.*, use the terms 'Ergastirakia' (Small Workshops) and 'Porto Ergastiria' (Bay of Workshops) to refer to the harbour.
173. Ph. Stephanopoulos, "Το νεοκλασικό Λαύριο", *Technika Chronika*, August 1976 (special edition), p. 18.
174. *Ibidem.*
175. D. N. Papayiannopoulos, *op. cit.*, p. 853.
176. Ph. Stephanopoulos, *op. cit.*, p. 19.
177. D. N. Papayiannopoulos, *op. cit.*
178. Ph. Stephanopoulos, *op. cit.*, p. 20.
179. See Th. Vellianitis, entry "Λαυρεωτικά", *MEE*, vol. XV, p. 848.
180. Ph. Stephanopoulos, *op. cit.*, p. 22.
181. See D. Philippides, *Αρχιτεκτονικές Μεταμορφώσεις*, vol. 1, 2006, p. 58.
182. D. N. Papayiannopoulos, *op. cit.*, pp. 853-4.
183. M. D.Vatalas, entry "Χαλκίς", *MEE*, vol. XXIV, p. 427.
184. M. Synarelli, *op. cit.*, pp. 189-190.
185. J. Petropulos and Aik. Koumarianou, "Περίοδος βασιλείας του Όθωνος 1833-1862", *Ιστορία του Ελληνικού Έθνους*, vol. XIII, p. 177.
186. L. Ross, *op. cit.*, pp. 272-273.
187. I. S. Sarris, entry "Εύριπος", *MEE*, vol. XI, p. 770.
188. *Athina*, 279/5.10.1835.
189. *Athina*, 477/9.10.1837.
190. *Athina*, 611/29.4.1939.
191. A. Karadimou-Yerolympou, *Επανασχεδιασμός και ανοικοδόμηση της Θεσσαλονίκης μετά την πυρκαγιά του 1917*, 1985, p. 108.
192. Publication in the Government Gazette (nos. 14-15). Δημοσίευση στην *Εφημερίδα της Κυβερνήσεως* (nos. 14-15) on the plan to design a *proasteio* (extension) at Chalkida (*Athina*, 933/11.7.1842).
193. *Aion*, 2780/4.5.1872.
194. T. A. Kalatheris, *Ένας άγνωστος Άγγλος περιηγητής στην Χαλκίδα του 1874*, 1989, p. 20, note 26.
195. *Ibidem*, pp. 4-5.
196. M. D. Vatalas, entry "Χαλκίς", *MEE*, vol. XXIV, p. 427.
197. See, for example, a report of the discovery in an excavation of a mosaic with Dionysos seated on a leopard (*Athina*, 1439/28.8.1847).
198. The plan for the west part of the town is included in the ESEP catalogue, 1984.
199. J. Travlos and A. Kokkou, "Πολεοδομία και αρχιτεκτονική", in G. Christopoulos and J. Bastias (eds.), *Ιστορία του Ελληνικού Έθνους*, vol. XIII, 1977, p. 517. Previously published in the PETE catalogue, *op. cit.*, p. 85.

200. *Athina*, 230/20.3.1835.

201. As is admitted at the beginning of the relevant founding decree "Concerning the settlement of Psarianoi at Eretria" 1836 (A. Karadimou-Yerolympou, *Επανασχεδιασμός και ανοικοδόμηση...*, *op. cit.*, p. 100).

202. If I count correctly, the Peloponnese had 37 settlements that were given a plan, some of them in three successive phases (See relevant map, ESEP catalogue, *op. cit.*).

203. A. Karadimou-Yerolympou, *Επανασχεδιασμός και ανοικοδόμηση...*, *op. cit.*, p. 101.

204. A map of the old settlement is included in ESEP, 1984.

205. E. Papayiannopoulou, *Η διώρυγα της Κορίνθου*, 1989, p. 70.

206. Decree relating to the new site of Corinth, *Athina* 2651/28.3.1858. The "Plan for the new town of Corinth" (Royal Decree 26.6.1858) was included in ESEP, 1984.

207. Chr. Daskalakis, entry "Κόρινθος (Νέα)", *MEE*, vol. XIV, 1930, p. 887.

208. E. Papayiannopoulou, *Η διώρυγα της Κορίνθου*, 1989, pp. 65-67.

209. See "Street plan of the town of Philiatra", 1876, and "Street plan of the town of Gargalianoi", 1881 (included in ESEP, 1984).

210. I. Sarris, entry "Αίγιο", *MEE*, vol. II, p. 492.

211. A. Panayiotarea, "Aigio: tradition 'to be demolished'", *I Kathimerini*, 25.6.1995.

212. There is another old square (Platanou Square) near the sea, with twelve fountains and perennial trees (A. Karakatsani and Th. Stathakopoulou, *Αχαΐα - Ηλεία*, 1973, p. 20).

213. I. Sarris, *op. cit.*, p. 491.

214. *Ibidem*, p. 492.

215. There is a special reference to the Panayiotopoulos mansion, which suffered damage, in M. Biris, "The treasures of Aigio", *I Kathimerini*, 6.8.1995.

216. "Plan of the New Town of Patra", 1829 by St. Voulgaris, as printed in *Souvenirs de Stamati Bulgari*, Paris 1835 (published in the PETE catalogue, *op. cit.*, p. 157). "Pianta della citta di Patrasso" by St. Voulgaris, no date, "Plan of the Town of Old Patra", 1831-36; "Plan zu der Erbauung eines neuen Molo's...", 1837 (all these included in ESEP, 1984).

217. D. E. Moustakas, entry "Patra", *MEE*, vol. XIX, p. 789.

218. Chr. Papadatou-Yiannopoulou, *Εξέλιξη του σχεδίου πόλεως των Πατρών 1829-1989*, 1991, p. 17.

219. *Ibidem*, p. 29.

220. We may note at this point that Pausanias describes a similar situation on the coast of Patra, with sanctuaries amidst vegetation (*ibidem*, p. 30).

221. *Ibidem*, p. 15.

222. *Ibidem*, p. 31 (where a not very convincing interpretation is offered).

223. *Ibidem*, p. 33. The difficulties involved in reading a necessarily schematic map naturally give rise to a large number of hypotheses which are hard to confirm. To this category belongs the view of J. Dimakopoulos that Voulgaris was inspired by the design of Roman army camps ("Ρωμαϊκές αναβιώσεις στην Ελλάδα του Καποδίστρια. Η Πάτρα του Σταμάτη Βούλγαρη", *Νεοκλασική πόλη & αρχιτεκτονική*, *op. cit.*, pp. 68-83).

224. *Ibidem*, pp. 23-24.

225. *Ibidem*, p. 34. The assessments of Ch. Papadatou-Yiannopoulou are based on the oldest surviving street plan of the Municipality of Patras (1858) and the plans that followed. ESEP (1984) publishes an "Extract of the approved plan for the town of Patra" (1866), which, like that of 1865, "brought [its predecessor] to perfection" (*MEE*, vol. XIX, p. 789).

226. See a debate in Parliament on a bill to compensate for properties in the Old Town by exchanging them for building plots in the New Town (*Athina* 2655/12.4.1858).

227. *Athina*, 1299/14.3.1846.

228. *Athina*, 1733/20.1.1851.

229. "Patra", *Athina*, 1654/2.2.1850.

230. *Aion*, 3680/22.10.1881.

231. M. Synarelli, *op. cit.*, p. 144.

232. D. E. Moustakas, entry "Πάτραι", *MEE*, vol. XIX, p. 790.

233. "Diagram of a settlement on the coast of Kyparissia", 1871 (included in ESEP, 1984).

234. Ch. E. Daskalakis, entry "Κυπαρισσία", *MEE*, vol. XV, p. 397.

235. *Athina*, 743/21.8.1840.

236. For the breakwaters in the harbour from 1865, see M. Synarelli, *op. cit.*, p. 195.

237. "Plan de la ville basse de Navarin ...", 1831 (published in the PETE catalogue, *op. cit.*, p. 323 and included in ESEP, 1984, with the wrong date).

238. As with many defence works in the Peloponnese, which received successive interventions from the Ottoman Turks and the Venetians down to the latest by the expeditionary force of N. Maison (the 'famous' east fort).

239. "Plan of the town of Neokastro", 1861 (included in ESEP, 1984).

240. Published in the PETE catalogue, *op. cit.*, p. 322 and included in ESEP, 1984.

241. G. Saitas, "Μάνη", *EPA*, vol. 5, p. 191 and *MEE*, vol. X, p. 104.

242. Included in ESEP, 1984.

243. G. Saitas, "Μάνη", *op. cit.*, p. 132.

244. G. D. Kapsalis, entry "Γύθειον", *MEE*, vol. VIII, p. 755.

245. G. D. Kapsalis, entry "Σπάρτη", *MEE*, vol. XXII, p. 200.

246. The road from Sparti to Gytheio was of great importance: the planning of it began in 1837, but its construction was still not completed in 1868 (M. Synarelli, *op. cit.*, pp. 45-47).

247. P. Kalogri and B. Tsokopoulos, *op. cit.*, p. 437.

248. *Athina*, 500/15.1.1838.

249. "Review of issues regarding the town of Sparta under erection", *Athina*, 493/11.12.1837.

250. A refugee settlement developed on the south boundary of the town, beyond the tributary.

251. G. D. Kapsalis, entry "Σπάρτη", *op. cit.*

252. *Athina*, 459/4.8.1837. The toing and froing between the two settlements was to drag on, as is clear from a report on 22.8.1848 that the "annual fair of the municipality of Sparti" was held "at Mystras" (*Athina*, 1518/9.8.1848). The issue was finally settled two years later (*Athina*, 1969/30.4.1853).

253. *Athina*, 298/21.12.1835.

254. *Athina*, 322-323/25.3.1836.

255. *Athina*, 415/27.2.1837.

256. "The Road from Gytheio to Sparti under construction", *Athina*, 440/29.5.1837. The road was finally opened twenty-two years later (*Athina*, 2830/12.12.1859).

257. *Athina*, 500/15.1.1838.

258. *Athina*, 508/16.2.1838.

259. *Athina*, 493/11.12.1837.

260. *Athina*, 603/1.4.1839.

261. Euthyphron, "Concerning Sparti", *Aion* 220/22.12.1840.

262. *Athina*, 1154/13.9.1844.

263. The later image of Sparti is expressed in two of its plans: "Extract of the plan [...] showing its commercial squares and the warehouses built around it", 1856; and "Sparti", 1894 (1899) in two parts, designed by a foreman (included in ESEP, 1984).

264. In 1893 it was replaced by a new church, the modern Cathedral, also dedicated to the Evangelismos (G. D. Kapsalis, "Σπάρτη", *op. cit.*, p. 200). Cf. the brief description by E. About: "It is an administrative and commercial town, full of shops, barracks and offices" (*op. cit.*, p. 47).

265. *Ibidem*.

266. *Ibidem*, p. 205.

267. See D. Philippides, *Αρχιτεκτονικές Μεταμορφώσεις*, *op. cit.*, *pp.* 50-53.

268. See the map "Plan directeur de la ville de Nauplie", no date, probably 1828, by St. Voulgaris, and the later "Plan der Stadt Nauplia", 1834 (published in the PETE catalogue, *op. cit.*, p. 163).

269. L. Ross, *Αναμνήσεις*, *op. cit.* (cited in S. Karouzou, *op. cit.*, p. 68).

270. *Athina*, 126/1.7.1833. "[...] the only European city". (*Athina*, 214-215/26.1.1835).

271. S. Karouzou, *op. cit.*, p. 69.

272. *Ibidem*.

273. PETE catalogue, *op. cit.*, p. 325.

274. The renovation of the defence works in the second period of Venetian rule led to the earlier moat to the west of the town falling into disuse and being filled in; the Land Gate on the same side was demolished at an unknown date (S. Karouzou, *Το Ναύπλιο*, 1979, pp. 42-43).

275. See the following step, in accordance with the new town planning regulations: the designing of the Cemetery (Proasteio, Nafplio 1852. Extract of the plan "of the Suburb of the town of Nauplia", with the cemetery 1847. Published in the PETE catalogue, *op. cit.*, p. 331). See the description by L. Ross (*op. cit.*, p. 31) of the meeting of the Greek National Assembly here, in "a shack made of planed planks".

276. Ph. G. Kanellopoulos, "To the Municipal Council of Nauplia", *Athina*, 205/18.12.1834.

277. "Plan for the extension of enclosure and the regulating of the harbour of Nauplia", 1866 (included in ESEP, 1984).

278. The official designation of the old nucleus of Nafplio as a historical centre (1987) prevented its deterioration, so that today it is still a popular destination for excursions.

279. "In a census of 1913 [on Lesvos], 162 mechanically operated industrial establishments were recorded, the main bulk of which (113) are olive-presses. [...] According to the census of 1920, there were 47 tanneries on Samos" (N. Sifounakis, "Ανατολικό Αιγαίο. Η βιομηχανική κληρονομιά", in D. Philippides (ed.), *Νησιά του Αιγαίου*, 2003, p. 105). In a census of 1928, the olive-oil industry was 88% mechanised, and 141 factories, 340 hydraulic presses, and 3 olive oil refineries are recorded (P. N. Papas, entry "Μυτιλήνη", *MEE*, vol. XVII, p. 927). This flourishing local industry in the East Aegean suffered a serious blow in 1922 and then went into decline down to the Second World War.

280. N. Sifounakis, *op. cit.*

281. *Ibidem.*

282. Generally speaking, neoclassical towns in Greece appear to have developed in an atmosphere of devastation – material destruction, as on Chios, and ideological destruction, as of the old model of life.

283. In 1822-23, the refugees "found a home in Apano Chora, either in houses (the wealthier of them) or on the paved alleys of the township." (A. Th. Drakakis, "Οι πρώτοι Χιώτες πρόσφυγες που καταφύγανε στη Σύρα μετά την Επανάσταση του 1821", *Syriana Grammata* 6/1989, p. 104).

284. *Athina*, 785/18.1.1841.

285. *Athina*, 903/25.3.1842.

286. Cited in M. Synarelli, *op. cit.*, pp. 160-161.

287. *Ibidem*, p. 148. For the difference between Syros and Piraeus that led to the latter predominating, see P. Kalogri and V. Tsokopoulos, *op. cit.*, p. 436.

288. "Draft bill concerning the jetties to be constructed on Syros" *Athina*, 1613/2.8.1849.

289. M. Synarelli, *op. cit.*, pp. 162-163.

290. See Chr. Agriantoni, "Νεώριον Σύρου. Μια υπεραιωνόβια επιχείρηση" και "Βυρσοδεψείο Μενέλαου Κορνηλάκη, 1853-c.1970", in G. Polyzos and V. Panayiotopoulos (eds.), *op. cit.*, pp. 169, 279.

291. Th. Xenomanidis, "Concerning Hermoupolis", *Athina* 101/8.4.1833. Cf. *Athina* 457/28.7.1837.

292. "Plan de la ville d'Hermoupolis sur l'île de Syra", 1837 (PETE catalogue, *op. cit.*) and "Plan du nouveau lazaret de quarantaine à Syra", 1838, *Ιστορία του Ελληνικού Έθνους*, vol. XIII, 1977, p. 523.

293. *Athina*, 457/28.7.1837.

294. E. S., "The plan of Hermoupolis and its Mayor", *Athina*, 619/27.5.1839.

295. A. Kolezis, *Athina*, 1281/6.1.1846 (report-complaint).

296. *Athina*, 725/19.6.1840.

297. *Athina*, 726/22.6.1840.

298. *Athina*, 860/22.10.1841.

299. *Athina*, 982/9.1.1843. Cf. the revision of the plan for Hermoupolis, "due to the confined area of the place and the uneven nature of the ground", since provision had originally been made for large plots (*Athina*, 982/9.1.1843).

300. All these references and dates are taken from the exemplary monograph by J. Travlos and A. Kokkou, *Ερμούπολη*, 1980.

301. Republished from the *Enosis* of Syros (*Athina*, 2337/10.11.1855). Cf. the description of a paved square with music striking up "and the ladies pulling along their silk tails" in *Λουκής Λάρας* by D. Vikelas (1879).

302. "Erection of a municipal grocery store in Hermoupolis", *Athina*, 2272/13.6.1855. Cf. the comparison of the New Market in Hermoupolis with Athens, where nothing like it was to be found (*Aion*, 1552/26.8.1857). Would this optimism last long, though? An international crisis was to strike a blow at the town (*Athina*, 2611/6.11.1857).

303. *Athina*, 1947/3.2.1859.

304. Report from Syros (*Athina*, 2400/14.4.1856).

305. Report from Hermoupolis (*Aion*, 4559/22.9.1884).

306. See J. Travlos and A. Kokkou, *op. cit.*, pp. 102-183.

307. For exports of cocoons and silk, using the sizeable local fleet, and the dependence of the island on corresponding imports of 44% of its grain, see M. Synarelli, *op. cit.*, pp. 151, 156.

308. An early attempt was made in a report to Kapodistrias in 1828, following a local decision to construct a harbour (I. K. Voyiatzidis, *Γλώσσα και λαογραφία της νήσου Άνδρου*, 1957, vol. IV, pp. 35-36). Other fruitless endeavours followed in 1852, 1882 and about 1925 (D. P. Paschalis, *Ιστορία της νήσου Άνδρου*, vol. I, 1925, pp. 104-110).

309. "To the Minister for Public Education", *Syriana Grammata* 5/1989, pp. 38-41.

310. The earliest, though smaller, church of the Panayia Theoskepasti lies inside the Castle.

311. With marble along the extension in the town and with schist slabs in the old section.

312. Similarly, it proved impossible to construct a jetty at Chora so that ships could put in (J. Petropoulos and Aik. Koumarianou, "Περίοδος βασιλείας του Όθωνος 1833-1862", *Ιστορία του Ελληνικού Έθνους*, vol. XIII, p. 177).

313. R. E . Kasperson, *The Dodecanese: Diversity and Unity in Island Politics*, 1966, p. 72.

314. *Ibidem*, p. 75.

315. Three such extensions are mentioned in about the middle of the 19th century, two at the south (the earliest and most populous) and one, Neo Marasi, to the north of the Old Town (R. Matton, *Rhodes*, 1966, p. 75).

316. M. D. Volonakis, entry "Σύμη", *MEE*, vol. XXII, p. 523.

317. *Δωδεκάνησα*, Explorer Editions, 2002, p. 122.

318. K. Farmakidis και A. Karakatsani, *Σύμη*, 1975, p. 19.

319. *Ibidem*, p. 20.

320. See, for example, the relevant references in D. Porphyrios ("Classicism is not a style", Architectural Design and Academy Editions, 1982).

321. The main source of information for Chania is the study by Aim. Kladou-Bletsa, *Τα Χανιά έξω από τα τείχη*, 1978.

322. *Ibidem*, p. 19.

323. *Ibidem*, p. 24.

324. *Ibidem*, pp. 27, 29.

325. *Ibidem*, p. 30.

326. *Ibidem*, pp. 31-34.

327. *Ibidem*, p. 41.

328. *Ibidem*, pp. 48-49.

329. *Ibidem*, p. 33.

330. A. Agorapoulou-Birbili, *Η αρχιτεκτονική της πόλεως της Κέρκυρας*, 1977, p. 116.

331. Additional planning seems to have been used in parts of the town where buildings were demolished when the second enceinte of Corfu was erected (*ibidem*, p. 145).

332. *Ibidem*, pp. 105-108.

333. *Eadem*, "Κέρκυρα", *EPA*, vol. 1, 1982, p. 227.

334. A. Agoropoulou-Birbili, *Η αρχιτεκτονική της πόλεως της Κέρκυρας*, *op. cit.*, p. 123.

335. *Ibidem.*

336. *Ibidem*, p. 132.

337. *Ibidem*, pp. 139-141.

338. *Ibidem*, p. 128.

339. *Ibidem*, pp. 123, 141.

340. *Ibidem*, p. 75.

341. *Ibidem*, p. 146.

342. *Ibidem*, p. 116.

343. *Ibidem*, p. 33.

344. *Ibidem*, p. 87.

345. *Ibidem*, p. 146.

346. These were the work of the British colonel and engineer George Whitmore (*ibidem*).

347. The general information is from the guidebook *Επτάνησα*, *op. cit.*

348. D. Zivas, *Η αρχιτεκτονική της Ζακύνθου από τον ΙΣΤ΄ μέχρι τον ΙΘ΄ αιώνα*, 1970, pp. 26-28.

349. *Ibidem*, p. 31.

350. *Ibidem*, p. 34.

351. *Ibidem*, p. 35.

352. *Ibidem*, pp. 36, 40. Ayiou Markou Square was a social centre with many uses: as a meeting place for the noblemen and the seat of two churches, the Catholic cathedral, after which the square was named, and an Orthodox church (*ibidem*, p. 41).

353. A characteristic report of the time states that lightning struck a small gunpowder magazine and destroyed 120 houses (*Athina*, 624/14.6.1839).

354. A. Karadimou-Yerolympou, *Μεταξύ Ανατολής και Δύσης*, 1997, pp. 93-95.

355. *Ibidem*, pp. 96-97.

356. *Ibidem*, p. 98.

357. V. Chastaoglou, *Βόλος. Πορτραίτο της πόλης τον 19ο και 20ό αιώνα*, 2002, p. 54. Cf. Ch. V.[arlamidis], a doctor, "The plan of the town of Volos, from other points of view, but mainly from that of hygiene", *Aion* 3909/20.7.1882. Three plans ("Diagram of the street plan of the town of Volos – second section", 1882; "Diagram of the regulation of the fort of the town of Volos", 1887; "Diagram of the street plan of the fort of the town of Volos", 1888) are included in ESEP (1984).

358. V. Chastaoglou, *op. cit.*, p. 58.

359. *Ibidem*, p. 64.

360. *Ibidem*, pp. 64-65.

361. *Ibidem*, pp. 55-56.

362. *Ibidem*, p. 65.

363. *Ibidem*, p. 70.

364. P. Kalogri and V. Tsokopoulos, *op. cit.*, p. 436.

365. V. Chastaoglou, *op. cit.*, p. 73.

366. *Ibidem*, p. 71.

367. G. Kizis, *Πηλιορείτικη οικοδομία*, 1994, p. 57.

368. No source assigns a date to it. The neoclassical coffee-house and restaurant at the front of the square bears an inscription stating that it was built in 1903, when D. Ph. Alexiou was mayor.

369. According to its inscription, the famous old foundation at the back of the square was renovated in 1930, along with the square, by a private individual, the "merchant prince from Egypt", Z. A. Livanos (R. Leonidopoulou-Stylianou, *Μακρινίτσα*, 1982, p. 102).

370. *Ibidem*, p. 42.

371. At the back of the square there was a slightly raised 'hayati' for the exclusive use of the notables and wealthy, which no longer exists *(ibidem*, p. 102).

372. See *Ibidem*, p. 38.

373. Reduced to ruins by the 1955 earthquake, this church began to be rebuilt in 2005.

374. K. Makris, *Η λαϊκή τέχνη του Πηλίου*, 1976, pp. 52-53.

375. A contributing factor here is the existence of the old cosmopolitan Theoxenia Hotel (1910), which was burned during the German Occupation and is now being restored at a very slow rate.

376. Examples are the Kantartzis Mansion, Folklore Museum (1864?), The Athanasakeio Nursery School (K. Argyris, 1903), etc.

377. A. Karadimou-Yerolympou, *Επαναοχεδιασμός και ανοικοδόμηση..., op. cit.*, p. 97.

378. *Ibidem*, pp. 32-35.

379. A. Karadimou-Yerolympou, "Σχεδιασμός και ανάκτηση του χώρου της πόλης", *op. cit.*, p. 381.

380. A. Karadimou-Yerolympou, *Επαναοχεδιασμός και ανοικοδόμηση..., op. cit.*, p. 369.

381. *Ibidem*, p. 365.

382. *Athinai* 10.12.1917.

383. See A. Karadimou-Yerolympou, *Μεταξύ Ανατολής και Δύσης, op. cit.*, pp. 125-126.

384. *Ibidem*, p. 93.

385. D. Rogoti-Kyriakopoulou, "Γιάννινα", *EPA*, vol. 6, 1988, p. 200.

386. A. Karadimou-Yerolympou, *op. cit.*, pp. 110-111.

387. The Italian Guiccardini visited Ioannina in 1900 (cited in A. Karadimou-Yerolympou, *Μεταξύ Ανατολής και Δύσης, op. cit.*, p. 148, note 236).

388. Ch. I. Soulis, *MEE*, vol. XIII, 1930, pp. 374-376.

389. A. Karadimou-Yerolympou, *Επαναοχεδιασμός και ανοικοδόμηση..., op. cit.*, p. 19.

390. The construction of a harbour, e.g., was undertaken by the French engineer Edmond Bartissol on 8(20).7.1896 (S. E. Lykoudis, entry "Θεσσαλονίκη", *MEE*, vol. XII, p. 611).

391. A. Karadimou-Yerolympou, *Επαναοχεδιασμός και ανοικοδόμηση..., op. cit.*, pp. 37-38.

392. *Ibidem*, p. 39.

393. A. Adamantiou, "Θεσσαλονίκη", *MEE*, vol. XII, p. 620.

394. The corresponding legal provision had been instituted in Greece by the Royal Decree of 9(21).4.1836, to which reference has already been made.

395. A. Karadimou-Yerolympou, *Επαναοχεδιασμός και ανοικοδόμηση..., op. cit.*, pp. 41-44. Cf. a previous formulation of the interventions made in the period 1866-1900, in *eadem*, "Εκσυγχρονισμός και πολεοδομία στη Θεσσαλονίκη του 19ου αιώνα", *op. cit.*, pp. 54-67.

396. *Ibidem*, p. 53, σημ. 30.

397. *Ibidem*, pp. 117-122. The centre of Larisa, which burned down in 1882, was rebuilt under similar circumstances. The terms under which it received its new form are still unclear *(ibidem*, pp. 111-113).

398. A. Adamantiou, entry "Θεσσαλονίκη", *op. cit.*, p. 620

399. A. Karadimou-Yerolympou, *Επαναοχεδιασμός και ανοικοδόμηση..., op. cit.*, pp. 141-142.

400. *Ibidem*, p. 138.

401. *Ibidem*, pp. 139-140.

402. When the 'Macedonian Question' arose at the end of the 19th century, Thessaloniki became an apple of strife between Bulgaria and Greece. The Great Powers brought pressure for reform to bear on the Ottoman empire, and Thessaloniki was at the centre of things from 1897 on, when the Young Turk Revolution broke out there (1908). The rivalry between Greece and Bulgaria came to an end in 1912, when the Greek army entered Thessaloniki one day earlier than the Bulgarians, and the town was converted into an army camp.
The murder of King George I intervened, and three months later the Bulgarians were decisively defeated and retreated (A. Adamantiou, entry "Θεσσαλονίκη", *op. cit.*, p. 620).

403. A. Karadimou-Yerolympou, *Επαναοχεδιασμός και ανοικοδόμηση..., op. cit.*, p. 157.

404. *Ibidem*, p. 162. Law 1394/1918 on the implementation of the plan "was a general tool for intervention in an existing settlement" (p. 172), and did not meet "substantial opposition" to its essence (p. 183).

405. International Committee for the Study of the New Town Plan, *Η ανοικοδόμηση της Θεσσαλονίκης*, Athens, 1918 (cited in G. Th. Koutoupis, "Η αυτονομία του σχεδίου της πόλης. Σχέση μεταξύ των συνιστωσών της πολεοδομικής επέμβασης κατά τον επαναοχεδιασμό της Θεσσαλονίκης, μετά την πυρκαγιά του 1917", *Technika Chronika*, I, vol. 14, 1/1994, p. 281).

406. T. Mawson, "The new Salonica", *Balkan News*, 29-31/Jan. 1918 (cited in G. Th. Koutoupis, *op. cit.*).

407. N. Kalogirou, "Η ανοικοδόμηση της Θεσσαλονίκης από τον Ernest Hébrard, μια επέμβαση στον αστικό χώρο και την αρχιτεκτονική της πόλης", *Νεοκλασική πόλη & αρχιτεκτονική, op. cit.*, *p.* 84-96.

408. A. Karadimou-Yerolympou, *Επαναοχεδιασμός και ανοικοδόμηση..., op. cit.*, p. 225.

409. *Ibidem*, pp. 226-229. The first consequence related mainly to "those who lost most" as a result of the rebuilding, the Jewish population of the town *(ibidem*, p. 329).

410. R. Dreyfus, "La reconstruction de Salonique", *L'Architecture*, 8/1927 (cited in G. Th. Koutoupis, *op. cit.*).

411. D. E. Moustakas, entry "Θεσσαλονίκη", *MEE*, vol. XII, p. 605.

412. A. Karadimou-Yerolympou, *Επαναοχεδιασμός και ανοικοδόμηση..., op. cit.*, pp. 361-365. It may be noted that penetrating comments like these have not been made for any any place, even Athens.

413. *Technika Chronika*, 182/1939, pp. 213-225.

414. D. Zygomalas, "Ο Αριστοτέλης δίδαξε, η πλατεία Αριστοτέλους διδάσκει;", digital journal *Monumenta*, 01/2007, www. monumenta.org.

415. D. E. Moustakas, "Καβάλα", *MEE*, vol. XIII, p. 419.

416. The story of the Kavala harbour had many vicissitudes down to 1930 *(ibidem)*. In the end, the foundations of it were laid by E. Venizelos in 1929 (S. P. Angeloudi, "Ο νεοκλασικισμός στην Καβάλα", *Νεοκλασική πόλη & αρχιτεκτονική, op. cit.*, p. 42).

417. A. Karadimou-Yerolympou, *Μεταξύ Ανατολής και Δύσης, op. cit.*, *p.* 288.

418. *Ibidem*, p. 112.

419. *Ibidem*, pp. 113-114.

420. *Ibidem*, p. 244.

421. S. P. Angeloudi, *op. cit.*, pp. 40-42.

422. *Ibidem*.

423. See, for example, the design of Mitropoleos Square, which 'the interests' reduced to an "oven of Nasradin hodja" (*Athina*, 2888/30.6.1860). Similarly, see the design of Ayias Irinis Square (*Avgi*, 896/21.8.1861).

INDEX

Numbers in bold refer to figures.

MAIN SOURCES

Adami, M. (ed.), *Σταμάτης Βούλγαρης. Ο πρώτος Έλληνας πολεοδόμος*, Libro, Athens no date.

Νεοελληνική πόλη. *Οθωμανικές κληρονομιές και ελληνικό κράτος*, Proceedings of an International History Conference, Society for the Study of Modern Hellenism, Athens and Hermoupolis, 1984, Athens 1985.

Zivas, D., *Η αρχιτεκτονική της Ζακύνθου από τον ΙΣΤ΄ μέχρι τον ΙΘ΄ αιώνα*, publ. by the Technical Chamber of Greece, Athens 1970.

Karadimou-Yerolympou, A., *Επαναοχεδιασμός και ανοικοδόμηση της Θεσσαλονίκης μετά την πυρκαγιά του 1917*, academic annual of the Polytechnic School of Thessaloniki University, appendix 31, Vol. IX, Thessaloniki 1985.

Karadimou-Yerolympou, A., *Μεταξύ Ανατολής και Δύσης*, Trochalia, Athens 1997.

Kladou-Bletsa, Ai., *Τα Χανιά έξω από τα τείχη*, publ. by the Technical Chamber of Greece, Section for West Crete, Chania 1978.

Kyriazis P. (ed.), *Πρώτοι Έλληνες Τεχνικοί Επιστήμονες Περιόδου Απελευθέρωσης*, publ. by the Technical Chamber of Greece, Athens 1976.

Biris, K., *Αι Αθήναι από του 19ου εις τον 20όν αιώνα*, Melissa, Athens 1966.

Papageorgiou-Venetas, A., *Εδουάρδος Σάουμπερτ 1804-1860*, translated by T. Siepi, Odysseas, Athens 1999.

Rongoti-Kyriopoulou, D., "Γιάννινα", in *Ελληνική Παραδοσιακή Αρχιτεκτονική*, vol. 6, Melissa, Athens 1988.

Saitas, G., "Μάνη", in *Ελληνική Παραδοσιακή Αρχιτεκτονική*, vol. 5, Melissa, Athens 1988.

Νεοκλασική πόλη & αρχιτεκτονική, Proceedings of a Panhellenic Conference, History and Archaeology Seminar, Thessaloniki University, Dec. 1983, Thessaloniki 1984.

Travlos J. and Kokkou, A., *Ερμούπολη*, publ. by the Commercial Bank of Greece, Athens 1980.

Chastaoglou, V., Βόλος. *Πορτραίτο της πόλης τον 19ο και 20ό αιώνα*, Volos Municipal Centre for History and Documentation, Volos 2002.

PARTY OR GO HOME